Nancy

INSIDERS' FRENCH

INSIDERS' FRENCH

Beyond the Dictionary

Eleanor Levieux and Michel Levieux

The University of Chicago Press
Chicago and London

ELEANOR and MICHEL LEVIEUX are coauthors of *Beyond the Dictionary in French,* first published by Cassell's in 1967 and later known as *Cassell's Colloquial French.* A Franco-American couple, graduates of the Sorbonne and Cornell, they taught at the Institut d'études politiques ("Sciences Po") in Paris for many years. They have also taught French history and courses on contemporary France and Europe at the University of Oregon. Ms. Levieux is assistant professor at the British Institute in Paris (University of London) and is a professional translator.

The University of Chicago Press, Chicago 60637
The University of Chicago Press, Ltd., London
© 1999 by Eleanor Levieux and Michel Levieux
All rights reserved. Published 1999
08 07 06 05 04 03 02 01 00 99   1 2 3 4 5

ISBN (cloth): 0-226-47502-6
ISBN (paper): 0-226-47503-4

Library of Congress Cataloging-in-Publication Data

Levieux, Eleanor.
    Insiders' French : beyond the dictionary / Eleanor Levieux
and Michel Levieux.
        p.   cm.
    Includes bibliographical references and index.
    ISBN 0-226-47502-6. — ISBN 0-226-47503-4 (pbk.)
    1. French language—Glossaries, vocabularies, etc.
    2. French language—Spoken French.   I.   Levieux, Michel.
    II.   Title.
PC2680.L38   1999
443'.21—dc21   98-49005
                                                     CIP

♾ The paper used in this publication meets the minimum requirements
of the American National Standard for Information Sciences—
Permanence of Paper for Printed Library Materials, ANSI Z39.48-1992.
This book is printed on acid-free paper.

Pour Raphaël Lorenzo Roero de Cortanze

Preface

If you had been living in France between, say, 1993 and 1998, what would you have been hearing on the radio, seeing on television, reading in the papers? The great majority of the terms and phrases you would have encountered were not part of the French scene at all in 1970, or in 1980, or even in 1990. The country itself, and its perception of the world outside its borders and of itself in relation to that world, have changed tremendously. Many of the words used now are neither new nor imported from another language. *Exclusion, foulard,* and *insertion* are obvious examples; they have always been there, in the French language, but they have taken on new meanings or acquired new connotations.

This book is not a dictionary of the classic type. Nor does it dwell on slang or on proverbs and sayings. It is not a travel guide or a guide to restaurants or vineyards. It does not provide a complete bilingual glossary to computer terms. All of these specific aims can be better achieved by other authors.

What, then, is the aim of this book?

It tries to present a verbal snapshot of the France of the mid- and late 1990s. Oh, the France of *ooh, la la!* and *le beaujolais nouveau* still exists—*Dieu merci!* But today there are other Frances as well: a France of high unemployment, a France that is hooked on fast food but ambivalent about the country where it originated, a France that is about to experience the European single currency but is not at all certain what being part of Europe is going to entail, a France with a substantial and ever more controversial immigrant population, a France with a much diminished Communist Party and a provocative extreme Right, a France that cannot agree on what nationality and cultural identity mean.

We hope that this book will enable you to hear France from the inside, see France from the inside, and understand France from the inside as the country stands anxiously on the brink of the third millennium.

We have striven to be objective. As a result, some of our entries may even seem bland or tongue-in-cheek. Many of the examples we give express opinions. They are not our opinions; they are those we have heard (often from anonymous callers phoning in to a talk show) or read and have noted down. As a result, the

French we quote is not always perfectly grammatical, orthodox French. It is the genuine article, French as it is really spoken (and increasingly written in certain parts of the press). The register is often very *familier* on topics that are very grave.

Occasionally we have broadened the definition of media to include such modes of communication as the telephone (attitudes to which have changed radically in the past half dozen years), *baby-foot* and the game of *boules* (attitudes to both of which have changed virtually not at all), and *SDF* magazines (newcomers on the socioeconomic and journalistic scene).

Where words exist within clusters—the word *chômage,* for instance, immediately brings with it other words: *Assedic, ANPE, CDD, plan social,* and so on—we have cross-referenced from one entry to another. The word *foulard* refers the reader to *chador, Clovis, laïcité, tchador,* and *voile à l'école* because all of them relate to the central issue: is France essentially *un pays laïc,* a secular country, whose public schools are nondenominational, or is it essentially a country rooted in the Christian—and, specifically, Catholic—tradition? *Clivage d'opinion* and *loi Falloux* are also relevant to the same issue. Cross-referenced entries are always indicated in boldface.

We have included at least two phrases whose origins hark back to ancient Rome because they are still in common use today by politicians and journalists alike.

As in our previous books, we emphasize the context in which each word or phrase is used and generally add one or more sentences which provide relevant vocabulary.

A word on acronyms (*ANPE, Assedic, CNPF, Insee* and so on). Usage on this point in French can and does vary, sometimes within one and the same book. Generally speaking, those which are pronounceable as if they were words take a capital only on the first letter; those which are not pronounceable capitalize all of the letters. But this is not a hard and fast rule.

We have selected nearly a dozen cartoons because they are both funny and enlightening and because they prove that whatever problems France may face today, the French are still witty and still willing to laugh.

Vive la France!

Paris, November 1998

Acknowledgments

Our warm appreciation goes to Valérie Levieux for her patient reading and alert editing of various stages of the manuscript and her extremely pertinent comments and suggestions. Thanks also go to Terenia Jarzembowska for her vigilance as she perused an early draft of the manuscript.

We are very grateful to Drake McKenney for having done so much to make this book possible and to the Authors Guild, particularly Kay Murray, for their advice and support. We thank Michael Riccioli and Morad Samimi for their contributions concerning the Internet.

We thank the following cartoonists and periodicals for having granted us permission to use the cartoons that appear in this book:

Cardon, "Economie: c'est la reprise!" in *Le Canard enchaîné* (October 23, 1996)

EsCaro, "Fabrique nationale de pantoufles" and "Non à la consommation" in *Le Canard enchaîné* (February 2, 1997, and July 9, 1997)

Ghertman, "L'Eglise Saint-Bernard évacuée" in *Le Canard enchaîné* (August 14, 1996)

Lefred-Thouron, "Si vous n'achetez qu'une voiture" and "Y a-t-il de l'emploi sur Mars?" in *Le Canard enchaîné* (July 9, 1997)

Wojniak, "La police aux petits soins" in *Le Canard enchaîné* (August 14, 1996)

Plantu, "Vache folle" in *L'Express* (April 11, 1996)

Boll, "Ce qui est bon pour l'entreprise" in *Marianne* (July 7–13, 1997)

Loup, "J'ai la gauche qu'est trop gauche" in *Marianne* (May 19–25, 1997)

Nicoulaud, "Comment savoir ce que je pense?" in *Marianne* (May 19–25, 1997).

A

abaisser Another way of saying *baisser, réduire*. *"Quand va-t-on abaisser les charges patronales?"* demanded one panelist on *Le téléphone sonne*, a radio talk show, May 1997; "'How long must employers go on paying so much above and beyond wages?'" See **charges sociales**

Abbé Pierre An outspoken priest who for decades pioneered efforts *dans le domaine de l'humanitaire*, looking after the poor and the homeless. Opinion polls showed that he was the most widely admired living figure in France; his name was a household word. Early in 1996, however, when he was over eighty years old, he issued statements in support of an old friend, Roger Garaudy, who happened to be the prominent author of revisionist works denying the justification of the word *génocide* as applied to the killing of Jews during World War II. *La réputation de l'Abbé Pierre s'est trouvée par conséquent ternie;* "The Abbé Pierre's reputation suffered as a result."

abracadabrant(e) Adjective meaning far-fetched, unlikely bordering on the absurd. *Se trouver dans une situation abracadabrante*, to be in the most wildly unlikely situation.

abribus (m.) A coined word: a bus stop offering shelter from the elements (with a roof and walls on three sides). See **mobilier urbain**

absent This is what French diplomacy does not want to be, as in *"La France est un petit peu absente de ce processus de paix" (israélo-palestinien)*, a phrase used in 1995 by one commentator (and by others since then) on France's diminished role on the international scene.

abus (m.) *"L'abus d'alcool est dangereux pour la santé. Sachez consommer avec modération"*—the standard warning that must be included in every advertisement for alcohol and on every bottle.

   Abus de biens sociaux, one of the most common accusations brought in recent years against business executives accused of corruption: misappropriation of company funds or property.

   Abus sexuels contre les enfants: see **Ados 71; pédophilie**

académicien (m.) Member of *l'Académie française,* founded by Richelieu in 1634 and approved by Louis XIII in 1635. The forty members, *les immortels,* are prominent living Francophone writers; when one of them dies, candidates come forward or are nominated to occupy *son fauteuil.* Marguerite Yourcenar, although of half-Belgian, half-French origin and a naturalized American, reacquired French nationality and, in 1980 became the first *académicienne,* "woman member," ever.

académie (f.) For purposes of the *Ministère de l'Education nationale,* France is divided into regions called *académies.* All schools in *l'académie de Paris-Créteil-Versailles* will have their *vacances de la Toussaint,* their All Saints' Day (November 1) school vacation from, say, October 26 to November 6, whereas those in *académie d'Aix-Marseille* will have theirs from October 21 to November 2. The aim of staggering vacations this way is to avoid having overcrowded highways, trains, and airports on the dates when vacations begin and end. In addition, all schools within a given *académie* will have the same questions on the *Baccalauréat.* See **Bac + 2**

accession (f.) **à la propriété** The fact of becoming the owner of one's house or apartment. Government policy is to encourage individuals to own their housing instead of renting it. In 1995 it introduced an interest-free loan, *"le prêt à 0%,"* for prospective homeowners whose income was below a certain level. See **Plan d'épargne logement**

accords (m. pl.) **de Blair House** During the *négociations du GATT* at the end of 1992, there was much talk of these agreements between Washington and the European Commission. French delegates wanted to renegotiate the provisions limiting the amount of land to be planted with *les oléagineux,* "oilseed crops," and decreasing exports of subsidized crops. Southwestern France, for instance, has an abundance of *champs de tournesol,* "sunflower fields," because twenty years earlier *les cultivateurs* had been encouraged to plant sunflowers, for their seeds; now the same *cultivateurs* were being told that there was a glut of sunflowers, that they must stop growing them and *laisser leurs champs en friche,* "let their fields lie fallow." See **jachère; PAC; paysan(ne)**

accords (m. pl.) **d'Evian** The March 1962 agreement that ended the Algerian war of independence, known for a long time as *les événements d'Algérie,* now officially called *la guerre d'Algérie.* See **Algérie; harki; Papon, Maurice; porteurs de valises**

accords (m. pl.) **de Grenelle** Also called *le constat de Grenelle* (named after the Paris street on which the *Ministère de l'Industrie* is located), these agreements were reached in May 1968. They were landmark agreements among *le gouvernement, les syndicats, et le **patronat*** concerning *la hausse des sa-*

laires et la réduction du temps de travail, "salary increases and a shorter work week." The agreements came about as the result of the general strikes that paralyzed the country in May. Workers expressed their support for student protests but did not demonstrate or riot along with the students. See **événements de mai 68**

accro A shortened version of *accroché(e),* "hooked on something"—drugs, crossword puzzles, or whatever it may be. Originally rather slangy, it has become part of the spoken language. *Quand il s'agit des films de Woody Allen le public français est complètement accro—il ne peut plus s'en passer,* "The French public is completely hooked on Woody Allen films—they can't do without them."

acquis (m. pl.) **sociaux** Literally, the benefits that have been gained (acquired) in terms of *les mesures de protection sociale,* "social benefits dispensed by the central government": *congé* (m.) *maternité prénatal, congé maternité postnatal, crèches* (f. pl.) *municipales, cinq semaines de congés payés, retraite* (f.) *de la Sécu, allocations* (f. pl.) *familiales, allocations chômage, allocation rentrée* (for families with school-age children), *RMI* (m.), and so forth.

"Touchez pas aux acquis sociaux!" " 'Hands off our (hard-won) benefits!' " is a common slogan during *les manifestations contre les propositions de restrictions budgétaires,* "demonstrations against proposed cuts in government spending." See **critères de convergence; rentrée sociale; RMI**

actionnaire (m. or f.) Beginning in 1986–1988, when the newly elected center right *RPR-UDF* government began privatizing firms that had been nationalized by previous governments, and again in 1993–1997, under another *RPR* government, everyone was urged to *devenir actionnaire en achetant des actions* (f. pl.), "become a shareholder by buying shares." Taken as a whole, shareholders form *l'actionnariat (m.):* see **-ariat.** Individual shareholders, who each own only a handful of shares, as opposed to corporate shareholders, *les investisseurs institutionnels,* are referred to collectively as *les petits porteurs,* literally, "small bearers" (of shares). *Actionnariser,* to increase the number of shareholders in a firm. See **gros porteur; ni-ni; privatisation**

actualités (f. pl.) The old term for radio or TV news or for the newsreels that used to accompany the feature film at the movies. The term has been largely supplanted by *les* **informations** (both radio and TV) and by *le journal télévisé.*

adepte (m. or f.) Most often heard in the sense of a member of a sect: see **Ordre du temple solaire**

administré(e) Each person who lives in France, whether a citizen or not, is—from the standpoint of the government (the administration)—*un(e) administré(e)*. The passive construction of this word may have something very significant to say about the relationship between *l'Etat* and the individual. Similarly, see **contribuable**

admissible The aim of every student and especially of every candidate in *un* **concours** is *être admissible*, "to pass one stage in the exam and therefore be allowed to take the next part of it"; typically, to *réussir l'écrit* and so be eligible to *se présenter à l'oral.*

ado (m. or f.) In youngspeak, this is short for *adolescent*(e), "teenager." Of course, the practice of chopping off the last syllable(s) of a word has been around for a long time; the ancient Greeks called it *apocope*. Modern examples are everywhere: *vidéo(scope)*, *kilo(gramme)*, *pneu(matique)*, *photo(graphie)*, *ciné(ma)*, *moto(cyclette)*, *hétéro(sexuel)*, *homo(sexuel)*. *Promo(tion) spéciale, trois bouteilles pour le prix de deux.* See **accro.** But the young are among the most prone to indulge. *On va au ciné cet aprèm (après-midi)? On prend le métro(politain)? Non, il faut que je me trouve un appart(ment) près de la fac(ulté). On se retrouve demain pour le petit déj(euner)? Tu votes écolo(giste)? Manif(estation) géante demain. Remplir un formulaire de la Sécu(rité sociale). La récré(ation)* at school. *C'est super sympa(thique).*

Ados 71 Code name for *la campagne antipédophilie*, "antipedophilia campaign," run by *la gendarmerie* in the spring of 1997. See **pédophilie**

adouber A medieval image harking back to the days when noblemen were *adoubés*, "dubbed" and elevated to the knighthood. The idea carries over onto the modern political scene. *C'est un jeune espoir qui attend d'être adoubé par son parti politique;* "He's a young hopeful who's only waiting for the party to give him its official seal of approval."

AELE (m.) *Accord européen de libre échange*, European Free Trade Agreement (EFTA), created in 1960. Founding member countries included Austria, Britain, Denmark, Norway, Portugal, Sweden, and Switzerland; all but Norway and Switzerland have since become members of *l'Union européenne*, formerly called *la Communauté européenne*. See **ALENA**

aéronef (m.) Aircraft—a generic word. The more common word, of course, is *avion* (m.), "airplane," but it does not include *les hélicoptères. Avion à réaction,* jet plane. *Gros porteur* (m.), jumbo jet.

Aérospatiale (f.) Major aircraft builder, nationalized in 1936. It produced the Concorde in 1969. Like Snecma and Thomson-CSF, most of its capital comes from *l'Etat*. Among other major aircraft builders are **Airbus Industrie,** Dassault-Aviation, and Matra Défense Espace. See **avionneur**

affaires (f. pl.) A number of scandals involving corruption came to light during the late 1980s and early 1990s, while François Mitterrand, as head of *le Parti socialiste,* was president. **L'opposition,** chiefly *le RPR (Rassemblement pour la République),* gleefully called these *les affaires (l'affaire Carrefour du développement, l'affaire Urba,* etc.; see **vrai faux passeport**). But after Jacques Chirac, at the head of the *RPR,* was elected president in 1995, other *affaires* came to light, involving members of the former opposition *(l'affaire Juppé et les appartements de la Ville de Paris, l'affaire Tibéri et l'appartement HLM de son fils,* etc.).

In the legal sense, *une affaire* is "a case"; hence, *affaire classée,* "case closed," the verdict reached in some of these cases.

Un affairiste is "an unscrupulous businessman" but not necessarily one involved in *les affaires* in the political corruption sense.

affamer To starve. *Affamer les populations civiles à des fins politiques en ne distribuant pas l'aide alimentaire reçue de l'étranger (par exemple, au Rwanda, en Somalie, au Soudan, au Zaïre . . .);* "To starve civilian populations for political purposes by not distributing food donated from abroad (as, for instance, in Rwanda, Somalia, Sudan, Zaire, etc.)." *Est-ce que le sommet de la **FAO,** qui se tient cette année à Rome, se prononcera contre cette pratique?* "Will the FAO summit, meeting in Rome this year, come out with an official statement condemning that practice?"

afficher To post or display, to put up *affiches* (f. pl.), "posters." But also to announce or publish figures. *La société de gestion d'**Eurotunnel** affiche un déficit énorme pour l'année écoulée malgré de bons résultats d'exploitation;* "The accounts of the consortium operating the Channel Tunnel show a huge deficit for the year just ended despite positive operating figures."

Rester trois ans à l'affiche is said of a play that runs for three years.

Un colleur d'affiches, someone who puts up posters. *Il y a parfois des bagarres entre des colleurs d'affiches de partis politiques opposés;* "People who put up posters for one party have been known to clash with people putting up posters for another party."

AGED (f.) *Allocation pour garde d'enfant à domicile.* Much was heard of this policy in 1997 when the Socialist government decided to reduce it by 50 percent, but only by 25 percent for families with net incomes under 300,000F (approximately $50,000) a year. *L'AGED est versée aux couples dont les deux travaillent et qui font garder à domicile un enfant de moins de six ans par une personne légalement déclarée;* "This allowance is paid to couples both of whom work and who have an under-school-age child looked after at home by a legally declared person." See **mise sous condition de ressources**

Agessa *Association pour la gestion de la Sécurité sociale des auteurs,* the retirement and compensation fund into which self-employed artists and writers are required to *cotiser,* "pay a percentage of their earnings," just as salaried workers have contributions to the *Sécurité sociale* deducted from their paychecks. See **URSSAF**

agglomération (f.) *Lille est, avec Lyon et Marseille, une des trois agglomérations en dehors de Paris avec plus d'un million d'habitants;* "Along with Lyons and Marseilles, Lille is one of the three metropolitan areas, not counting Paris, to have a population of over one million." *Le code de la route impose de ne pas dépasser 50 à l'heure dans toute agglomération;* "The highway code sets a speed limit of fifty kilometers per hour (thirty miles per hour) in any built-up area."

But *aggloméré* (m.) does not refer to *un habitant d'une agglomération!*—it is "composition board, made from compressed wooden particles."

agriculteur (m.) Perhaps because France had an essentially rural economy for so long, there are several ways of saying "farmer" today. *Agriculteur(trice)* and *exploitant(e) agricole* are the terms most commonly used by government officials, journalists, economists, and the like; both terms refer to "a person who raises crops and may have some herds but not on a large scale." *Cultivateur(trice)* refers to "someone who grows crops and who may also have a few cows and pigs, as well as hens and rabbits." "A farm" in all of these cases is *une ferme* or *une exploitation agricole. Eleveur(euse)* refers to a "breeder"; he or she has *un élevage.* A *fermier(ière)* may be the "tenant or owner of *une ferme* generally related, even today, to the local *château.*" One of the major farmers' unions is the *Fédération nationale des syndicats d'exploitants agricoles* (*FNSEA*). The latter term is no doubt the most recent, dating from after World War II.

Farmers will often talk about themselves as *les paysans et la paysannerie* and consider that their natural enemies are **Bruxelles** and *les technocrates.* See **PAC; paysan; tourisme**

AIEA (f.) *Agence internationale de l'énergie atomique,* International Atomic Energy Agency. Neither French nor European, this agency was set up in 1957, chiefly to foster peaceful uses of atomic energy. It has 123 member countries and headquarters in Vienna.

airbag (m.) The English word is generally used, although the French term is actually *coussin (m.) autogonflable,* "self-inflating cushion," or *coussin gonflable de sécurité.*

Airbus Industrie (f.) An international aircraft consortium that is chiefly French and German, with about 20 percent participation by British Aerospace and about 4 percent Spanish participation. The original arrangement, dating from 1970, included the Netherlands.

aire (f.) **de repos** Rest area alongside *une autoroute* but without *une station d'essence,* "gas station." *Aire* (f.) *de service,* service area along an *autoroute,* with *une station d'essence, une boutique, une aire de piquenique,* and sometimes *un parcours de santé,* a fitness circuit set up outdoors with brief laps to run, hurdles, parallel bars, and the like, for drivers who wish to stretch their muscles.

Albertville In the Alps (*Savoie*) between Geneva and Grenoble; site of the 1992 *Jeux olympiques* (J.O.) *d'hiver,* "winter Olympics."

Albion (f.) Always preceded by *perfide,* to form a grimly humorous name for England. (Not all scars left by the Hundred Years' War have yet healed.) *La crise de* **la vache folle** *est encore un coup de la perfide Albion,* say some people, "With the mad cow scare the English have done it again." Not related to the ***Plateau d'Albion.***

ALENA (m.) *Accord de libre echange de l'Amérique du Nord,* North American Free Trade Agreement (NAFTA).

Algérie (f.) A French colony from 1830, when France brought Turkish domination to an end, until 1958, when the French government passed a law declaring that Algeria was an integral part of the French Republic; Algeria was divided into three *départements,* like the other *départements* of France. But the Algerian war continued, and in 1962 Algeria became independent. See **accords d'Evian; FIS; harki; intégrisme; Maghrébin(e); Papon, Maurice; parabole; pied-noir; terrorisme; Zeroual, Liamine**

alibi (m.) (fig.) Token, as in *Sur la photo des membres du Comité d'animation du quartier il y a toujours un* **beur** *alibi—ça fait bien;* "In the group photo of the district cultural and activities committee, there's always a token second-generation North African—that makes a good impression." *Avant que la notion de* **parité** *hommes-femmes ne fasse son chemin, on voyait très peu de femmes sur la scène politique française, plutôt des femmes alibi;* "Before the idea of equal numbers of men and women in politics began to gain ground, very few women took part in French political life, mostly token females." This use of *alibi* is, of course, an extension of the basic meaning, *avoir un alibi.*

allégé(e) Light—that is, with a lower fat content—as in *crème allégée* and *margarine allégée.*

allègement (m.) **des charges sociales** A step that the French **pa-**

tronat clamors for. *Les **charges sociales*** (or *charges patronales*) are what an employer pays to the government on each employee's salary over and above what the employee receives—Social Security health insurance, old-age pension, unemployment insurance, and so on. These charges add up to approximately 50 percent on top of the salary amount. The government offers a certain amount of *allègement,* "reduction" or "relief," to employers who hire various categories of unemployed individuals.

Allemagne (f.) **occidentale** The western portion of Germany, since reunification; a term used by international organizations, thinktanks, and economists but rarely by the man or woman in the street, who tend to say *Allemagne (fédérale).*

The country that was known in English, before reunification, as West Germany was *l'Allemagne de l'ouest* or, in official terms, *la République fédérale allemande (RFA);* in common parlance today, *l'ex Allemagne de l'ouest or l'ex RFA.*

La Virginie occidentale, West Virginia. See also **occidental(e)**

Allemagne (f.) **orientale** The eastern portion of Germany, since reunification. The country that was known in English as East Germany was *l'Allemagne de l'est* or, in official terms, *la République démocratique allemande (RDA)*; hence, in common parlance today, *l'ex Allemagne de l'est or l'ex RDA.*

L'Extrême Orient, the Far East; *le Moyen Orient,* the Middle East; *le Proche Orient,* the Near East.

allocation (f.) **parentale de libre choix** It was suggested in October 1993 that the government introduce this type of allowance with a view to encouraging families to have more children. The idea was to pay one-half of the **SMIC** to any mother who decided to stay at home and take care of her own child, instead of working outside the home and relying on a child care facility or hiring a caregiver at home; see **AGED.**

allocations (f. pl.) **familiales** First introduced in 1932 in an attempt to increase the birthrate, this government allowance increases with the number of children. A couple with three children or more is officially termed *une famille nombreuse* and is entitled to significantly higher allowances plus reductions on train fare and on the purchase of certain items such as shoes. *Toucher les "allocs" (allocations familiales),* "to receive a family allowance," is a cherished part of the **acquis sociaux.**

allopathie (f.) Ordinary—that is, nonhomeopathic—medicine. *Une pharmacie* will often display a sign saying that it carries both medicines relating to *allopathie* and those relating to **homéopathie** (f.).

amalgame (m.) *Faire un amalgame,* a commonly used reproach especially in political or economic analysis, is "to lump together facts, ideas, or aspects that should be kept separate" or "to make an unjustified connection among them." *Il faudrait éviter de faire l'amalgame entre les chiffres du **chômage** en France et les chiffres de l'**immigration.** *"Statistics on unemployment should not be taken in conjunction with statistics on immigration." *Certains syndicalistes ont tendance à faire l'amalgame entre des revendications légitimes et des revendications fantaisistes;* "Some union activists are inclined to confuse legitimate demands with more far-fetched ones."

*Lors de la commémoration de **Clovis** en 1996 on a vu un certain nombre d'intellectuels et de politiques faire un amalgame entre cet événement religieux et le principe de la **laïcité;*** "In 1996, when the 1,500th anniversary of Clovis's anointment was being observed, quite a few intellectuals and politicians tried to create a link between what had been a religious event and the republican principle of secularity."

américain A sharp distinction is made by some linguists, publishers, and others between British English (*l'anglais*) and American English (*l'américain*). French translations of American authors are generally marked *"traduit de l'américain."*

AMI (m.) *Accord multilatéral sur l'investissement,* Multilateral Agreement on Investment (MAI). *Au début de 1998, cet accord l'AMI était en train d'être négocié au sein de l'OCDE, une organisation intergouvernementale dont les 29 pays membres (y compris les Etats-Unis et la France) sont tous des pays industrialisés.* By early 1998, the MAI was being negotiated within the Organization for Economic Cooperation and Development (OECD), an IGO whose twenty-nine member countries (including the United States and France) are all industrialized nations.

*En France l'AMI a été vivement attaqué dans certains médias et par des cinéastes et autres créateurs, qui voyaient en cet accord un instrument pour protéger des multinationales et les investisseurs étrangers (surtout américains) contre les investisseurs à l'intérieur de chaque pays et pour bafouer les lois nationales et les règlements de la future Europe. L'accord paraissait comme la quintessence de la mondialisation prônée par les "néo-libéraux" et la **pensée unique** portant atteinte à la souveraineté des peuples, aux droits des citoyens et à l'**exception française;*** "In France the MAI came under fierce attack in some of the media and by filmmakers and other artists, who viewed the agreement as a tool to protect multinational corporations and foreign (especially American) investments against domestic investors in each country and to ride roughshod over national legislation and the future European regulations. The agreement appeared to epitomize the globalization favored by the 'neoliberals' and the **pensée unique,** endangering national sovereignty, citizens' rights, and French identity." By spring 1998, reaction against the MAI from France, the United States, and other countries had become so strong that the negotiations were postponed.

amiante (f.) Asbestos. See **désamianter**

amnistie (f.) Amnesty. *Les Députés viennent de se voter une amnistie dans toutes les affaires de corruption de ces deux dernières années;* "The members of the *Assemblée nationale* have just voted into law an amnesty for themselves concerning all the corruption scandals of the last two years."

amont, en Upstream. *Souvent les fabricants cherchent à fusionner avec leurs fournisseurs en amont ou à contrôler une part importante de leur capital;* "Manufacturers often try to merge with their suppliers upstream or to acquire a controlling share in their capital." Downstream is *"en aval."*

amphétamine (f.) Amphetamine.

anabolisant (m.) Anabolic steroid.

ancien combattant (m.) War veteran. *Tous les ans, au 11 novembre, les anciens combattants de la grande guerre sont à l'honneur;* "Every year on Armistice Day, World War I veterans are honored."

anglo-saxon If you are reading this book in English, you are presumably *un(e) anglo-saxon(ne).* Any native English speaker is one, although the term once referred to the British more than to Americans. One radio station offers *une revue de la presse anglo-saxonne* every morning, including the *International Herald Tribune,* the *New York Times,* the *Washington Post,* and the *Wall Street Journal* as well as the British press. There is *la littérature anglo-saxonne, la culture anglo-saxonne,* and so on. However, there is no such phrase as *la cuisine anglo-saxonne* since, *"par définition, les anglo-saxons ne savent pas faire la cuisine"* (*sic*).

annualisation (f.) **de l'emploi** This demand was made by the *CFDT* (see **syndicat**) in the mid-1990s on behalf of dockworkers in Marseilles who were being hired only on an occasional or seasonal basis; the *CFDT* wanted them to be hired on a full-year basis. The word was again in the news in 1997, in connection with the **Conférence nationale sur l'emploi, les salaires, et le temps de travail,** a top-level gathering of unions, employers, workers, and government officials.

See also **la mensualisation**

ANPE (f.) The *Agence nationale pour l'emploi,* created in 1967, to assist people who are looking for work, professional training, or advice and to foster *la mobilité géographique et l'adaptation aux emplois.* Today, anyone who becomes unemployed must register with the *ANPE* before he or she can be entitled to receive *des allocations chômage* or to do a paid training period in any branch (*faire un stage d'informatique, par exemple*).

antidépresseur (m.) Antidepressant; also *euphorisant* (m.). *Tranquillisant* (m.), tranquilizer. *Somnifère* (m.), sleeping pill. Statistics show that the French are the largest consumers of such products in all of Europe.

antigang (adj. and f.) *La brigade de recherche et d'intervention,* a part of the police more familiarly known as *la brigade antigang* (or *l'antigang*), "the gangbusters."

août The missing month in the French calendar because so many people go away on vacation; they become *des aoûtiens* (pronounced "ah-oo-sien"). Signs on shop doors will inform you, *"Fermeture annuelle du 1er au 28 août";* a few factories shut down for the month. *Les parcmètres à Paris sont gratuits au mois d'août;* "You don't have to put money in the parking meters in Paris in August." But try to get your shoes repaired or your clothes cleaned in August. Try to find *une boulangerie ouverte, une boucherie ouverte, un marchand de vins ouvert* in August. Try to order wallpaper, take delivery of a new car, or have the *électricien* or the *menuisier* come in August: you'll probably have to wait until *la rentrée* (i.e., September).

On the last weekend in July or the first one in August, the media will warn about *le chassé-croisé des juilletistes et des aoûtiens,* "the two-way pattern of very heavy traffic" as many people come back from vacation while equally many leave on vacation.

apaiser To appease, cool things down; *calmer les esprits* is another way of saying it. *Dans les négociations avec les routiers, le gouvernement a joué l'apaisement dans la fermeté à cause du climat social tendu;* "When bargaining with the teamsters, the government tried to defuse the situation yet remain firm because the labor relations situation is so tense."

apnée (f.) *La plongée en apnée,* skin diving without an oxygen supply.

Apostrophes Perhaps the best-known literary talk show on French TV. It began in the late 1970s and ran for over fifteen years. Its formula was very simple: the host, Bernard Pivot, invited three or four authors and questioned them on their own and each other's latest books. His name became a household word. There were and still are other shows along similar lines (*Ex libris, Jamais sans mon livre, A quel titre,* etc.). After a brief pause, Pivot launched a new show called *Bouillon de culture* that tried—briefly—to get away from books per se and cover other types of entertainment, but it quickly bowed to *la demande générale* and now uses *une formule quasi-identique à l'ancienne.* See **dictée; orthographe**

appel (m.) **de Cochin** A speech made by Jacques Chirac, then mayor of Paris, in 1978, at a time when he had broken his leg and was forced to enter *l'hôpital Cochin* in Paris. The speech was a manifesto against the pro-European policy of then President Valéry Giscard d'Estaing, whose *Premier ministre* Chirac had been from 1974 to 1976. In 1978 Chirac was resolutely opposed to *la **construction de l'Europe*** and to France's submersion in it; see **inféoder.** The speech was dubbed *l'appel de Cochin* by analogy with *l'**Appel du 18 juin*** by Charles de Gaulle.

Appel (m.) **du 18 juin** In mid-June 1940, after German armed forces entered France and overpowered the French army, an armistice was declared. Charles de Gaulle, then a colonel, refused to accept the armistice and left for England to form a free French government in exile. From London, by radio, he issued an appeal to the French people, saying, among other things, *"La France a perdu une bataille, mais elle n'a pas perdu la guerre";* "'France has lost a battle, but it has not lost the war'." Although very few people in France heard the speech on the day it was broadcast, it has been invoked countless times since as exemplifying the French resistance spirit, particularly by those *qui se réclament du Gaullisme,* "who claim to continue in the Gaullist tradition."

See **Pétain, Philippe**

apport (m.) **personnel** When you wish to buy a house or apartment, this is the down payment you must be able to make from your own funds (*ce que vous apportez*), 10 or 20 percent of the total price, in addition to whatever loans you may obtain.

apprécier Both to appreciate (to be grateful) and to appreciate in value. *Le franc s'apprécie par rapport au DM;* "The franc is increasing in value against the deutsche mark."

après-guerre (m.) With reference to events concerning France, this generally means the post–World War II period; it is not usually related to *la guerre d'Indochine,* which ended in 1954, or *la guerre d'Algérie,* ended in 1962. *Après* has, however, become the prefix in a number of more recent words coined in the same way: *l'après-de Gaulle, l'après-Mitterrand, l'après-Dayton (accords de paix en ex-Yougoslavie, négociés à Dayton dans l'Ohio en 1995).*

aquaplaning (m.) *Faire de l'aquaplaning* is not a sport! It is what a car is said to do *quand elle dérape,* "when it skids" on water kicked up by the car ahead of it or by rain on the road.

Arabe (m. or f.) Because of the very strong influx of people from the former French colonies in North Africa, an Arab population of approximately two and a half million is now living in France. *Arabe* is often used interchangeably with *musulman(e).* When said by certain French persons, *Arabe* can be distinctly scornful, as in *Les Arabes sont tous les mêmes, Qu'est-ce que viennent faire les Arabes chez nous?* and so forth.

Le petit Arabe du coin refers—semitolerantly, semicondescendingly—to "the little grocery shop at the corner" that is almost invariably run by Tunisians or Moroccans and stays open until *22 heures* or *23 heures* (and often on Sundays), whereas in town *le supermarché* or *la superette* will close at about *19h30* or *20h* on weekdays and at *13h* or all day on Sundays. See **Maghrébin(e)**

ARC (f.) *Association pour la recherche sur le cancer.* The association was the subject of a major scandal in 1994 when it was alleged that a disproportionately large percentage of the funds donated to this nonprofit organization, ostensibly devoted to research and preventive treatment, had been used to cover its running expenses and/or embezzled by its director. *D'autres organismes caritatifs et de recherche avaient peur d'être éclaboussés par ces accusations contre l'ARC;* "Other charitable and research organizations were afraid of being suspected of similar misdoings and therefore of receiving fewer donations." See **caritatif(ive)**

argent (m.) **sale** Money that needs to be laundered, money derived from dubious sources. See **blanchir**

Ariane (f.) *Le programme Ariane* is the European space rocket program. *La base de lancement des fusées Ariane est située à Kourou, en Guyane française;* "The Ariane rockets are launched from Kourou, in French Guiana." *Le pas de tir,* launching pad. *La fenêtre de tir, durée pendant laquelle le lancement de la fusée est possible,* period of hours or days during which the rocket can be launched. See **programme spatial**

-ariat or **-at** A useful masculine suffix when you want to form a collective noun. *Le salariat* comprises all wage earners, considered as a whole. *Le partenariat,* "partnership," as, for instance, between *l'Etat* and private enterprise in launching a given project. *Le patronat,* "employers" (patrons) as a whole; *le CNPF* is the influential *Conseil national du patronat français. Le lectorat,* "readership" (of a journal or periodical). *L'assistanat* (m.), the fact of relying on government allowances—that is, *être assisté(e)(s)* in order to survive. *Vedettariat* (m.), all *vedettes,* "stars"; or the status of being *une vedette.*

Arlésienne (f.) Something that is invisible or that never materializes is said to be like *l'Arlésienne* in the opera of the same name (music by Bizet, book by Daudet) because she never appears on stage.

armée (f.) **de métier** An army of career soldiers, as opposed to an army of *appelés sous les drapeaux*—that is, *conscrits;* "draftees." Early in 1996 President Jacques Chirac announced that he intended to do away with *le service militaire,* "the draft," before the end of the century. Two of the main reasons for the change were *une réduction des dépenses* and *une restructuration.* Another aim was to achieve *la professionnalisation de l'armée* on a volunteer basis. *La durée du service militaire obligatoire* had gradually been reduced from about two and a half years in the period ended by the **accords d'Evian** to ten months at the time of Chirac's announcement.

He further announced that he wished to replace *le service militaire* by some form of *service civil,* which would involve women also. Each young person would have to take part in a week-long *rendez-vous* (m.) *citoyen* involving instruction in civics. Until then, each prospective draftee had had to appear before *un conseil de révision,* "draft board," and *faire "ses trois jours."* This preliminary usually lasted a day and a half; the prospective draftee took *des tests d'aptitude* and indicated *dans quelle arme il voulait faire son service,* in which branch he wanted to do his stint. Once actually *incorporé,* "inducted," the draftee had to *faire ses classes,* go through three months of military training and theory, then complete the remainder of the ten-month period.

The law voted in late 1997 *concernant la suppression du service militarie en 2002 et la professionnalisation de l'armée* stipulated that *les appelés disposant d'un emploi seraient dispensés du service,* "draftees who had a job would be exempt from the draft." Nothing more was said about *un rendez-vous citoyen* or about women.

Les armes sont l'armée de terre, "army"; *l'armée de mer* or *Marine nationale,* "navy"; *l'armée de l'air,* "air force"; and *les chasseurs* (m. pl.) *alpins,* "mountain infantry." *La grande muette* is an unofficial name for "the army."

armes (f. pl.) Weapons. *Armes à feu,* firearms, guns. *Armes blanches,* knives, swords, and the like. *La détention d'armes et le port d'armes sont soumis à déclaration ou à autorisation;* "You cannot own a gun or carry a gun unless it has been registered or unless you have a permit" (*un permis de* **port** **d'armes**). *Les personnes qui sont détentrices d'armes à feu sont invitées à se mettre en règle,* "Individuals owning guns are requested/required to report them to the authorities." *Armes nucléaires,* nuclear weapons. *Armes conventionnelles,* conventional weapons. *Arme de poing,* handgun.

Armor The old Celtic name, now nostalgic, for the coastal part of the region that corresponded to today's Bretagne. *Côtes d'Armor* (called *Côtes du Nord* until 1990), one of the present-day *départements* comprising Brittany. *Arcoat* referred to the forest, but the word has dropped out of use today. *Armorique,* name of Brittany as a whole until the seventh century. *Radio*

France Armorique, a Breton radio station today. *La Bretagne bretonnante,* the part of Brittany (essentially the west) where Breton is still spoken to some extent.

arnaque (f.) A swindle. *Une des plus grandes arnaques, du point de vue des chômeurs, disent certains économistes, est le fait que les étudiants sont de plus en plus nombreux à effectuer des stages non rémunérés dans les entreprises—ce qui dispense les patrons d'engager des personnes sur une base rémunérée pour faire le même travail;* "One of the biggest ripoffs from the standpoint of jobless people, say certain economists, is that there are more and more students doing unpaid internships in companies—which means that those companies don't need to hire anyone on a paid basis to do the work."

arraisonner To board and inspect a vessel because of official suspicion of wrongdoing or potential health problems. *Un chalutier espagnol accusé d'avoir pêché dans les eaux territoriales françaises a été arraisonné par la marine française;* "A Spanish fishing boat accused of having fished in French territorial waters was boarded and inspected by French naval officers."

arrestation (f.) **musclée** A euphemism for what occasionally happens in response to a protest movement. *Au cours de la manifestation les forces de l'ordre ont procédé à quelques arrestations musclées,* "During the demonstration, the police used physical force or intimidation when taking individuals into custody." See **bavure**

arrêt (m.) **de travail** If you are sick or injured and therefore unable to go to work, your doctor will give you an *arrêt de travail de 48 heures, de huit jours,* or whatever period. During that time you must stay home and are allowed to go out only between 10 A.M. and noon and between 4 P.M. and 6 P.M.—that is, long enough to do your food shopping or pick up your prescription but not long enough to go to the movies. This is (theoretically) so that an inspector from the *Sécurité sociale* may come around and check that you really have a valid medical reason for not being at work.

arroser To water plants; and by extension, to pay a bribe, *verser un pot de vin.* For instance, *un entrepreneur peut être tenté d'arroser des conseillers municipaux,* "a contractor can be tempted to bribe the town councillors."

Of course, *arroser* also means "to celebrate with wine or champagne." *Une bonne nouvelle! Ça s'arrose!*

Arte Franco-German television channel conceived as a public service cultural channel that would carry no advertising. The aim is to create greater understanding between two countries that were at war with one another three times (1870, 1914–1918, and 1940–1945) in three generations.

First there was *La Sept (Société d'édition et de programma-*

tion de télévision), created in 1986; then *Arte* (Association relative aux télévisions européennes) in 1990. The German end of *Arte* was created in 1991, and in 1992 *Arte* was launched in France. *En principe* all films are shown *en version originale,* "undubbed"; thus, a Chinese film will be subtitled in French in France and in German in Germany. It will be shown at the same time on the same day in both countries.

Article 49.3 (m.) *Si le gouvernement invoque l'Article 49.3,* that means the government is using that section of the Constitution to try to force passage of a bill through *l'Assemblée nationale.* The article provides that if the government decides to stake its survival on the passage of a given bill, the measure is adopted without even having been voted on in the parliament unless a motion of censure is deposited within twenty-four hours and passed by an absolute majority of *les Députés.* Between 1958, when *la Cinquième République* began, and 1995, successive governments made use of this vote-of-confidence mechanism nearly eighty times.

arts (m. pl.) **martiaux** The martial arts: *l'aïkido* (m.), *le judo, le karaté, le tae kwendo, le tai chi,* and so forth. *Ceinture* (f.) *noire,* black belt.

Assedic (f.) *Associations pour l'emploi dans l'industrie et le commerce,* stemming from a 1958 agreement between the **CNPF** (the **patronat**) and the **syndicats** to create a form of unemployment insurance; the full name is virtually never used. Today *l'Assedic* manages the payment of *les allocations chômage,* "unemployment benefits." *Toucher les Assedic* is a widespread though unofficial way of saying *recevoir une allocation chômage. Les bureaux de l'Assedic* have become a sadly familiar feature of most *arrondissements* in Paris and every major *commune* throughout France. See **ANPE; chômage; revendications sociales des chômeurs**

assiette (f.) **fiscale** Tax base (nothing to do with *une assiette plate, assiette creuse, assiette à dessert,* and other items of tableware).

assistanat (m.) Collective noun covering *tous les **assistés.** Une société fraternelle qui refuse l'assistanat, c'est ce que réclament ceux qui déplorent la disparité entre les riches et les pauvres;* "A (more) brotherly society in which no one has to be on welfare is the goal of people who reject the gap between rich and poor."

assisté(e)(s) *Un(e) assisté(e)* is a welfare-dependent person, *une personne qui ne vit que d'allocations.* French farmers, protesting vigorously against European legislation requiring them to plant less and let fields lie fallow in exchange for a government allowance, have stated, *"Nous ne voulons pas avoir une mentalité d'assistés."*

assouplissement (m.) To make something less stringent. *L'assou-*

plissement des **critères de convergence** *est une des grandes questions du jour;* "Whether to make the **Maastricht** criteria less demanding is one of the major issues of the day." In the physical sense, *l'assouplissement* can be "gymnastics" or "any physical exercise to make muscles less stiff."

ATOS (m. pl.) *Les administratifs, techniques, ouvriers de service—* that is, ancillary, nonacademic employees in the education system.

atteinte (f.) An attack on or attempt to harm something. *Les commentaires de Jean-Marie Le Pen en septembre 1996 sur* **les iné-galités de race** *ont été dénoncés par les organismes antiracistes comme une atteinte à la dignite humaine;* "In September 1996, when Jean-Marie Le Pen made his comments on the inequalities between the races, they were denounced by antiracism associations as an attack on human dignity."

attentat (m.) The meaning that comes most readily to mind today is "terrorist attack." See **Algérie; Port Royal**

audimat® (m.) TV ratings. *Hier soir, la finale hommes à Roland Garros a atteint 34,3 (trente-quatre virgule trois) à l'audimat alors que le discours présidential n'a atteint que 12,6;* "Last night the men's finals in tennis at **Roland Garros** got a TV rating of 34.3 whereas the President's speech got only 12.6."

The word *audimat* derives from *Audimétrie* (f.) *foyer,* a system introduced in 1981 that, on the basis of 650 *foyers,* "households," measured the number of those households watching any given TV show but was not designed to indicate the type or number of individuals involved. In 1989 the present system, *l'audimétrie individuelle,* was introduced; it relies on 2,300 households comprising nearly 5,700 individuals aged four or over. The word *audimat* has remained in use. *La part d'audience,* "audience share," is expressed in percentages (12.6 percent, 34.3 percent, etc.); 1 percent is taken to be 514,500 individuals aged four or over.

auteur (m.) Used much more widely than in English, to mean not only a writer but also the person responsible for or having originated something in any field. *Il n'y a aucune indication sur les circonstances de ce meurtre ni sur son (ses) auteur(s),* "There is no clue as to the circumstances in which this murder took place or who committed it." *Qui est l'auteur de ce projet farfelu?* "Who's behind this goofy idea?"

automobile (m.) Car manufacturing as a whole. *L'automobile est un secteur en crise.*

autonomes (m. pl.) People who take part in a demonstration without being affiliated with a specific union or student organization. Also, *les travailleurs autonomes,* self-employed persons.

autoroute (f.) Expressway or superhighway. All of them require payment of *un péage,* "a toll." *Faire l'appoint,* to have exact change. *Sortie* (f.), exit. *Bretelle* (f.), access road. *La vitesse est limitée à 130 kilomètres heure par temps sec, à 110 en cas de pluie;* "The speed limit is eighty miles per hour in good weather and about seventy miles per hour when it rains." *Contrôle* (m.) *radar,* radar speed check. *Péage* (m.) *à 800 m;* "Toll booth ½ mile." *Il est interdit de rouler sur la bande d'urgence;* "No driving allowed in the emergency lane." *Rétrécissement* (m.) *de la chaussée;* "Road narrows ahead." *Travaux—Rouler lentement;* "Work going on ahead—Drive slow." *Route* (f.) *à six voies,* six-lane highway. *Essence* (f.) *sans plomb, super* (m.) *sans plomb 98, super sans plomb 95,* unleaded gasoline. *Super,* leaded gasoline. *Gas-oil* or *gazole,* diesel. *GPL, gaz pétrole liquéfié. Vérifier l'huile* (f.) *et la pression des pneus,* to check the oil and the tire pressure. See **aire de repos**

autoroutes (f. pl.) **de l'information** Information superhighways. *Circuler sur les autoroutes de l'information.* See **Internet**

avion (m.) **furtif** Stealth plane.

avionneur (m.) Commonly used term for aircraft manufacturers, instead of *fabricant d'avions.* See **Airbus Industrie; Aérospatiale**

Avoriaz Ski resort in the French Alps (*Haute Savoie*) and host to an annual *festival* (m.) *du film d'horreur.*

avortement (m.) Abortion. The medical term is *une interruption volontaire de grossesse (IVG). Avortement spontané,* the medical term for a miscarriage—a natural (i.e., noninduced) abortion. In layperson's terms, to have a miscarriage is *faire une fausse couche. Commando* (m.) *anti-IVG,* group of antiabortionists that enters or tries to enter a clinic or hospital so as to obstruct procedures or damage equipment.

Some key dates: 1971: *le Manifeste des 343 françaises reconnaissant nommément s'être fait avorter,* a manifesto by 343 Frenchwomen who admitted that they had had an abortion was published, giving their names, in the weekly news magazine *le Nouvel Observateur.* 1972: in *le procès de Bobigny,* a young woman who had had an abortion after having been raped was tried at Bobigny along with her mother, considered her accomplice; they were acquitted. 1974: *la loi Veil autorise l'IVG,* the (Simone) Veil law made abortion legal. 1982: *la loi Roudy: l'IVG est remboursée par la Sécurité sociale,* the cost of an abortion would be refunded by the *Sécurité sociale.* 1987: *premiers commandos anti-IVG,* the first anti-abortion groups took action. 1993: *la loi punit toute entrave à l'avortement,* any attempt to hinder an abortion was made a punishable offense.

An abortion must be performed in a hospital or clinic and generally before the end of the tenth week of pregnancy, but it may be carried out at any stage if two doctors certify that the pregnancy is dangerous for the woman or the infant. In nonurgent cases the woman goes through *trois consultations de médecin successives et trois périodes de réflexion* before the final decision is made. Doctors can opt to refuse to perform an abortion (*la clause de conscience*). See ***IVG***

axe (m.) **franco-allemand** Diplomatic partnership between France and Germany, considered by French officials to be the linchpin of European diplomacy and political development.

axe (m.) **rouge** A traffic control measure introduced in Paris in the early 1990s; a street designated as *un axe rouge* is a main artery on which all parking is strictly forbidden at all times. If you are rash enough to park there anyhow, *votre voiture risque fort d'être emmenée à la fourrière,* your car is likely to be towed away to the pound.

B

babyfoot® (m.) Miniature soccer, like U.S. foosball; a standard feature of many a café and playground. Two or more players gather on either side of a sort of table slightly smaller than a pinball machine; each player maneuvers the projecting end of a rod linking a number of miniature soccer players, about eight inches high; several rods make up an eleven-man team, and each team tries to get the ball through the goal of the opposite team, facing it. See **ballon rond**

Bac + 2 or + 3, etc. *Le Bac* is *le Baccalauréat,* the nationwide exam that all *lycéens* must take, in two parts: *le Bac français* at the end of *la première* (eleventh grade), and then the exam in all other subjects at the end of the next year, *la terminale* (twelfth grade). Early in the 1990s the government announced that its goal was to see *80% de lycéens réussir leur Bac. Par conséquent, le fait d'avoir son Bac ne suffit plus pour rendre un jeune apte à l'emploi;* "As a result, the fact of having le Bac is no longer enough to qualify young people for jobs." *Il faut qu'ils aient un Bac + 2;* "They must be able to demonstrate that they have studied at university level for two years after getting their Bac"; or *Bac + 3,* for three years, which generally takes them through le ***DEUG*** or *la Licence;* or *Bac + 4,* and so on.

   La BAC (Brigade Anti-Criminalité) is a section of the police; its members volunteer for this special duty and are trained to deal with violence in *les **banlieues.***

bain (m.) **de foule** *Prendre un bain de foule* is said of a politician who "works" a crowd. *Jacques Chirac n'est jamais aussi heu-*

reux que quand il prend un bain de foule et il serre la main à tout le monde; "Chirac is never so happy as when he plunges right into the crowd, shaking hands with everyone."

baisser le pantalon A pretty vulgar phrase, meaning to give in, show weakness, be made a fool of. During the GATT negotiations in December 1993, one commentator said heatedly, *"Pour la France il s'agit de ne pas baisser le pantalon devant les Américains."*

baissier (m.) A bear, *quelqu'un qui pense que les cours de la Bourse vont baisser,* "someone who believes that stock market prices are going to decline." *Par contre, un haussier is a bull, puisqu'il estime que la tendance à la Bourse est à la hausse.*

baladeur (m.) The name officially bestowed on the Walkman® by the *Délégation générale de la langue française,* the French government committee in charge of devising—and stipulating the use of—words in French to supplant or prevent the use of words borrowed from English. Although a pleasing word, from *se balader,* "to stroll or go on an excursion," it has not caught on enough to oust *un walkman, des walkman.* See **Conseil supérieur de la langue française**

This term should not be confused with Edouard Balladur, prime minister from 1993 to 1995; because he was the leader at that time of the *UDF* party, it was widely assumed that he would be *le candidat unique de la droite* in the 1995 *elections présidentielles*—until Jacques Chirac, leader of the *RPR* and mayor of Paris, came from behind and became a candidate as well *au premier tour du scrutin,* "on the first round of voting," then *le seul candidat de la droite au deuxième tour.*

balayer devant sa porte To clean up one's own act. Talking about *l'intégrisme en Algérie et en Irak,* one commentator said, *"Ici en France il faut balayer devant notre porte."*

balbutier To stammer, to be in infancy. *Dans l'industrie en France, comparée à d'autres pays, la sous-traitance est balbutiante;* "French industry, compared with industry in other countries, is only just beginning to subcontract."

ballon (m.) **rond** Ball used in European football (soccer). *Ballon ovale,* ball used in American football or in rugby.

ballottage (m.) The situation that arises in an election when none of the candidates has a clear or sufficient majority, so that a further round of voting—*tour* (m.) *de scrutin*—is needed. *Etre en ballottage se dit principalement pour un(e) candidat(e) sortant(e) ou pour un(e) candidat(e) qui a été parachuté(e) et qui est une personnalité connue;* "The phrase is used chiefly when the candidate is an outgoing officeholder or when he or she has been slotted into the district by the party and is a well-known figure." (See **parachutage.**) *Le candidat écologiste est en ballottage favorable après le premier tour;* "The environmentalist candidate must face a second round of voting but looks likely to be elected." *Etre en ballottage difficile* or *défavorable,* to seem to stand little chance of winning on the second round.

banaliser To make something banal, ordinary. *"La libération des moeurs banalise le désire,"* declared the weekly *Marianne* in July 1997; "'Sexual freedom makes desire just run of the mill.'" *Une voiture banalisée,* an unmarked (police) car.

bande (f.) **annonce** Preview of a coming film. *Prochainement,* coming soon.

bande (f.) **dessinée** Comic strip. *Album de bandes dessinées,* comic book. *Le festival de la bande dessinée a lieu tous les ans à Angoulême, dans la Charente;* "A comic strip festival takes place in Angoulême, in the *Charente* region, every year."

bande (f.) **de Gaza** The Gaza strip.

bande (f.) **son** Soundtrack.

banderole (f.) Streamer bearing a slogan; what demonstrators (*des manifestants*) carry with them as they march to express their demands. For instance, *Réduction du temps de travail* or *35 heures,* shorter working week (so as to permit the creation of more jobs).

banlieue (f.) Once a relatively neutral word, meaning "suburb" and even "a desirable residential suburb" (*"Ma banlieue, ma banlieue a des charmes que rien ne remplace,"* boasted one old song). In recent years, however, *le terme banlieue(s) est devenu fortement connoté,* "has taken on a heavy connotation," designating housing developments that are just beyond the city limits, that are noted for drab post–World War II architecture, are inhabited almost exclusively by first- and second-generation immigrants, chiefly from former French colonies in Africa, and suffer from a higher-than-average *taux de chômage,* "unemployment rate." It has become a commonplace to say that *la population des banlieues est composée essentiellement de marginaux et d'exclus.* See **exclu(e); marginal**

If someone wishes to say that he or she lives in the suburbs in the old sense of the word, he or she will say, *"J'habite une banlieue résidentielle"* or *"J'habite en dehors de* [or *tout près de*] *Paris, de Toulouse, de Lyon,* etc."

banqueroute (f.) Not just *une faillite* but *une faillite frauduleuse. La banqueroute a été requise contre le PDG de la société;* "A verdict of bankruptcy and fraud was sought against the firm's director."

Barbie, Klaus A World War II German officer in France, known as *le boucher de Lyon,* "the butcher of Lyons," because of the number of people he had arrested and turned over to the Gestapo. See **Jean Moulin**. *En 1983 Barbie a été retrouvé en Bolivie et extradé en France. Pendant son procès, à Lyon, il a refusé* *de parler;* "In 1983 Barbie was traced to Bolivia and extradited to France; during his trial in Lyons, he refused to speak." In 1987 he was sentenced to *la prison à perpétuité,* and in 1991 he died a natural death in prison.

barbouze (f.) Colloquial term used in the 1960s and 1970s for "secret agent."

barbus (m. pl.) Disrespectful and informal name given (by non-Muslims) to *les intégristes,* "fundamentalists," in Muslim countries.

bas de gamme (adj.) Down-market, low end of the quality range. *Haut de gamme* is, of course, the opposite.

bas (m.) **de laine** A woolen sock or stocking; a traditional way of saving money was to put coins aside in *un bas de laine.* Today it has a figurative meaning, as in *Il faudrait que les gens puisent dans leur bas de laine afin de consommer davantage;* "People are being urged to dip into their savings so as to buy more consumer goods."

base (f.) The rank and file. *Le leader syndicaliste est d'accord pour annuler la grève; c'est très bien, mais est-ce qu'il peut se faire obéir par sa base?* "The union's leader has agreed to call off the strike; that's all well and good, but can he get the rank and file to go along with him on that?"

bassin (m.) **Pacifique** Pacific basin. *Le pourtour du bassin Pacifique,* Pacific rim.

bassin (m.) **parisien** A geological and hydrological term for the Paris area.

Bastille The new *Opéra Bastille* was built on the eastern side of the *Place de la Bastille,* in whose center the winged *Génie de la Bastille* is poised high on top of a column. *L'Opéra*'s presence has transformed *le quartier en général,* leading to a certain amount of gentrification.

bâtiment (m.) Short for *l'industrie du bâtiment,* the construction industry. *Quand le bâtiment va, tout va,* the saying goes: "When the building industry is doing all right, everything's going all right." *Le secteur BTP, bâtiment et travaux publics,* construction and public works.

bavure (f.) A euphemism for a regrettable mistake, incident, slip-up, especially *une bavure policière. Le nom de **Malik Oussekine** est parfois évoqué bien que la bavure remonte à la fin de 1986 lors d'une manif dans le Quartier Latin contre une proposition de loi (la loi Devaquet) visant à réformer certains aspects de l'enseignement supérieur; cet étudiant d'origine nord africaine est mort après l'affrontement entre les étudiants et la police;* "The name of Malik Oussekine is sometimes invoked although the incident goes back to late 1986, during a demonstration in the Latin Quarter against a bill (the Devaquet bill) outlining certain reforms concerning higher education; a student of North African origin, he died following the clash between students and the police."

Une bavure can also mean "friendly fire."

BCBG *Bon chic bon genre,* referring to your hair style, choice of clothing and accessories, car, country house, golf course, school, club, and so forth. Associated chiefly with the *16e arrondissement* in Paris and with Neuilly, adjacent to the *16e.* A cross between preppy and yuppie, perhaps. Not to be confused with *le BCG,* the tuberculosis vaccination.

BCE (f.) *Banque centrale européenne,* European Central Bank. Located in Frankfurt, its mission is to manage the euro and keep prices stable throughout the European Union.

BD (f.) *La bande dessinée; un album de BD,* comic book. *Un(e) bédéphile,* someone who loves comic strips; the word is a dubious pun on **pédophile.**

beauf Short for *beau-frère* but can be applied to anyone you consider uncultivated, reactionary, racist, smug, vulgar, dull, or dismally devoted to the delights of the consumer society.

Beauvilliers Although located in the region called *la Beauce,* 20 kilometers from Chartres and 85 kilometers from Paris, it appeared in June 1996 to be the leading contender for the site of the third Paris airport, tentatively scheduled to be built around the year 2015. In the meantime, this project would require setting land aside, *le gel de 3,000 hectares de terres beauceronnes.*

bébé (m.) **éprouvette** Test-tube baby.

Bébête Show, le A TV puppet show of devastating satirical impact that began while François Mitterrand was president. (In some quarters it was even held partly responsible for the death of **Pierre Bérégovoy.**) Its targets were politicians. Mitterrand, dubbed *"Dieu"* because of the way he seemed to conceive his own position, was a wide-mouthed, disdainful frog; Jacques Chirac, his then prime minister during two quasi-bellicose years of "cohabitation" between the Socialist president and the *RPR* leader, was an impatient bird of prey dubbed "Black Jack"; Michel Rocard, a Socialist prime minister who incurred the president's disfavor, was a crow who went around croaking *"Je le hais!"*; Raymond Barre, economics professor and ex–prime minister, a chubby and somewhat sleepy teddy bear; Jack Lang, minister of culture with abundant curly fleecelike hair, a billy goat; Georges Marchais, the Communist Party leader whom the cartoonists loved to hate, was a bourgeois sow with piggish snout and long strands of pearls; and so it went. The show spawned others along similar lines; see *Guignols de l'Info.*

BEI (f.) *La Banque européenne d'investissement.* One of the less known European institutions, it lends money (over 150 billion francs each year, stated the *Nouvel Observateur* in June 1997) to major projects such as high-speed trains and the Channel Tunnel but also to thousands of innovative **PMEs** within the European Union, and it also finances job creation programs.

Belgique To some French people, there is nothing funnier than a Belgian. Belgian eating habits (*"une frite et une moule"*), a Belgian accent, Belgian turns of phrase (*"une fois"*), and so on, are considered fair game. The height of humor is said to be *une histoire belge;* the point is always to emphasize how stupid Belgians are. Puns, even weak ones, are part of the joke. For instance, *Quand un Belge va à la piscine, pourquoi est-ce qu'il aime bien nager sous l'eau? Parce qu'au fond les Belges c'est pas si bête;* "When a Belgian goes to a swimming pool, why does he like to swim underwater? Because at bottom the Belgians are not so dumb."

Other French people realize what Francophone culture owes to Belgian grammarians, writers (Georges Simenon, Hergé), and entertainers (Jacques Brel, Raymond Devos), among others.

belote (f.) A card game. *Belote et rebelote,* a phrase derived from that game, is used by politicians and journalists to mean, "Here we go again" or "Doesn't this sound familiar?"

bémol (m.) A flat, in music; or a deintensifier, as in *"L'Etat restera détenteur de 51% des actions de Renault, ce qui met le bémol à la polémique sur sa privatisation"* (radio news commentator, July 1994); "'The state will continue to own 51 percent of the shares in Renault, which puts a damper on the quarrel over the firm's privatization.'"

bénéficier d'un non-lieu To have your case dismissed for lack of evidence; a phrase often heard in the course of various **affaires.** *Monsieur Untel, actuel Ministre et ancien maire, accusé d'avoir fait faire d'importants travaux dans sa maison de campagne aux frais de la commune, a bénéficié d'un non-lieu;* "The case against Mr. X, currently a minister and former mayor, accused of having extensive work done on his country house at the expense of the local taxpayers, has been dismissed for lack of evidence."

bénévole Both adjective and noun, meaning volunteer (i.e., unpaid). *Une association de médecins bénévoles. Elles sont venues nous aider à titre bénévole. Faire du bénévolat,* to do volunteer work.

Bercy A district of eastern Paris, on the Right Bank, to which the *Ministère des Finances* moved from its grand offices in one wing of the Louvre along the *rue de Rivoli,* when the dusty old *musée du Louvre* was transformed into *le Grand Louvre.* Hence, the word *Bercy* itself is used informally to designate *les Finances,* just as *le quai d'Orsay* stands for *le Ministère des Affaires étrangères; l'Elysée* means the president's offices and official residence in the *Palais de l'Elysée; Matignon* means those of the prime minister at *l'Hôtel Matignon; rue de Valois, le Ministère de la Culture;* and so on.

The government wishes to develop Bercy and the rest of eastern Paris. The site chosen for the new **Bibliothèque de France** is at Tolbiac on the Left Bank, across the Seine from *les Finances,* and the *Palais Omnisports,* built in 1984 to replace the old *Vél d'hiv* (*Vélodrome d'hiver*), of sinister memory, demolished in 1959.

Bérégovoy, Pierre A Socialist prime minister during Mitterrand's second term as president. A self-made man of humble origins, he was widely respected and largely untainted by suspicion of major involvement in *les **affaires.*** His suicide on May 1, 1993, stunned the public.

Bérézina (f.) A river in (present-day) Belarus that Napoleon's troops, *la Grande Armée,* had to cross in November 1812 during *la retraite de Russie,* their retreat from Russia, which was fatal to so many of them. By extension today, *C'est la Bérézina* means "It's harrowing," "It's an ordeal/a defeat." When the value of shares in **Eurodisney** was plummeting in 1994, the *Nouvel Observateur* noted, *"La direction pourtant s'évertue à minimiser cette Bérézina,"* "Yet management is doing all it can to play down the calamity."

berger (m.) *La réponse du berger à la bergère* is the last word of an argument or debate; today, the phrase is used chiefly in a humorous mode, to describe a politician or top business executive replying to another.

best of In the early 1990s, among record and cassette companies, there was a rage for compilations of the work of rock singers and groups. These collections of songs were titled *Best of . . .* or *The Best of . . .* or *Le Best of. . . .* (The French word that might well have been used a few years earlier was *un florilège.*) Fast-food chains got into the act, offering *"un menu Best of."*

A compact disc is *un disque compact* or *un CD,* as opposed to *un disque vinyl, un 33 tours, un disque 30 centimètres,* or *un disque noir. Cassette* (f.) is often written as it is pronounced, *K7.*

bête (f.) *Une bête de scène* is "a born actor" or "a performer who simply cannot possibly keep away from a stage and footlights." Similarly, *une bête de l'informatique* is "a born computer wonk."

béton (m.) Literally, concrete. Figuratively, guaranteed, 100 percent reliable, carved in stone. *La Redoute,* a well-known mail-order house, promised one-day delivery with this slogan: *"24 heures chrono, c'est du béton."*

Bétonner, en termes de football, "in soccer terms," means "to position most of the team in front of *le but* (the goal)."

Le béton is also a synonym for all of the frantic construction of apartment buildings, hotels, and so on, with little or no regard for zoning regulations, along the *Côte d'Azur* and in other resort regions once enjoyed for their unspoiled natural beauty. *Les promoteurs ont bétonné toute la Côte; il n'y a presque plus un mètre carré qui soit intacte;* "Developers have put up high-rises all along the Riviera; there's hardly one square foot that hasn't been spoiled." *Les écologistes déplorent la bétonnisation des stations de ski. Les promoteurs sont atteints de bétonnite.*

beur (m. or f.); sometimes **beure or beurette** (f.) Second-generation **Maghrébin(e)** in France. *De jeunes beurs ont manifesté pour exprimer leur attachement à la nationalité française;* "Young second-generation North Africans staged a demonstration to show how deeply they care about having French nationality." *Un jeune beur a été interpellé par la police;* "A young North African born in France was called in for questioning by the police." *En cherchant un emploi, les beurs doivent lutter contre des stéréotypes et des préjugés;* "When young North Africans born in France go looking for a job, they have to contend with people's preconceived ideas [of Arabs in general]." See **bleu blanc rouge.**

The word *beur* is an example of *le verlan,* a type of language developed in *les banlieues, où tout est dit à l'envers,* where everything is said backward. The word *verlan* itself is the word *l'envers* backward. *Beur* is *Arabe* backward.

bibendum (m.) The Michelin tire company logo, a roly-poly, round-eyed, round-faced figure made of tires; also called *le bonhomme Michelin.* Also, any person shaped in somewhat the same way.

Bibliothèque (f.) **de France** Official name of the new national library, at Tolbiac, on the left bank of eastern Paris, intended to supplement the venerable *Bibliothèque nationale,* on the *rue de Richelieu* on the right bank of central Paris. The new library is unofficially dubbed the *Très grande bibliothèque* (*TGB*), by analogy with the high-speed train, the *train à grande vitesse* (*TGV*).

big (m.) An example of semiassimilated English, as when one chain of hamburger eateries advertised *Offre spéciale: Un big + une frite + une boisson gazeuse;* "One giant burger plus one French fries plus one soft drink."

billet (m.) **vert** The U.S. dollar.

bio (adj.) Organic, as in *la nourriture bio* and *le marché bio.*

biodégradable (adj.) Biodegradable.

bip (m.) **sonore** On telecommunications devices, this is the beep announcing that you can begin to talk. Your friends' *répondeurs,* "answering machines," for instance, may say, *"Soyez gentil de laisser votre message après le bip sonore."*

BIP *Bibliothèque d'Information Publique,* the free public library at the *Centre Georges Pompidou,* better known as *Beaubourg,* in Paris. Each *arrondissement* has its *bibliothèque* open free of charge to residents of the *arrondissement,* but the *BIP* was the first in Paris to be open free of charge to all comers, whereas the old *Bibliothèque nationale* is open essentially to academics and other researchers, and the new *Bibliothèque de France* is not free of charge.

BIRD (f.) *Banque internationale pour la reconstruction et le développement* (the IBRD); pronounced *la beard.*

bison (m.) **futé** An invention of *la prévention routière,* the traffic control and safety authorities: the wise buffalo that finds alternative routes carrying lighter traffic than the autoroutes. *Bison futé vous conseille de partir en vacances avant 16 heures cet après-midi ou après 22 heures. Bison futé vous conseille d'éviter l'autoroute A6 et de prendre l'itinéraire suivant.* One recent ad for the **RATP** showed a bison standing up in a Paris Metro car, wrapped nonchalantly around a pole, and the caption was *"Bison futé."*

black blanc beur See **beur; bleu blanc rouge; pluriel(le)**

blanchir Not simply to bleach. *Blanchir l'argent* is "to launder money"; *le blanchiment de l'argent.* One controversial book, accusing Swiss banks of playing a key role in such operations, was titled *La Suisse lave plus blanc* (a parody of ads for soap powders, *des lessives*). See **argent sale**

blancs et nuls In an election, *les bulletins blancs et nuls* are blank ballots and ballots that are void for various reasons.

bleu blanc rouge The traditional description of *le tricolore,* "the French flag." To describe the demographic pattern of today's France, resulting from immigration, the phrase has been updated by some commentators to *black blanc beur.* See **beur**

bleus (m. pl.) The French soccer team, *"équipe* (f.) *de football,"* at international events such as *la **Coupe du monde,*** and *les Jeux olympiques (J.O.).* See **onze tricolore**

blocage (m.) Similar to *barrage;* see **transports routiers.**

Another meaning can be psychological: *avoir un blocage,* to have a mental block. *Il y a un certain nombre de blocages catégoriels de la société française.*

boeufs-carottes (m. pl.) These are *la police des polices, l'Inspection générale de la police nationale (IGPN),* the disciplinary officers within the police force itself, as distinct from ordinary police, known to the public as *les policiers* or *les agents de police* (familiarly, *les poulets* or *les flics*). To round out the culinary approach to the officers of the law, a police van is familiarly called *un panier à salade!* (Officially it is *un fourgon de police* or *un car de police.*)

However, when you wish to ask *un policier* or *une femme*

policier for directions or other information, you address him or her as *Monsieur/Madame l'agent.*

bogue (m.) **de l'an 2000** The Y2K bug. *Le Monde,* on August 20, 1998, noted: *Les décideurs appréhendent les effets du 1er janvier 2000 sur le fonctionnement des ordinateurs . . . Des "M. Bogue de l'an 2000" ont été nommés dans les grandes entreprises françaises . . . ;* "Each large French firm has put someone in charge of the problem." *Mais la mobilisation semble moins forte dans les petites et moyennes entreprises, par manque d'une communication et d'une information suffisantes.* On July 3, *Le Monde* wrote, *. . . le groupe d'assurances Allianz soulignait la préparation insuffisante des entreprises aux effets du bogue qui, estime-t-il, coûteront 3 600 milliards de francs, soit plus de deux fois le budget de la France;* "The bug's effects, judged the Allianz insurance group, would cost 3,600 billion francs, that is, twice as much as the French national budget."

boisson (f.) **gazeuse** Soft drink; it is sold either *en canette* (f.) (i.e., *en boîte alu*), "in aluminum cans," or *en bouteille.*

boîte (f.) Short for *boîte de nuit,* "nightclub." *Aller danser en boîte. On va en boîte.*

bombe (f.) **à retardement** Time bomb, in both the literal and the figurative senses. *Le maintien de colons sur ce territoire est une bombe à retardement;* "The policy of keeping settlers in those areas is a time bomb."

bonjour les dégâts A phrase that caught on like wildfire around 1985, borrowed from a campaign to urge people to drink moderately: *Un verre de vin ça va, deux verres bonjour les dégâts,* which could be roughly translated as "One glass of wine is OK; two and the damage is here to stay." Variants sprang up instantly: *Bonjour les ennuis, Bonjour les problèmes* ("What a load of problems" or "That's when the problems began"), *Bonjour l'accueil* ("What a bad reception we got"). All very spoken French, somewhat like *Je te raconte pas les dégâts/les ennuis/l'accueil,* which is in use chiefly among the younger generation.

bonnet (m.) **phrygien** This is what **Marianne** always wears. She is cartoonists' shorthand for France (i.e., the French Republic), because *Marianne* was the name of a prorepublican secret society during the Second Empire (1851–1870).

bonus (m.) If you have not had any automobile accidents in the past year, you will be entitled to *un bonus,* "a reduction," on your insurance premium. But if you have had an accident, you'll have to pay *un malus,* "a higher premium."

Bosnie (f.) Much in the news from 1992 on, of course, *à cause de la guerre en ex-Yougoslavie. Bosniaque,* both the people and the adjective. *La Croatie; croate* (adj.). *La Serbie; serbe* (adj.). *Serbo-Croate. La Slovénie; slovène* (adj.). *La Forpronu, force*

de protection des Nations unies, United Nations forces. See
casque bleu

bouchon (m.) *"Faisons le point sur les bouchons en Ile-de-France,"*
croons the radio cheerily every weekday morning until about
9 o'clock: "Here's the latest check on traffic jams in the
greater Paris area."

boucler *Boucler un dossier,* to settle a matter. *Est-ce que le dossier
du **sang contaminé** sera un jour bouclé?*
   Also, to shut off, seal off. *Après chaque attentat en Israël,
on assistait au bouclage des territoires occupés;* "Every time
there's been a terrorist incident, the next step was to shut off
the occupied territories."

bouffe (f.) A very informal term for a meal you prepare yourself.
*Faisons une petite bouffe entre copains. On va se faire une pe-
tite bouffe.*

bouger, se Highly informal version of *se remuer,* "to make an all-
out effort to obtain something." *Tout le monde essaie de se
bouger pour obtenir l'implantation du stade de foot,* said one
commentator in 1993, when several towns were competing to
be chosen as the site of the huge new stadium to be built for
the **Coupe du monde** *de football* en 1998. (Saint-Denis, on the
northern edge of Paris, was selected.) Possibly related to
Bouge de là, an expression of impatience and frustration
(roughly, "get a move on," "do something about it") made
popular by MC Solaar, the best known of *les rappeurs,* "rap
singers," to emerge in the 1990s.

bougnoule (m.) Extremely pejorative word for Arab.

boui-boui (m.) Originally a humble or low-life theater or café concert; today the word designates a very ordinary or dubious restaurant.

Boulogne-Billancourt A suburb on the western edge of Paris, long
synonymous with Renault vehicles because the main Renault
plants were on *l'île Seguin* in the Seine, in Boulogne. They
were closed at the beginning of the 1990s. See **Sochaux**

bousculer To upset the scheduled time frame for something. *Les
Israéliens souhaitent bousculer le calendrier d'Oslo;* "The Is-
raelis want to alter the timetable agreed on in Oslo for reaching a peace agreement."

Bousquet, René During the Vichy period, he was secretary-
general to the head of government for police affairs; although
he was accused after the war of having taken harsh measures
against the *Résistance* and being responsible for the arrest of
many foreign Jews in France by French police officers, he was
given only a suspended sentence. He was later pardoned by
President Pompidou and was a visitor at Mitterrand's country
home at Latché. By 1993 he was one of the few prominent
Vichy figures still alive and free; pressure to bring him to trial

was building up, but he was assassinated at his Paris home in June. See **Papon, Maurice; Touvier, Paul**

braquage (m.) A hold-up. *Braquer une banque.* See **casse**

bras (m.) **de fer** Arm wrestling and, by extension, a struggle to the finish or showdown between political rivals, between labor and management (*les syndicats et les patrons*), and so forth.

bricoler In a positive sense, to be a do-it-yourself specialist; *un bricoleur; le bricolage. C'est un bricoleur de génie; il peut tout créer, tout réparer.*

In an adverse sense, to lack an overall plan, to do something in bits and pieces. *Le dernier projet du gouvernment, c'est du n'importe quoi, c'est du bricolage; il n'y a aucune stratégie d'ensemble;* "The government's latest scheme isn't really a scheme at all; they're just trying a little of this and a little of that."

brigade (f.) **des stups** The narcotics squad; *stups* are *les stupéfiants,* "drugs." *La brigade des stupéfiants a réalisé hier sa plus grosse prise depuis cinq ans: 800 kg d'héroïne pure à l'aéroport de Marignane;* "Yesterday, at the Marseilles airport, the drugs squad seized two thousand pounds of pure heroin, its biggest catch in five years."

brique (f.) Ten thousand francs—that is, *un million d'anciens francs.* Informal term, used to describe large sums, such as the grand prize in a lottery or the price of real estate. *C'est une bagnole sensationnelle, mais évidemment elle coûte vingt briques;* "It's a terrific car, but, then, it does cost two hundred thousand francs/twenty million old francs." Although the shift from *anciens francs* to *nouveaux francs* was made in 1960, by simply dropping two zeroes from every figure in *anciens francs* (i.e., dividing it by 100), older people are still prone to speak in *anciens francs.*

Bruxelles The devil incarnate. It is the headquarters of the *Commission européenne,* nerve center of the *Union européenne.* The commission's decisions regulate every aspect of economic life—including even how *pâté de foie* must be made, what ingredients it should and should not contain, to what temperature they should be heated, and so on—and are therefore perceived by many French people as blatant interference. There was a great outcry at its rumored intention to prohibit all *fromages au lait cru,* "cheeses made from raw milk."

Buba (f.) *La Buba* is the German Bundesbank, closely watched in France by bankers and those responsible for French monetary policy. *La politique du franc fort est étroitement liée à la politique monétaire de la Buba.*

Burger King Fast-food chain that in July 1997 succumbed to the dominant position in France of McDonald's and Quick, a Franco-Belgian chain, and announced that it was withdrawing from the French market. The headline in *Le Monde* was *"Burger King jette l'éponge"* ("throws in the towel"). See **fast food; McDonald's; néfaste food; restauration rapide**

BVP (m.) *Bureau de vérification de la publicité,* an independent self-regulatory body responsible for seeing that ethical standards are maintained in the advertising profession.

C

CAC 40 (m.) Pronounced "cack quarante." *A la Bourse,* "on the Paris stock exchange," *CAC* 40 is the stockbrokers' main index—*indice* (m.) *des compagnies d'agents de change*—indicating the ratio between the instant market valuation of forty leading securities and their reference valuation; it is adjusted twice a minute throughout the day. It is given daily by the media, along with the Dow Jones and several key exchange rates: between the dollar and the yen and between the French franc and the deutsche mark, the pound sterling, the Swiss franc, and the dollar.

Caillou (m.) *Le Caillou* is an unofficial name for *la Nouvelle Calédonie,* a *TOM (un territoire d'outre-mer,* "overseas territory") in the South Pacific.

caisse (f.) Checkout in *un supermarché, un hypermarché, une grande surface,* or *une superette. Caisse à la sortie.* Also, of course, cash register, and cash desk or payment point in any store or shop. The employee who works there is *un(e) caissier(ière).*

    Passer à la caisse, to cough up, pay your debts, literally or figuratively; also, to collect your last paycheck, when you've been dismissed.

caisse (f.) **de retraite** Pension fund to which both employee and employer contribute; but see **fonds de pension.** *Les caisses de retraite sonnent l'alerte dès maintenant: vu l'allongement de l'espérance de vie et l'augmentation du nombre de personnes sans emploi et par conséquent ne cotisant plus aux diverses caisses, elles ne seront peut-être plus en mesure d'assurer le plein versement des retraites au-delà de l'an 2010;* "Pension funds are already beginning to warn the public that what with the increase in life expectancy and in the number of people who are jobless and therefore no longer paying in to the funds, they may not be able to pay out full pensions after the year 2010."

caisse (f.) **noire** Slush fund. *On a parlé de caisse noire à propos* *de certains dirigeants d'équipe de football professionnel;* "The managers of certain professional soccer teams were accused of having slush funds."

calendrier (m.) **de Maastricht** Timetable for completing each step laid down in the 1992 **Traité de Maastricht** for achieving complete European union and launching the single currency, *la monnaie unique,* in 1999.

Calment, Jeanne Died in Arles in 1997 at the age of 122; she was born in Arles in 1875 and spent her entire life there. Until then the French media had proudly called her *la doyenne de l'humanité,* "the oldest living human being in the world."

calmer les esprits (pl.) Also *calmer le jeu,* "to cool things off." *Le gouvernement a fait un geste pour calmer les esprits;* "The government made a gesture to keep the situation from becoming explosive."

caméscope (m.) Camcorder; video camera.

camouflet (m.) Slap in the face. When the European authorities ruled that Renault could not simply shut down its Belgian factory as it had announced (see **Vilvoorde**), the decision was reported in France as *un camouflet pour Renault.*

camper sur ses positions To remain firm, not change one's attitude. *Dans cette dispute entre la France et les Etats-Unis sur la défense du sud de l'Europe dans le cadre de l'**OTAN,** chacun campe sur ses positions, et le compromis semble exclu;* "In this dispute between France and the United States on NATO's defense of southern Europe, neither side is prepared to budge an inch, and compromise seems to be out of the question."

camps (m. pl.) This has nothing to do with summer camp, *une colonie de vacances. Les camps* always refers to *les camps de concentration.*

Canaques (m. pl.) The Melanesian population of *la Nouvelle Calédonie;* also written *Kanaks. Les Caldoches* (m. pl.), the white New Caledonians.

candidat(e) unique When there are several factions or splinter groups within a party or political movement, each with its own candidate in a given election, they (or some of them) attempt sooner or later to select a single candidate, *un(e) candidat(e) unique,* so as to have some chance of winning a useful percentage *des suffrages exprimés,* "of the votes recorded." *Les candidats en surnombre se désistent en faveur d'un candidat unique;* "The surplus candidates withdraw in favor of a single candidate."

Canebière (f.) The most famous avenue in Marseilles, as identifiable to any French person as *les Champs-Elysées* in Paris or *la Croisette* in **Cannes.**

Cannes Site of a major *festival de cinéma tous les ans au mois de mai. Les médias regorgent de photos des vedettes sur la*

Croisette, qui longe la mer comme la promenade des Anglais à Nice.

canon (m.) **à eau** Water cannon, which may be used to discourage or disperse a crowd *quand une manif déborde,* "when a demonstration gets out of hand."

CAO (f.) *Conception assistée par ordinateur,* computer-aided design. See **PAO; TAO**

carambolage (m.) A term borrowed from billiards but most often used to designate a mass pile-up of cars. *Le brouillard serait à l'origine du carambolage qui s'est produit sur l'A10 ce soir, à hauteur de Saintes;* "Fog seems to have been responsible for a mass collision tonight on the A10 expressway, near Saintes."

carburant (m.) Generally refers to liquid fuel for cars and airplanes, including *l'essence sans plomb,* unleaded gasoline; *le super,* leaded gasoline; and *le gazole/le gas-oil/le diesel. Le prix des carburants augmentera de 3% à partir du 1er juin;* "Gasoline prices will go up 3 percent as of June 1." Gasoline is sold by the liter in France, and consumption is measured in *litres au cent kilomètres. En ville ma voiture consomme dix litres au cent, mais sur autoroute ça descend à huit litres seulement;* "In town my car uses up ten liters per 100 kilometers, but on the expressway it uses only eight liters." Gasoline in France costs between three and four times as much as in the United States; over 80 percent of its price consists of taxes.

carcan (m.) Anything that is rigid or constraining. Some economists talk about *le carcan des marchés,* meaning that in shaping their employment policies, companies feel bound, above all, to obey what the stock market seems to demand; see **pensée unique**

caritatif(ive) Charitable, as in *une organisation caritative.* See **ARC**

carnet (m.) **de commandes** Order book. *Pour maintenir l'emploi, il est impératif que les entreprises puissent remplir leur carnet de commandes;* "If companies are to avoid shedding jobs, they must be able to fill their order books." *Grâce à ce nouveau paquebot, les chantiers navals de St. Nazaire auront leur carnet de commandes rempli pour les deux années à venir;* "Thanks to this new ocean liner, the shipyards in St. Nazaire will be working to full capacity for the next two years."

Carpentras Small city in Provence that belonged to the papacy for over five centuries (until 1791) and has a sizable Jewish community dating back to that period. The entire country, therefore, was shocked when in 1990 several tombs in the Jewish cemetery were *profanées,* "desecrated." The *Front national* was immediately suspected. Later it was said that some *lycéens* were responsible instead. At the end of July 1996, *coup de théâtre,* "a dramatic surprise": *un skin(head), membre d'un* *parti néonazi, a avoué que lui et d'autres personnes d'extrème droite étaient responsables;* "a skinhead who was a member of a neo-Nazi party came forward and admitted that he and other individuals on the far right were to blame."

carré (m.) **blanc** A white square at the bottom of your TV screen used to mean that the film you were watching was meant for adult viewing only. Now replaced by *une nouvelle signalétique.*

Carrefour (m.) **du développement** At the center of one of the *affaires retentissantes* (see **affaires**) in 1986. Charles Pasqua, then *Ministre de l'intérieur,* was accused of having issued (or having had issued) a passport in the course of the *affaire* to one of the main figures involved. It became famous as *le vrai faux passeport.*

carte (f.) **à mémoire, carte à puce** Memory chip card.

carte (f.) **de crédit, carte bancaire** It is linked directly to your **compte courant,** and functions as a debit card, in that the full amount of your purchase is deducted from that account at one time, either on the date of purchase or at the end of the month.

Le crédit can mean simply "borrowing" (*demander un prêt, emprunter, faire un emprunt*) or "installment buying," not necessarily involving a credit card. See **surendettement**

carte (f.) **grise** Registration paper for your car. It does not need to be renewed every year. See **vignette automobile,** however.

carte (f.) **magnétique** Magnetic card (i.e., personalized microchip) card replacing keys for the purpose of opening garage doors, office doors, and so on; *l'utilisateur place la carte dans la fente du dispositif de sécurité qui la "lit";* "the user places the card in the slot of a security device that 'reads' it."

carte (f.) **vermeil** A card that entitles persons aged sixty or more to reductions on train fares, movie tickets, and certain goods.

carte (f.) **verte** Automobile insurance certificate entitling you to coverage while driving in Europe outside France.

cas (m.) **échéant** Although this phrase uses the present participle of an almost vanished verb, *échoir,* "to fall (on a given date)," it is thoroughly alive and kicking; it means "if that is the case" or "as the case may be." It does have a legal or paralegal ring to it. See, for instance, **copropriété.** When utilities or maintenance charges on an apartment are to be paid at the end of a month or quarter, they are *payables à terme échu;* if they are to be paid at the beginning of the period, they are *payables à terme à échoir.*

cas-par-cas (m.) On an individual basis; one case at a time. *Les demandes de papiers des immigrés de l'**Eglise Saint-Bernard** seront traitées au cas-par-cas.*

casque (m.) **bleu** Member of the United Nations peacekeeping forces.

casse (m.) Note the gender when the word is used in this slang sense: *faire un casse,* to break into a shop or other premises with a view to burglary. (The official term would be *entrer avec effraction.*) *Braquer/Faire un braquage,* to hold up (a shop, bank, etc.).

La casse is a familiar word for "breakage," "destruction," as in *Pendant la manif il y a eu de la casse.* See **casseur**

cassette (f.) Cassette tape. *Cassette audio; cassette vidéo. Cassette vierge,* blank tape.

casseur (m.) The word—and the concept—are very heavily laden with sociological meaning and seem to have no exact, neat equivalent in English. "Troublemaker," "thug," "hooligan," "hoodlum," "rowdy"—these are only part of the idea. The word refers to the individuals who join in a demonstration (*une manifestation*) but who are not themselves demonstrating for or against the cause; they come along in order to smash windows and loot stores, perhaps burn and overturn cars. Nowadays they are invariably assumed—and usually said, by the media—to come from the **banlieues.**

cata (f.) Short for *catastrophe. C'est une vraie cata.*

catéchisme (m.) When the Vatican published the new catechism in 1992, the first language in which it was published was French, a source of pride to a number of French people.

Le mercredi après-midi les enfants des écoles primaires ne vont pas en classe; ils sont donc libres d'aller au catéchisme si leur famille le désire; "On Wednesday afternoon grade school children do not have class, so they are free to attend Catholic religious instruction (outside the school) if their families want them to."

cathodique (adj., n.) Anything having to do with a cathode ray tube (i.e., with television). *On appelle parfois la télé la grande messe cathodique;* "TV is sometimes called the great cathode-tube mass" (a pun, of course, between *cathodique* and *catholique,* in a country that still has a predominantly Catholic tradition; see **catéchisme; Clovis**). In July 1996, in a somewhat sarcastic article about TV anchorpeople who resigned, got fired, were overpaid, and/or accepted favors from politicians, *L'Express* called them *des cathodiques anxieux qui vérifient qu'ils ont toujours un coeur qui bat sous l'électron,* "anxious TV stars checking to see that beneath all those electrons they still have a heart that beats."

CCP *Compte de chèques postaux,* postal checking account. *La Poste rivalise avec les banques pour un certain nombre de fonctions—compte de chèques, caisse d'épargne, **Plan d'épargne logement,** and so on.*

CDD (m.) *Contrat à durée déterminée,* contract for a predetermined period of time. By far the most common form of contract offered today when an employer hires a new employee. At the end of the specified period, the employer can choose not to renew the contract, thus effectively terminating the employee's job without having to pay any compensation. The employer is then free to hire someone else, on the same basis.

CEA (m.) France's *Commissiariat à l'Energie atomique.*

CEI *Communauté des Etats indépendants,* the Commonwealth of Independent States (CIS) formed when *l'Union des républiques socialistes soviétiques (l'URSS),* "the Soviet Union," broke up.

"cela fait" plus noun without definite article. Convenient little phrase, as in *Cela fait problème;* "That's a problem." *Cela fait désordre:* an ironic way of saying, "That's kind of messy/not very neat/not very proper."

cellule (f.) **de crise** Crisis unit. *Suite au détournement d'un avion en provenance d'Alger, les autorités ont mis en place une cellule de crise pour s'occuper des familles qui attendaient des nouvelles;* "When an airplane coming from Algiers was hijacked, the authorities set up an emergency unit to look after the passengers' relatives as they waited for further information."

celui/celle par qui le scandale arrive A set phrase designating the person who, whether inadvertently or not, triggers an incident or development. Said, for instance, in 1996 of a TV anchorman, *un présentateur à la télévision,* whose overgenerous salary led to an investigation of his contract and ultimately to *la démission du président de la chaîne en question,* "the resignation of the director of the channel involved."

centrale (f.) **nucléaire** Nuclear power station. Most of France's electricity is produced from nuclear energy. *Il y a une vingtaine de centrales nucléaires situées dans différentes régions, à Fessenheim, Flamanville, Golfech, etc. L'utilisation du nucléaire est cependant très controversée;* "But the use of nuclear energy is very controversial." See **Superphénix**

Cercle (m.) *des poètes disparus* The French title of *The Dead Poets Society,* which was a cult film among French teenagers in the early 1990s. See *Grand bleu*

certaine idée (f.) **de la France** From a very young age, de Gaulle later wrote, he was imbued with *une certaine idée de la France,* "an idealized concept of France and of France's role." In June 1940, when the country was occupied, his *certaine idée* impelled him to come to its rescue from abroad and encourage the French to rescue themselves; see **Appel du 18 juin.** The phrase *une certaine idée de la France* is still quoted by *les hommes politiques qui se réclament du gaullisme,* "politicians who consider themselves de Gaulle's spiritual descendants."

César (m.) France's answer to the Hollywood Oscar. *Les Césars sont décernés tous les ans depuis 1976 au meilleur acteur de* *cinéma, à la meilleure actrice, au meilleur metteur en scène, au meilleur compositeur, au meilleur scénario, et ainsi de suite.* The equivalent for the theater world is *le **Molière**.* See also **Louis Delluc**

cessation (f.) **de paiement, être en** Said of a firm when it is unable to meet its bills and pay its employees; a euphemism for *être en faillite.*

chador (m.) Also spelled *tchador.* This is the head scarf worn by most Muslim women in France and many Muslim girls. *Il y a toute une polémique sur le port du chador à l'école;* "There is keen debate over the question of whether Muslim girls should be allowed to wear the *chador* in school." The government has taken the position that public schools in France are *des écoles laïques, attachées aux vertus républicaines* (i.e., they are non-denominational). (See **Clovis.**) The question first arose in 1989; in 1994 the *Ministre de l'Education nationale,* François Bayrou, issued a decree forbidding *des signes ostentatoires d'appartenance religieuse à l'école publique,* "the wearing of visible signs of religious affiliation at state schools," while tolerating, however, *des signes discrets.* It was immediately asked whether crosses worn by Catholic students, or yarmulkes (kippas) worn by Jewish students, constituted des *signes ostentatoires.* See **foulard; intégration; laïcité; tchador, voile à l'école**

chaîne (f.) **à péage** Pay or subscription TV channel.

chaîne (f.) **de haute fidélité** Or *chaîne hi-fi* (pronounced "eee-fee") or *chaîne stéréo,* hi-fi or stereo system. *Haut-parleur* (m.), loudspeaker. *Enceinte* (f.) *acoustique,* enclosed loud-speaker. *Baffle* (m.), baffle.

chaîne (f.) **de montage** Assembly line, *où les pièces détachées sont montées,* "where parts are assembled."

chalutiers (m. pl.) **de pêche espagnols** Spanish fishing boats, which sometimes get into the news when they stray into *les eaux territoriales françaises.* See **arraisonner**

chambardement (m.) A big upheaval, both figuratively and literally; quite familiar but correct. *Le Monde* used it in October 1993 in discussing the way individuals had been appointed to head nationalized firms: *le chambardement à la tête des entreprises nationalisées en 1981 et 1986.*

Chancellerie (f.) The administration of *le système judiciaire,* as seen from on high, from the offices of *le Garde des Sceaux,* the minister of justice. See **parquet**

changement (m.) **climatique** Climate change, as observed and/or predicted by *les scientifiques* and discussed by *les écologistes, les économistes, et les planificateurs dans tous les domaines.*

changement (m.) **de cap** A change in course or direction. A phrase that *RPR* politicians often use, as in *Le cap est bon; il faut le tenir;* "We're moving in the right direction; we must steer straight ahead." Conversely, *Un changement de cap est souhaitable/urgent/à conseiller.*

charentaises (f. pl.) A pair of big, comfortable, patterned, old-fashioned, decidedly unglamorous carpet slippers; very **beauf** or **France profonde.** See the cartoon on **sondages**

charges (f. pl.) **sociales** Also called *cotisations* (f. pl.) *sociales* or *retenues* (f. pl.), these are deducted directly from your pay-check and total approximately 20 percent of *le salaire brut,* "the gross salary": *Sécurité sociale* (two different deductions, one for *maladie* and one for *vieillesse*), **Assedic,** and *retraite complémentaire.* The employer pays approximately twice as much as the employee, particularly for *la Sécurité sociale.* (What the employer pays are called *charges salariales* or *patronales* or *la part employeur* or *la part patronale.*) The employee alone, however, also pays the **CSG** and the **RDS.** See also **cotisations**

L'impôt sur le revenu n'est pas prélevé sur le salaire; "Income tax is not deducted at source." See **tiers provisionnel**

charrette (f.) This word reaches back to the French Revolution, since *charrettes* were the tumbrils in which groups of people to be guillotined were taken from their prison to the place of execution. Hence, in today's economic context, *Les gens ont peur de faire partie de la prochaine charrette;* "People are afraid of being included in the next batch of layoffs."

charter (m.) 1. A charter flight. 2. A synonym for the government's policy with regard to undocumented immigrants, called *les illégaux, les **sans-papiers,** les (immigrés) clandestins.* In official terms, they are not expelled, *expulsé(e)s;* they are *reconduit(e)s à la frontière et renvoyé(e)s dans leurs pays d'origine par charter,* "accompanied to the border and sent back to their country of origin by charter flight." See also **Eglise Saint-Bernard.** Human rights groups find this incompatible with the traditional role of France as *une terre d'asile,* "a land of asylum," providing a safe haven for refugees. Hence, the front-page headline of *Le Canard enchaîné* dated August 14, 1996, at the height of the *Eglise Saint-Bernard* episode: *"France, charter d'asile!"*

chasse (f.) Hunting. *Les chasseurs constituent un lobby puissant en France. Mécontents à cause d'une directive de Bruxelles limitant la chasse aux espèces migratoires en Europe, les chasseurs français ont manifesté à Paris en février 1998. Pourtant en France on chasse davantage d'espèces migratoires que dans aucun autre pays d'Europe.* "Hunters are a powerful lobby in France; angry over a directive from Brussels limiting the hunting of migratory birds throughout Europe, French hunters demonstrated in Paris in February 1998. Yet more species of

migratory birds are hunted in France than in any other European country." See **poils**

Chasse, pêche, nature et tradition is the name of a relatively
small but influential and conservative political movement,
generally opposed to the various *partis politiques écologistes.*

chassé-croisé (m.) A simultaneous two-way movement, as at the
end of July and the beginning of August, when the media may
warn about *le chassé-croisé des juilletistes et des aoûtiens*—
people who took their vacation in July are coming back home,
and people who are about to take their vacation in August are
on their way.

chasseur (m.) **de têtes** Headhunter; *cabinet de chasseur de têtes,*
head-hunting firm or agency. *Se faire repérer, rechercher par
des chasseurs de têtes,* to be head-hunted.

chauffard (m.) A reckless or sometimes hit-and-run driver; there
is no feminine form of this word. The suffix *-ard* is generally
pejorative or condescending: *un(e) pantouflard(e),* an unad-
venturous, stay-at-home person; *un(e) banlieusard(e),* a suburban dweller, not necessarily a commuter.

chef (m.) **d'entreprise** The person at the head of a company or
firm; the feminine form is *une femme chef d'entreprise.* She or
he is *un(e) responsable* or *un patron ("une patronne"* is a bit
casual and is used chiefly in connection with a restaurant),
from the management point of view; *un employeur (une
femme employeur),* from the point of view of her or his *em-
ployés(ées)* or *salariés(iées).*

cheminot (m.) Railway worker; *SNCF* employee. *Les cheminots
ont lancé une grève massive vers la fin de 1995 parce que le
gouvernement voulait modifier leur droit à la retraite à 50 ans;*
"The railway workers went on strike nationwide because the
government wanted to alter their right to retire at fifty." *Pendant l'après-guerre les cheminots étaient auréolés de gloire et
gagnaient beaucoup de sympathies à cause du rôle souvent important qu'ils avaient joué dans la Résistance;* "In the after-
math of World War II, the railway workers were wreathed
in glory, and lots of people were on their side because they
had often played an important role in the Resistance." See
traminot

chèque (m.) **emploi-service** A device launched by the government
in December 1994 in an attempt to discourage people from
hiring household help (*des femmes de ménage, des gardes d'enfant,* etc.) on an undeclared basis, *au noir.* See **travail au noir.**
*Les personnes qui sont payées en liquide et ne reçoivent pas de
bulletin de salaire ne bénéficient d'aucune protection sociale;*
"Individuals who are paid in cash and receive no paycheck
do not get any benefits" (health insurance, old age pension

contributions, etc.). People are therefore urged to pay such part-time employees with *un chèque emploi-service* (available at all banks) instead of in cash; when the employee brings the check to the bank or deposits it in his or her account, the government thus credits the employee with the relevant employment period while the employer pays in the corresponding **cotisations** and benefits from a tax reduction.

chèque (m.) **en bois** A check that bounces. The more formal term is *un chèque sans provision. Quand vous écrivez un chèque sur un compte non approvisionné, votre compte est à découvert (vous avez un découvert);* "When you write a check on an account that does not have adequate funds, you are overdrawn (you have an overdraft)."

chevrons (m. pl.) The double inverted V symbolizing Citroën cars. *La marque du chevron signale une baisse des ventes de 3,5% par rapport au même trimestre de l'année dernière;* "Citroën reports that sales have dropped 3.5 percent compared with the same quarter last year." See **lion**

chiant(e), chier One of the most common vocabulary groups among today's younger generation. *Chier* is literally to shit, defecate. *On m'a piqué tous mes papiers, c'est chiant! Me taper vingt heures de cours par semaine, ça me fait chier. Tais-toi, t'es chiant(e).* The boundary line that barred such vocabulary from use by the media has long been breached. A couple of generations ago the same grievances might have been expressed through words such as *agaçant* and *casse-pied.* See **con(ne)**

chic et choc During the late 1980s, the Paris public transport authority, la *Régie autonome des transports parisiens (RATP)* launched a campaign to persuade potential customers that it was trendy and smart (*chic et choc*) to leave their cars at home and take the Metro or bus. Accordingly, it dusted off its image and created *des boutiques RATP* in which to sell a variety of articles (key rings, scarves, etc.) matching what were then the *RATP*'s colors (Metro and bus tickets were yellow with a brown stripe down the middle). The phrase *chic et choc* became an easy one to parody. By the early 1990s the *RATP* revamped its logo and switched to a turquoise green.

chiffre (m.) **d'affaires** Turnover. Often abbreviated *CA. Impôt sur le chiffre d'affaires,* turnover tax.

chiner This verb seems by and large to have lost one of its meanings, "to tease or kid." It now means "to go looking for bargains" *chez les antiquaires ou les brocanteurs, dans les foires, ou au marché aux puces.*

chirurgie (f.) **esthétique** Plastic surgery. *Chirurgien* (m.) *esthétique,* plastic surgeon. *Culotte* (f.) *de cheval,* saddlebags. *Liposuccion* (f.) or *lipo-aspiration* (f.), liposuction. *Poches* (f. pl.) or *valises* (slang, f. pl.) *sous les yeux,* bags under the eyes. *Rides* (f. pl.), wrinkles. *Un lifting,* a face-lift. *Avoir la fesse triste/tombante* (vulgar), to have drooping buttocks.

choc (m.) **pétrolier** Oil crisis; generally refers to the first one, in 1973. For another kind of crisis related to oil, see **marée noire.**

chômage (m.) Unemployment. The key word in France in the 1990s. *Plus de 12 et demi % de la population active se trouve au chômage;* "Over 12.5 percent of the labor force is unemployed." *Le nombre de chômeurs de longue durée a augmenté de 0,9% en janvier;* "The number of people who have been jobless for over a year rose by 0.9 percent in January." There are various categories of *chômage—conjoncturel, structurel, technique, partiel,* and so on. *A cause des grèves en France en décembre 1995, des ouvriers d'une usine de montage Opel en Allemagne se sont trouvés au chômage technique parce que les pièces fabriquées en Espagne n'ont pas pu être acheminées à travers la France;* "Because of the strikes in France in December 1995, workers at an Opel car assembly plant in Germany were temporarily laid off because parts produced in Spain could not be shipped through France to Germany." See **ANPE; Assedic; CDD; CIE; compression du personnel; conjoncture économique; dégraisser; délocaliser; eurogrève; intérimaire; suppression d'emploi**

Among euphemisms connected with *mettre au chômage* are such phrases as *redéployer les potentialités, réallocation des ressources humaines, recentrage des compétences, reéquilibrage des effectifs* (*Marianne,* July 1997).

Chouannerie (f.) Refers to a bloody and long-overlooked chapter in French history; interest in it revived in 1989, in contrast to the official celebrations and commemorations glorifying the French Revolution and marking *le bicentenaire,* "the bicentennial," of the beginning of it. Starting in 1793, *les Chouans,* royalist and devoutly Catholic counterrevolutionaries, chiefly in Brittany and in the **Vendée,** rebelled against the revolutionary generals and their troops, who succeeded in "pacifying" the region, by and large, by 1795, but at the cost of very heavy losses among the Chouans. The Revolution has been accused of carrying out *une politique d'extermination à l'égard des Chouans;* the word *génocide* (m.) has been used.

chouette One of the more enduring adjectives, still around after many years: "great," "terrific," "nice," "neat." *Une chouette* is still "an owl," of course.

chrysanthèmes (m. pl.) If you have been invited to dinner and are about to bring a bouquet of chrysanthemums to your *hôtesse,* you should be aware that they are *fortement connotés:* they are the flowers you lay on a grave or plant at the foot of it on *le Jour des morts,* "the Day of the Dead," *le 2 novembre,* when it is the custom to go to the cemetery and visit the tombs of your relatives and friends. The previous day, *le 1er novembre,* is *la Toussaint,* "All Saints' Day," and is always a public holiday. The eve of it however, October 31, which is Halloween, was never marked by any ceremony or imagery, whether public or private, until 1996, when commercial interests suddenly began to try to make Halloween popular.

Furthermore, *chrysanthèmes* are associated with *les Présidents de la République* who preceded de Gaulle. Until the current *Cinquième République* was created in 1958 and a very strong role was given to the presidents of it in the constitution (which de Gaulle wrote), French presidents had been essentially figureheads or, in the standard phrase, *tout juste bons à inaugurer les chrysanthèmes,* "just about able to cut the ribbon at official openings."

CHU (m.) *Centre hospitalier universitaire.* All medical students do part of their training and studies in a *CHU.* There are nearly a dozen such hospitals in Paris and twice as many *en province.* In 1997 *les internes des CHU* stayed out on strike for several months to protest against an administrative reform concerning relations between the *Sécurité sociale* and doctors and the way patients would be treated as a result. *Nous voulons une médecine plus humaine,* said the interns; "We want health care to be more humane."

cibler To target, pinpoint. *Pour discuter valablement, il faut cibler les problèmes;* "You have to define the problems if you want to have a worthwhile discussion."

CIE (m.) *Contrat d'initiative-emploi.* A measure introduced after Chirac was elected president in 1995, for the purpose of encouraging companies to create new jobs, but deemed unsuccessful and phased out by the fall of 1996. *"Formule un peu futée d'aide à la création d'emplois nouveaux par exonération de charges et versement de subventions aux patrons embaucheurs. . . . Les chiraquiens pur sucre étaient bien les seuls à y croire"* (*Canard enchaîné,* August 1996); "Not a very clever idea for boosting job creation; the idea was to exempt employers who hired new people from coughing up their *charges sociales* and to pay them subsidies. . . . Only diehard Chirac followers had any faith in it."

cinéma (m.) **d'art et d'essai** An art movie theater, and the corresponding part of the film industry itself. This kind of theater will invariably show foreign films *en v.o., en version originale sous-titrée,* "in the original language with subtitles," instead of *en v.f., en version française.* When a foreign film is shown in French, it has been dubbed, *doublé; le doublage,* dubbing. Actually, in Paris, it is common for certain foreign films to be shown in *v.o.* in some theaters and simultaneously in *v.f.* in others. *Qu'est-ce qu'ils donnent (Qu'est-ce qui passe) cette* *semaine?* "What are they showing (what's on) this week?" *Dépêchez-vous de voir ce film—il ne va pas rester longtemps à l'affiche;* "Better hurry to see that film—it won't be on for long." *Le mercredi c'est le jour de sortie des nouveaux films;* "New films come out on Wednesdays." *La séance comprend généralement une vingtaine de minutes de pub et d'aperçus de films à paraître, suivie du film lui-même;* "A showing usually starts with about twenty minutes of advertising plus trailers for coming films, followed by the film itself."

Cinq, la A TV channel that disappeared in 1992 but was then resurrected in a different form: as an educational channel, *la chaîne éducative,* in the afternoons and as the channel on which Arte broadcasts its programs in the evenings.

Cinquième République (f.) The one begun by Charles de Gaulle in 1958 and lasting up to the present day. *La Première République* lasted from 1792 to 1804; *la Deuxième,* from 1848 to 1852; *la Troisième,* from 1870 to 1940; and *la Quatrième,* from 1946 to 1958.

Cintegabelle The town in the *Haute Garonne* (southwestern France) from which Lionel Jospin became a *Conseiller général* in 1988. Prime Minister Tony Blair of Britain visited him there while on vacation in France in the summers of 1997 and 1998.

circonscription (f.) Electoral district. *Un(e) candidat(e) peut être parachuté(e) par son parti dans n'importe quelle circonscription, là où le parti estime qu'il est utile qu'il ou elle se présente;* "A candidate can be assigned by his or her party to any district in the country, wherever the party feels that it is useful for him or her to run." *"J'ai changé plusieurs fois de circonscription,"* was the candid admission of one politician in a 1997 radio interview; *d'abord Sarcelles in 1993, puis Cannes en 1995, puis Paris en 1996.* I've run for election from several different districts: first Sarcelles (working class suburb north of Paris), then Cannes, then Paris. See **parachutage**

cité (f.) A large apartment building or development *en **banlieue*** inhabited chiefly by immigrants.

clandestin (m.) *Un clandestin* is *un immigré clandestin,* "an undocumented immigrant." *Des **sans-papiers*** is a more colloquial word for *des clandestins.*

classe (f.) **politique** Politicians considered as a whole; see **crédible.**

classes (f.) *Faire ses classes,* to do the training period at the beginning of *le service militaire. Les classes durent normalement deux ou trois mois,* "typically last two or three months."

On a résumé (*un CV, curriculum vitae*), a young man will specify that he is *libre de ses obligations militaires,* he "has done his military service," "has been drafted and got it over with." See **armée de métier**

classes (f. pl.) **préparatoires** Also known as *prépa* (f.). These are the special courses that students can begin after their *Bacca-lauréat* and that prepare them for the competitive entry exams, *les **concours** d'entrée,* for the *grandes écoles.* Only students with top marks on the *bac* and the best *livrets scolaires* (high school report cards) are *admis(es),* "accepted," in a *prépa,* which lasts two years.

clavier (m.) Keyboard, whether that of *un ordinateur* (*clavier français,* AZERTY; *clavier anglais,* QWERTY) or *un instrument de musique. Une touche,* a key.

clignotants (m.) The turn signals on a car and, by extension, the warning signals in any context; *les clignotants politiques, sociaux,* and so forth.

climat (m.) **social** Nothing to do with being sociable or popular. *Le climat social* refers to the atmosphere or relations between management, *le patronat,* and labor, *les ouvriers, les salariés, les syndicats. Le climat social se dégrade d'année en année;* "Labor relations are getting worse every year." *De mémoire de syndicaliste, a-t-on jamais connu un climat social aussi tendu?* "As far back as any union member can remember, has the labor situation ever been so tense?" See **plan social; social**

clip (m.) Short for *vidéoclip.*

clivage (m.) **d'opinion** A sharp or unbridgeable difference of opinion—for instance, *le clivage d'opinion qui oppose l'école publique à l'école privée,* "the eternal quarrel between those in favor of free, state schools and those in favor of private (usually parochial) schools." *Ce clivage dure depuis la séparation de l'Eglise et l'Etat en 1905.* See **Clovis; laïcité; loi Falloux**

cloner To clone. *Le clonage en 1997 de la brebis nommée Dolly a fait la une de tous les journaux. On a tout de suite évoqué les problèmes d'ordre éthique que soulève ou que pourrait soulever cette manipulation génétique. Le Président Chirac a demandé qu'il y ait une résolution contre le clonage humain.* "The cloning of a ewe named Dolly in 1997 made front pages everywhere. The ethical problems that this genetic manipulation involves or could involve were raised; President Chirac urged that a resolution be passed forbidding the cloning of human beings."

Clovis King of the Franks, who was converted to Christianity by his wife Clothilde and was baptized in the year 496. He has long been considered *le fondateur de la nation,* "the founder of France," which in turn was considered for centuries (or considered itself) *la fille aînée de l'Eglise,* the eldest daughter of the Church of Rome. *Gesta Dei per Francos, les actes de Dieu par les Francs,* "the Franks as defender of the Church."

En 1996, pour fêter le mille cinq centième anniversaire du baptême de Clovis par l'évêque Rémi de Reims, le Pape est venu en France; "In 1996, to celebrate the 1,500th anniversary of

Clovis's baptism by Remy, bishop of Reims, the pope came to France." *D'où une controverse énorme: Est-ce que ces célébrations étaient contraires au principe de la laïcité qui définit la France depuis la Révolution? Est-ce que la république française devait recevoir un chef religieux et est-ce que le contribuable français devait payer les frais de sa visite en France?* "This gave rise to heated argument: Were those celebrations incompatible with the secular principle that has defined France since the Revolution? Should the French Republic receive a religious leader, and should the French taxpayer foot the bill for his visit to France?" See **chador; clivage d'opinion; foulard; laïcité; tchador; voile à l'école**

CNJA (m.) *Centre national des jeunes agriculteurs.*

CNPF (m.) *Conseil national du patronat français,* national employers' federation. Recently renamed *le Mouvement des entreprises de France* (*MEDEF*).

CNTS (m.) *Centre national de la transfusion sanguine.* See **sang contaminé**

COB (f.) *Commission des opérations boursières;* stock exchange regulatory body; the French equivalent of the Securities Exchange Commission (SEC). It was created in 1967.

cochonnet (m.) *Ah, le cochonnet!* This is the plain little wooden ball, smaller and lighter than a golfball, which you try to hit when you play *boules.* Each *boule* is about the size of a tennis ball; the classic version is made of steel, but lighter and cheaper *boules* made of plastic are now common, especially for use at the beach. Even today, whether *sur la place du village en province* or in the *Champ de Mars* in Paris, a hundred yards from the Eiffel Tower and its horde of tourist buses, at least 99 percent of *boules* players, and even onlookers, are men. Jackets will be hung on the branches of the nearest tree, and a yardstick or measuring tape, *un mètre à ruban,* is ever present, ready to put an end to argument by determining whose *boule* has landed nearest the *cochonnet.*

code (m.) **barre** The bar code identifying every item for sale in any shop or store.

code (m.) **confidentiel** A four-digit personal identification number (PIN) that you must be able to punch in when using your *carte de crédit au restaurant, dans une station service ou station d'essence, au supermarché,* and so on. Its use makes your signature unnecessary. For another kind of *code,* see **concierge.**

code (m.) **de la nationalité** Governs the status of foreigners in France, the conditions for entering the country, obtaining residence and work permits, and acquiring French nationality. It was reformed in 1993 so as to make all of these more difficult. For example, it took two years instead of six months under the previous law to acquire French nationality after marrying a French national; foreigners in France could no longer request French nationality for their children under legal age born in France; if children born in France of foreign parents born abroad wished to acquire French nationality, they had to explicitly express that wish between the ages of sixteen and twenty-one. The *loi Pasqua* of 1989 and that of 1993 were designed chiefly to stem the flow of illegal immigration and facilitate expulsion, *la reconduite à la frontière.* See **charter; droit du sol**

In 1997 *le rapport Weil* recommended that the provisions of this code be made more lenient, with the long-term goal of facilitating *l'intégration des immigrés.* It recommended reintroducing the concept of *droit* (m.) *du sol,* whereby a person born on French soil is French.

cohabitation (f.) Period of more or less peaceful coexistence or power sharing between political parties that may occur because of a feature in the Constitution: *le mandat présidentiel est de sept ans mais les élections législatives ont lieu tous les cinq ans,* "the president is elected for seven years, but legislative elections take place every five years." *La première cohabitation* occurred between 1986 and 1988. In 1981 Mitterrand and the Socialist Party swept into power; in the 1986 legislative elections, however, the *RPR* won and the Constitution required Mitterrand to appoint *un Premier ministre* from the winning party; it was Jacques Chirac. See **quinquennat; septennat.**

The second occurred between 1993 and 1995. In 1988 Mitterrand was reelected; but in 1993 the legislatives again went to *l'opposition,* and again he had to appoint *un Premier ministre* from the winning party; this time it was Edouard Balladur.

The third began in 1997. In 1995 Chirac (*RPR*) was elected president, but in 1997 the Socialists won *les législatives anticipées* and Chirac appointed Lionel Jospin (PS) prime minister. *De temps à autre, comme pour marquer son territoire, le Président fait des discours sur la politique étrangère et critique les politiques du gouvernement dans les domaines intérieurs;* "Now and again, to make it clear where his territory lies, the president makes speeches about foreign policy and criticizes the government's policies on domestic issues."

cohésion (f.) **sociale** Harmony between the different segments of society; specifically, between the haves and the have-nots (i.e., the employed and the unemployed). Achieving this is one of the major goals proclaimed by the present government. See **fracture sociale**

Cohn-Bendit, Daniel Also remembered as "Dany le Rouge" because of his auburn hair. One of the most prominent leaders of *les événements de mai 68;* half-German and half-French. By the early 1990s, a quarter century after having challenged the authority of the French government, he had become deputy mayor of Frankfurt, Germany. See **Nous sommes tous des juifs allemands**

collaboration (f.) Both the most positive and the most guilt-laden of words.

A businessperson, attending a meeting with his or her *homologues* (m. pl.), "opposite numbers," may well say, *"Je vous présente mes collaborateurs (-trices);"* "'Let me introduce my colleagues (or 'fellow workers' or 'members of my team')." Thanking people for their help, you may well say, *"Votre collaboration nous a été très précieuse." "Téléfilm réalisé avec la collaboration de la Télévision suisse."*

But referring to the Vichy period, 1940 to 1944, *collaboration* has only one meaning, which is political: collaboration with the Germans, *collaboration avec l'occupant. En 1945 certains collabos (collaborateurs) ont réussi à s'enfuir en Espagne.* With regard to French women accused of having slept with German officers or soldiers it was said, *"Elles ont fait de la collaboration allongée,"* "horizontal collaboration." The Vichy period still haunts France; book after book, film after film allude to or portray events and situations from those years. See **Bousquet, René; Papon, Maurice; Touvier, Paul**

collecte (f.) **sélective** *La collecte sélective des ordures,* involving the sorting, *le tri,* of trash (*le verre, le papier, le plastique,* etc.) and its collection on that basis.

collectivité (f.) **locale** A very common though administrative way of saying "the local authorities," "the local community." *La collectivité,* the community in general, society in general.

collège (m.) Definitely not "college" in the American sense. Instead, it is *le premier cycle,* the first four years of secondary school, from *la sixième à la troisième.* They are followed by *le second cycle,* from *la seconde à la terminale* (see **CP**).

College in the American sense is *l'université* (f.) or *la fac.*

colleur (m.) **d'affiches** Bill sticker; specifically someone (usually young) who puts up political campaign posters. *Une bagarre s'est produite entre des colleurs d'affiches de différents partis politiques, mais qui a provoqué qui?* "There was a fight between people putting up posters for various parties, but who started it?"

collimateur (m.) *Avoir quelqu'un dans le collimateur,* to take aim at someone, have someone in your sights. A phrase commonly used in discussing the political scene.

Colombey-les-deux-Eglises The tiny village in eastern France in which Charles de Gaulle had a family estate, *La Boisserie,* where he died in 1970. Because he was buried in the village cemetery, it is the site of an annual *pèlerinage* (m.), "pilgrimage," by leaders of the *RPR, qui se réclament du gaullisme,* "who claim to perpetuate the Gaullist tradition." See **certaine idée de la France**

colorant (m.) Dye of any sort; when it is used in food, it is required to be listed among *les ingrédients* by an international standard classification number, usually preceded by *E.*

combustible (m.) Fuel. *Combustible fossile,* fossil fuel. *Le combustible fossile n'est pas une source d'énergie renouvelable, alors que l'énergie éolienne, géothermique, nucléaire, solaire, et des marées sont des sources renouvelables;* "Fossil fuel is not a renewable energy source, whereas the wind, geothermal and nuclear sources, the sun, and the tides are."

comité (m.) **d'entreprise** The existence of such a committee is required by law in any plant or firm with fifty or more employees. They elect the members of this committee, which represents them in their dealings with management; the head of the firm likewise sits on this committee. It may organize summer camps, Christmas parties, and so forth, for employees' children.

commando (m.) **anti-IVG** Antiabortion group that breaks into a clinic or hospital to disrupt its activity and/or damage equipment. See **avortement; IVG**

commémoration (f.) Ceremony or holiday to mark past events. *Souvent controversée; par exemple, est-ce une bonne idée de commémorer la fin de la première guerre mondiale en 1918 et de la deuxième guerre mondiale en 1945 en faisant du 11 novembre et du 8 mai des jours fériés? Cela ne fait-il que perpétuer un vieil antagonisme? En Angleterre, par exemple, ni le 11 novembre ni le 8 mai n'est férié.* "Often controversial; for instance, is it a good idea to commemorate the end of World War I in 1918 and the end of World War II in 1945 by making November 11 and May 8 legal holidays? Or does that just keep old antagonisms alive? In Britain, for instance, May 8 and November 11 are not public holidays." See **lieu de mémoire**

communautarisme (m.) A tendency that emerged in the mid-1990s: a move to demand special rights for cultural, racial, or religious minorities (e.g., Muslim girls wearing head scarves to school). *Certains prétendent que cette tendance va à l'encontre des valeurs républicaines (applicables à tous) et à la laïcité. D'autres rétorquent, comment faire vivre ensemble les minorités? C'est ça la démocratie; elle est plurielle ou elle n'est pas.* "Some people feel this view is contrary to France's republican values (applicable to all) and secular principles. Others retort, how can minorities live together? That is democracy; it is many-faceted."

complicité (f.) **de corruption** One of the most common accusations arising from the investigations and trials brought about by the wave of **affaires** involving prominent political and business figures in the late 1980s and the 1990s.

composer This is what you do when you dial a telephone number, whether on a touch-tone phone (*un téléphone à touches*) or an old dial phone (*un téléphone à cadran*).

Most public pay phones in France today require the use of *une télécarte* in place of coins; you buy a card at the post office, or in *un tabac* or *une maison de la presse*, "a newspaper shop." *Introduisez votre carte*, "insert your card," the screen in the *cabine téléphonique* will tell you. *Patientez*, "wait." Next the screen will tell you how many prepaid units are left on your card. Then, *composez le numéro de votre correspondant*, "dial your party's number." The screen tells you *au fur et à mesure*, "as your conversation proceeds," how many units you have left. When you finish, you hear a beep and the screen reminds you, *"Retirez votre carte."*

If your party's number has changed or the line has been disconnected, a recorded voice will tell you, *"Le numéro de votre correspondant n'est plus en service actuellement; nous regrettons de ne pouvoir donner suite à votre appel."* If all lines are busy, you will hear, *"Suite à un encombrement, nous ne pouvons donner suite à votre appel; veuillez rappeler ultérieurement."*

composter To punch a hole or indentation in your Metro ticket (or bus or train ticket) so as to make it valid. This used to be done manually by people called *poinçonneurs* (*-euses*) on the Metro station platforms and *receveurs* in the buses and trains. *"Ah, des p'tits trous, des p'tits trous, toujours des petits trous, des trous de 1ère classe, des trous de 2e classe,"* said *Le poinçonneur des Lilas*, the song by Serge Gainsbourg. But automated turnstiles and machines were installed in stations and on board buses starting in 1968, thus winning one of the earliest and most visible victories of technology over employment in France. *Si on ne composte pas son billet de train, on risque une amende;* "If you do not punch a hole in your train ticket, you may get a fine."

compression (f.) **du personnel** Reduction in the number of employees; a euphemism for mass layoffs. See **licencier; plan social; suppression d'emploi**

compte (m.) **à rebours** Countdown. *C'est le compte à rebours jusqu'à l'entrée en vigueur de la **monnaie unique;*** "The countdown until the single currency comes into effect has begun."

compte (m.) **courant** Or *compte de chèques*, your checking account at the bank; or at the post office, *comptes de chèques postaux (CCP)*. *Compte rémunéré*, interest-bearing account.

con(ne) Vulgar but same remark as for **chiant(e), chier.** Use of this category of language used to lie only within the male province and to emerge especially in such emotionally charged circumstances as traffic accidents: *Quel con! Hé connard! Quelle connerie!* Today the root word and its derivatives have become democratized, the casual property of all speakers, men and women alike, and are no longer edited out of interviews in the media.

"To hell with consumption!" Party Convention menu: Consommé—Cucumbers—Confit of duck—Concoillotte cheese—Confitures (jam)—Co(n)gnac.

In the short-tempered days of June 1997, when the hastily decided dissolution of parliament had made so many RPR and UDF députés unexpectedly lose their seats, one of them, at a gathering of his fellow party members, decided to avoid the scheduled luncheon: *Le Canard enchaîné* quoted him as saying, "I'd rather have lunch at home. The food'll be better, and I'm under no obligation to eat with a bunch of *cons,* especially when they're hysterical."

by EsCaro in *Le Canard enchaîné,* July 9, 1997

concierge (m. or f.) Today it is more common to say *un(e) gardien(ne).* The function is often carried out by a couple together. The formidable powers of the old-time *concierge* have almost vanished. It is exceedingly rare today for the mail to be brought upstairs and placed under the doormat of each apartment; individual mailboxes have made their appearance on the ground floor of almost every building. Similarly it is now unheard of to call out your name or tiptoe past the *concierge*'s loge when you come in after 10 P.M.; doorcodes—*codes* (m.) *porte* or *digicodes* or *visiocodes*—have been installed in virtually all buildings.

Until the 1960s a *concierge* was almost always French. Then, reflecting the sources of immigration into France, came a period of Spanish *concierges,* followed, from the 1980s on, by a period of Portuguese *gardien(ne)s.*

concours (m.) A competitive exam. That is, candidates compete for a number of admissions that has been limited in advance. *Il peut y avoir 3000 candidats pour 150 places, par exemple. Le concours d'entrée à Sciences Po, le concours d'entrée à HEC (Hautes études commerciales),* and so on. *Concourir,* to take a competitive exam. *Préparer un concours; se présenter au concours. Réussir le concours* or *être reçu(e) au concours,* to pass. *Rater le concours,* to fail. See **sélection**

concrètement One of the present generation's favorite adverbs, meaning "in practical terms." *Et maintenant, après la signature du cessez-le-feu, qu'est-ce qui va se passer, concrètement?* "And now that the ceasefire has been signed, what's going to actually happen?"

concubin, -ine A status recognized in case law though not in the *Code civil,* designating the person with whom you live but to whom you are not married. Obtaining an official *certificat de concubinage* can bring certain insurance and other benefits to both partners. See **contrat d'union civile et sociale**

condition féminine It is not the condition itself that is feminine; this expression refers to all aspects of the conditions in which women live and work and to their legal status. The first *Secrétariat d'Etat à la condition féminine* was created by the Giscard d'Estaing government in 1974. The position was upgraded in later governments to *un Ministère de la Famille et de la Condition féminine,* but since there was no feminine form of the word *ministre,* even *le Ministre de la Condition féminine* was *Madame le Ministre.* However, once the Jospin government was formed in June 1997, with an unprecedentedly large number of women ministers, they insisted on being addressed as *Madame la Ministre.*

conditions (f. pl.) **carcérales** Conditions in prison. *Une commission a été nommée pour enquêter sur les conditions carcérales. Incarcérer,* to put in jail. *Son incarcération n'a duré que trois mois;* "He or she spent only three months in jail."

Condom The name of a town in southwestern France. It is not the usual word for a condom, which is *un préservatif.* In 1997, however, it was reported that the town was planning to open *un musée du préservatif.* See **contraception**

Conférence (f.) **nationale sur l'emploi, les salaires et le temps de travail** Also called *Conférence de Matignon,* it was held in October 1997; the prime minister announced that businesses with over twenty employees had until the year 2000 to adopt a thirty-five-hour workweek at thirty-nine-hour pay. This measure was intended to create more jobs; see **temps choisi.** The head of the **CNPF** resigned in protest. See **tueur**

conforter This, of course, means "to comfort someone"; but it also means "to strengthen or reinforce one's own position or ideas." *Les bons résultats de fin d'année affichés par la société Machin-Chouette vont conforter sa position en bourse;* "The good end-of-year results announced by the X company will strengthen its position on the stock exchange." *Les commentaires injurieux proférés par le Député de . . . me confortent dans l'idée que je me fais de son caractère.* "The nasty comments made by the *Député* from . . . confirm my impression of the kind of person he is." *Les derniers succès du PSG confortent les espoirs de leurs supporters;* "The Paris Saint-Germain's recent victories give their fans reason to hope." See **PSG**

congé (m.) **annuel** Annual vacation. The first *congés payés* were introduced in 1936, under the *Front populaire* government. Today workers are entitled to *cinq semaines de congé annuel.* There are other types of *congé. Le congé maternité* is one of the benefits brought by *la Sécurité sociale;* it includes *le congé prénatal,* which starts six weeks before the expected date of birth and *le congé postnatal,* which lasts for eight weeks afterward. The term *congé parental* has come into use in recent years, as fathers sometimes assume child-rearing responsibilities while mothers *travaillent à l'extérieur. Un congé maladie* is "sick leave." It is triggered by an **arrêt de travail,** "a doctor's certificate." An employee can also request *un congé (non-rémunéré) pour convenance personnelle,* "special (unpaid) leave for personal reasons." *Un congé* (m.) *de conversion* is retraining leave, for an employee.

congédier A verb that is hardly used any more; it meant "to dismiss a servant, an employee, or a lover." Today, *licencier, renvoyer,* or, more familiarly, *mettre à la porte* means "to dismiss or to fire."

conjoncture (f.) **économique** Economic situation, particular set of economic circumstances. *La conjoncture actuelle est bonne/mauvaise/difficile/critique. Chômage conjoncturel,* "unemployment caused by/linked to/justified by the economic situation."

conscription (f.) The draft; military draftees are *les conscrits.* See **armée de métier**

Conseil (m.) **supérieur de la langue française** Official government body appointed in 1989 for the purpose of attempting to regulate (and stem) the use of foreign words in French, chiefly by devising alternative words or expressions in French to replace foreign words or obviate the need for them; see **baladeur.** The *Délégation générale de la langue française,* created the same year, has similar functions. See **francophonie**

Conservatoire (m.) **du littoral** A government agency whose mission is to protect France's coasts and shores from overdevelopment or *la construction sauvage,* "unregulated development." It can buy up land but does not manage it and works closely with local officials in determining the *Plan d'occupation des sols* (*POS*), "zoning regulations," in each town. In September 1994, on *Le téléphone sonne,* a phone-in radio talk show, a *Conservatoire* official indicated that at that time some 43,000 hectares (just over 100,000 acres) had been acquired; only 2 to 3 percent of the acquisitions had come about through expropriation.

console (f.) *Console de jeux vidéo,* videogames display unit.

consommer This is what the government urges everyone to do, to stimulate the economy: *encourager la consommation pour donner un coup de fouet à la production et remplir les* **carnets de commandes,** "encouraging consumption so as to stimulate production and fill up the order books." *La société de consommation,* consumer society. *Consommateur(-trice).*

"*Sachez consommer avec modération,*" however, is the standard health warning on every bottle of alcohol; see **abus.**

constructeur (m.) **automobile** Car manufacturer. For decades, *la construction automobile* has been a leading sector of activity in France and hence a major source of employment. *Mais aujourd'hui la concurrence touche tous les constructeurs—français, européens, américains, japonais, asiatiques en général;* "But today, competition is affecting all makes—French, other European, American, Japanese, and other Asian." *Il est devenu courant de dire que sur les trois constructeurs français il y en a maintenant un de trop;* "It has become a commonplace to say that out of the three French manufacturers, there is now one too many."

construction (f.) **de l'Europe** The phrase commonly used to embrace all the phases leading up to the achievement and completion of the European monetary union, with a single currency, *la monnaie unique.* It covers all of the adjustments or rethinking that is being done or may need to be done among all of the member countries in areas such as *la fiscalité, la législation du travail, la protection sociale, et ainsi de suite,* "taxation, labor legislation, welfare, and so forth."

contaminé(e) See **sang contaminé**

contentieux (m.) Topic of disagreement, bone of contention. *Le contentieux entre Alain Juppé et son Ministre de l'Economie et des Finances, Alain Madelin, s'est soldé par le départ de celui-ci;* "The disagreement between then Prime Minister Alain Juppé and his Finance Minister (Secretary of the Treasury) Alain Madelin led to the latter's departure."

In a firm, *le service du contentieux* is "the legal department."

contester To challenge. *Lors des* **événements de mai 68** *tout à coup tout le monde contestait tout; tout le monde était contestataire. Mais aujourd'hui, période de crise économique, il y a moins de contestation;* "Suddenly, in May 1968, everyone was busy challenging everything, but today, what with the economic recession, there is less challenging going on."

contraception (f.) Contraception. *La pilule anticonceptionnelle est devenue disponible en France sur ordonnance en 1966;* "The pill became legally available in France, by prescription, in 1966." *Le stérilet,* intrauterine device (IUD). *La méthode Ogino,* abstinence on certain days of the cycle. *Le préservatif,* condom. *Le contrôle des naissances,* birth control. *Les centres de planning familial proposent des conseils sur les meilleures façons de pratiquer la contraception.*

contractuel(le) (m. or f.) A traffic warden who distributes parking tickets and fines.

contrat (m.) **d'insertion professionnelle (CIP)** The Balladur government proposed this early in 1994, as a measure intended to help young people find jobs: since they could be hired, *embauchés,* at 80 percent of the **SMIC** for two years, employers would not be loath to hire them, and young people would thus acquire some professional experience. *Mais les jeunes, surtout les élèves de première et de terminale et les étudiants, ont manifesté dans la rue;* "But young people, especially high school and college students, demonstrated against the measure," deriding it as *le SMIC jeunes* and saying that it did not open up any useful outlook for them, since employers would be able to dismiss them after two years and hire other young people on the same basis, and so on, indefinitely. The government withdrew the measure.

contrat (m.) **d'union civile et sociale (CUCS)** This bill was proposed in the *Assemblée nationale* in 1997, partly to improve the legal situation of homosexual couples by granting each partner in the couple greater rights concerning taxation, inheritance, housing, pensions, and social protection than those available through *un certificat de vie commune* or *de concubinage,* established locally by a mayor. The bill was also intended to cover other categories of individuals living together, such as elderly people or brothers and sisters. It was not intended, however, to establish the marriage of homosexual couples or to allow them to adopt children. Some months later it was suggested that *un Pacte d'Intérêt commun (PIC)* or *Pacte civil de solidarité (Pacs)* be created.

contrefaçon (f.) Counterfeiting, forgery. A source of major economic concern in a country known, among other things, for such items as *les foulards Hermès, les sacs Louis Vuitton, les parfums Chanel,* and the like. *Tous ces produits de luxe sont vulnérables devant l'activité des contrefacteurs, et la balance commerciale du pays peut en pâtir;* "All of these luxury products are vulnerable when cheap imitations are produced, and the country's trade balance can suffer from them."

contre-la-montre (m.) *C'est du contre-la-montre;* "It's a race against time." *Satisfaire aux **critères de conversion** est maintenant une question de contre-la-montre.*

contre-manifestation (f.) A demonstration held to protest against another demonstration or meeting (m.). In September 1997, for instance, when the *Front national* held its *fête des bleu-blanc-rouge* at *la Pelouse de Reuilly* (in the Parc de Vincennes, just east of Paris), *une contre-manif* marched between *la République* and *Bastille* with slogans such as *Le Pen fait la fête, préparons sa défaite,* and *A bas le fascisme et le racisme.* One *contre-manifestant,* interviewed that evening on the radio, called the counter-demonstration *"une sorte de harcèlement démocratique,"* "'democratic harassment,'" and *"un réveil citoyen,"* "'an act of civic awareness.'"

contre-performance (f.) An uncharacteristically poor performance by a sports(wo)man or athlete or—by extension—by individuals in other fields also.

contre-pouvoir (m.) The idea of checks and balances. In recent years *les juges, les magistrats* (who are appointed, not elected), have been acquiring more and more powers of investigation, *si bien que le judiciaire est parfois appelé un contre-pouvoir vis-à-vis de l'exécutif et du législatif,* "so that it is sometimes said the judiciary function has become more independent of the executive and the legislative." See **parquet**

contribuable (m. or f.) Taxpayer. A euphemistic but official term related to the notion of *contributions* (f. pl.) *directes,* "direct taxes," and *contributions indirectes,* "indirect taxes." The more common term for taxes is, of course, *impôts* (m. pl.). See **administré(e); tiers provisionnel**

contrôle (m.) A test or check-up of any kind. *Contrôler; être contrôlé(e). Lors des derniers championnats cet athlète a été contrôlé positif—on a trouvé des traces de dopage au cannabis;* "At the last championship meet, this athlete tested positive— they found traces of cannabis."

contrôle (m.) **d'identité** A random police check that can require anyone walking down the street, sitting at a café, or whatever, to produce *une carte d'identité, un passeport,* or *un permis de séjour,* "residence permit for foreigners." *Un permis de conduire,* "driver's license," is not accepted as *une pièce d'identité.* Such *contrôles* tend to be carried out especially if there has been a terrorist incident or threat or in an attempt to catch *des **clandestins*** or individuals suspected of cooperating or sympathizing with *des intégristes dans les pays d'Afrique du nord.*

contrôle (m.) **de sécurité** Security check, as *dans un aéroport.*

convention (f.) **collective** *Convention collective en matière syndicale et patronale,* collective agreement among union organizations and employers' organizations in a given professional branch, entailing the obligation to hold negotiations periodically on salary policy, professional training, working hours, and so on.

conventionné(e) Said of a doctor or establishment who/that has signed *une convention,* "an agreement," with *la Sécurité sociale* whereby the physician or organization will not charge more than a certain fee for a visit, an operation, or other medical services. In practical terms, this means that the doctor's retirement benefits will be paid for by *la Sécu*. A doctor who is *non conventionné(e)* charges higher fees; that is, his or her retirement benefits are in effect being paid for directly by the patient.

convoi (m.) **humanitaire** This phrase came into use as of 1992 with *la guerre en ex-Yougoslavie,* to designate a convoy of vehicles carrying food, medical supplies, or other types of aid. *Couloir* (m.) *humanitaire,* "passageway, through enemy or contested territory, created and acknowledged so that *des convois humanitaires* can get through." See **ingérence**

coopération (f.) *La coopération* is a nonmilitary form of national service and lasts about two years. Often carried out in some developing country or area of the world, it can involve working with a French firm or bank abroad or with an embassy. *Faire sa coopération; être coopérant.*

coordination (f.) Less formal than a labor union, this is an attempt by strikers to organize in order to express their grievances and support their strike movement. During the second Mitterrand presidency, French nurses, *les infirmières,* formed *une coordination* and went on strike for better pay, shorter hours, and higher status in recognition of the increasingly technological nature of their duties. Students, too, may form *une coordination.*

copropriété (f.) Condominium. Each unit in a building or group of buildings belongs to a different owner, but *les parties communes* (*toiture, entrée, cour, jardin, escalier, palier, ascenseur, couloir des caves, loge de la gardienne le cas échéant et ainsi de suite*) belong *conjointement,* "jointly," to all the owners. *Tous les copropriétaires partagent les frais d'entretien et de réparation de ces parties communes;* "Together the copropriétaires share the costs of upkeep and repairs of the common areas of the building." They hold an annual *assemblée générale* to make decisions concerning them.

coq (m.) **gaulois** Symbol of France; literally, the Gallic rooster. *Pousser/Lancer des cocoricos,* to crow cock-a-doodle-doo (i.e., to be chauvinistic).

corbeille (f.) The central enclosure at *la Bourse,* "the stock exchange."

corporatisme (m.) *Une corporation,* in the Middle Ages, was a guild. Today, the phrase *pratiquer le corporatisme* is often used accusingly, as a lofty way of saying "to give preference to the old-boy network." *Par exemple, un ingénieur Polytechnicien recrute un autre Polytechnicien, et ainsi de suite;* "For instance, an engineer who has graduated from l'Ecole polytechnique will hire another Polytechnique graduate, and so forth."

Corrèze (f.) The *département* from which President Chirac hails. It is in the western part of the *Massif Central,* an essentially rural region.

corruption (f.) **passive** Like **complicité de corruption,** a common accusation brought in the course of investigations into the connections between political and business figures.

Corse (f.) Corsica, often called *l'Ile de Beauté.* The first *département* to be *libéré* from the Axis forces; liberation was achieved in September 1943, almost a year before Paris was liberated. Divided into two *départements* in 1974. In recent years pressure in favor of Corsican independence from France has been stepped up by a minority using terrorist means (*bombes, voitures piégées,* etc.), chiefly against police stations and other government buildings and offices. By mid-summer 1996 the violence had reached such a point that Raymond Barre, an *UDF* former prime minister known for not speaking out rashly, exclaimed, *"S'ils veulent leur indépendance, qu'on la leur donne!"* "'If they want their independence, let's give it to them!'" In February 1998 *le Préfet de Corse,* appointed by Paris, was assassinated.

There have been *règlements de compte,* "bloody attempts to settle scores," between various factions of the *Fédération de libération nationale de la Corse* (*FLNC*) and other groups. One radio talk show in late 1996 deplored *la dérive de certains mouvements nationalistes corses vers le banditisme et la dérive mafieuse et le fait qu'ils tiennent des conférences de presse cagoulées,* "the fact that some Corsican nationalist movements were drifting off course into banditry and Mafia-type pressure and tactics, and wore hoods and masks while holding press conferences." Said one speaker, *"Est-ce que la Corse est encore un état de droit? Si les organisations clandestines se dissolvent, vous aurez demain des petites bandes dans les micro-régions";* "'Is Corsica still ruled by law? If the secret organizations break up, next thing you know you'll have lots of miniregions each with its own gang(s).'"

In the mid–eighteenth century Corsica belonged to Genoa, but Genoa sold the island to France in 1767; two years later Napoleon Bonaparte (Buonaparte) was born there.

COS (m.) *Coefficient d'occupation des sols,* land planning or zoning density.

cosmonaute (m. or f.) A word used interchangeably with *astronaute* and *spationaute.*

cote (f.) **d'amour** *Cote* always conveys the idea of a measurement, a level, a rating. *Avoir la cote d'amour,* to be very popular. *La cote d'amour de Lionel Jospin est en hausse, d'après le dernier sondage réalisé;* "Lionel Jospin's popularity rating is rising, according to the latest poll."

cotisations (f. pl.) Generally speaking, these are the dues that you pay to an association, club, or the like. However, *cotisations sociales* are **charges sociales.**

couche (f.) **d'ozone** Ozone layer. *Le trou dans la couche d'ozone suscite beaucoup de soucis;* "The hole in the ozone layer is causing a great deal of concern."

couloir (m.) **autobus** On a city street, this is a lane that only buses (and sometimes taxis) can use; *souvent il va dans le mauvais sens dans une rue à sens unique,* "it often goes the 'wrong' way in a one-way street." *Couloir pour vélos,* a narrower lane for use only by bicycles; more such lanes are being created, in an attempt to encourage people to use bikes instead of cars.

couloir (m.) **humanitaire** See **convoi humanitaire; ingérence**

couloir (m.) **rhodanien** An elaborate, geopolitical way of saying "the Rhone valley." Similarly, there is *le bassin rhodanien,* "the Rhone River basin." See **Rhin-Rhône**

coup (m.) **de frein** *Il faut un coup de frein sur les dépenses de la Sécu;* "We have to slow down (put the brakes on) spending by the *Sécurité sociale.*"

Coupe (f.) **Davis** Davis Cup, won by the French team in 1991 for the first time since 1932. The French won again in 1996, still coached by Yannick Noah. See **Noah, Yannick; Roland Garros; saladier d'argent**

Coupe (f.) **d'Europe** The European soccer championship.

Coupe (f.) **du monde** The World Cup, the international soccer tournament held every four years. In 1998 it took place in France. *L'équipe de France, entraînée par Aimé Jaquet, a gagné, et tous ses membres ainsi que l'entraineur ont été nommés Chevaliers de la Légion d'honneur.* See **Mondial; plurielle; Stade de France**

couple (m.) **franco-allemand** In unofficial diplomatic language and in journalese, this refers to the unique relationship between France and Germany. The concept dates from after World War II—which began with the third invasion of France by German troops in three generations (1870, 1914, 1940)—and is intended to promote peace between the two countries and a shared European leadership role. Konrad Adenauer and Charles de Gaulle were the first "couple" to personify the relationship; Willy Brandt/Helmut Schmidt and Valéry Giscard d'Estaing were another, followed by Helmut Kohl and François Mitterrand/Jacques Chirac.

coup (m.) **médiatique** A media scoop. *Par exemple, le débarquement des troupes américaines en Somalie a été un sacré coup médiatique.*

coureur (m.) **cycliste** Anyone who takes part in *une course cycliste,* a bicycle race, from the Tour de France on down. *Coureur automobile,* racing car driver. *Un coureur* (without any adjective) is anyone who runs in a race of any kind—*le 100 mètres haies, le 400 mètres, le Marathon de Paris.*

couronne (f.) *La petite couronne* and *la grande couronne* refer to the outlying districts around Paris. The entire Paris region constitutes *l'Ile-de-France,* whose inhabitants are *les Franciliens(iennes).* It comprises several *départements:* 75 (Paris proper—i.e., the 20 *arrondissements*), 77 (*Seine-et-Marne*), 78 (*Yvelines*), 91 (*Essonne*), 92 (*Hauts de Seine*), 93 (*Seine-Saint-Denis*), 94 (*Val de Marne*), and 95 *Val d'Oise.*

courrier (m.) **électronique** E-mail, which is often also called *E-mail* even though the French government decreed that its official name in French would be *mél* (m.), meaning *message électronique.* The word *courriel* (m.) has also been coined. See **Internet**

cousu main Hand-stitched. *C'est du cousu main* applies not just to fabric or clothing but to any field: "it's top notch, first-rate."

covoiturage (m.) Car pool. The word may exist in the minds of city planners and traffic engineers, but the actual system is more of *un voeu pieu,* "wishful thinking," at this stage.

CP *Cours préparatoire,* the first year of *l'école primaire.* It used to be called *la onzième,* since years in the French primary and secondary school system are numbered backward. *CP* is followed by two years of *Cours élémentaire, CE1 and CE2* (formerly called *la dixième* and *la neuvième*), then by two years of *Cours moyen, CM1 and CM2* (formerly *la huitième* and *la septième*). By this time pupils are about ten or eleven years old and move up to *le collège* (from *la sixième* to *la troisième*). At fourteen or fifteen they go on to *le lycée,* consisting of three years: *la seconde, la première,* and, finally, *la terminale.* See **collège**

crèche (f.) Day care center. Many *futures mamans* who work or plan to work hope to find *une place dans une crèche (municipale ou de quartier) pour leur enfant,* but to do so, they (almost) have to apply for it even before they are pregnant. *La crèche parentale (familiale)* is a variation on the theme, whereby the parents themselves take turns running the *crèche* and looking after all the children. Another alternative is *une nourrice agréée,* "a woman who is licensed by the local health authorities to look after infants (*des nourrissons*) and very young children."

During the **événements de mai 68,** students who were occupying *le théâtre de l'Odéon, la Sorbonne,* and other public buildings in Paris and *en province* set up *des crèches sauvages*—that is, improvised child care centers for their children. See **sauvage**

crédible *D'après le dernier* **sondage** *Sofres, 57% des Français trou-*

vent que la classe politique n'est plus crédible; "According to the latest Sofres poll, 57 percent of the French people feel that politicians are no longer credible."

créer *Créer 700.000 emplois* was one of the Socialist Party's campaign promises in 1997. *La création d'emplois concernerait surtout les collectivités locales et la fonction publique;* "Jobs would be created chiefly at municipal level and in the civil service."

Creys-Malville Site, in eastern France, of *le surgénérateur Superphénix.*

crime (m.) **contre l'humanité** A phrase made famous by the Nuremberg trials at the end of World War II and applied since then to events in *l'ex-Yougoslavie.*

crise (f.) *Un des mots clé de cette dernière décennie;* "One of the key words in the past decade." *La crise* refers to *la situation économique en général, la **mondialisation**, le **chômage**,* and to the resultant atmosphere—*la morosité, la sinistrose. Sortir de la crise, tel est le but du gouvernement, du monde des affaires, et de tout un chacun,* "such is the aim of government, business, and everyone else."

crispation (f.) State of physical tension or contraction; its use in the figurative sense has now become common. *Une crispation sur le nationalisme,* a dogmatic approach or hard line with regard to nationalism. *Le ton n'est pas à la négociation; le ton est à la crispation.*

critères (m. pl.) **de convergence** These are the economic criteria with which the various member countries of *l'Union européenne,* "the European Union," had to comply by 1998 if their currencies were to be replaced by *la monnaie unique,* "the European single currency," as laid down by the Maastricht Treaty of 1992. The criteria related, among others, to the budget deficit; it was not supposed to exceed 3 percent of the *produit intérieur brut (PIB),* "gross domestic product (GDP)" in each country. To date, there is only *une monnaie commune,* "a common currency," in Europe; once called the ecu, it has been renamed the **euro.** But since all European countries continue to use their individual currencies, the *euro* is not yet *la monnaie unique,* as it will be under full monetary union.

Dans les rangs des anti-Maastricht, on clame que les gouvernements successifs, dans leur désir excessif de satisfaire aux critères de convergence, négligent le social ou le sacrifient carrément; "The opponents of **Maastricht** proclaim that one government after another, falling all over itself to meet the convergence criteria, has neglected or quite simply sacrificed social legislation and the human dimension of employment."

Croisette (f.) See **Cannes**

croissance (f.) *Un autre mot clé,* referring to *la croissance écono-*

mique. Le taux de croissance, the rate of growth. *Encourager/ atteindre/améliorer la croissance.*

Croissant (m.) **rouge** Red Crescent, the Muslim version of the Red Cross.

croix (f.) **et la bannière** This term conveys the idea of immense effort, tantamount to a veritable Crusade. *Pour convaincre le directeur de changer de tactique, c'est chaque fois la croix et la bannière;* "It takes a huge struggle every time to get the manager to use a different approach."

CRS (f.) *Compagnie républicaine de sécurité,* the riot squad. *Hier soir à Paris les manfestants ont voulu atteindre le **Palais Bourbon**, mais les CRS leur ont barré le chemin;* "The demonstrators in Paris last night tried to get as far as the *Assemblée nationale,* but the security police barred the way."

crypté(e) Encoded. *Notre première chaîne de télévision cryptée pour abonnés,* "our first encoded subscription TV channel." *Décrypter,* to decode.

CSA (m.) *Conseil supérieur de l'audiovisuel,* created in 1989; one-third of its members are appointed by *le Président de la République,* one-third by *le Président du Sénat,* and one-third by *le Président de l'Assemblée nationale.* The watchdog over radio and TV broadcasting, it is meant to be an independent body (its members cannot hold elective office or hold interests of any kind in any commercial firm involved in radio, TV, films, publishing, the press, advertising, or telecommunications), whose functions are to defend freedom of communication, protect children and young people, propose ways to improve broadcasts, foster competition, uphold use of the French language, and so forth.

CSG (f.) *Contribution sociale généralisée,* a new direct tax introduced early in the 1990s and deducted at source, at the rate of 0.95 percent of 1.01 percent of gross income. It is meant to help fund the *Sécurité sociale* (see **trou**) and is said to be democratic since it is levied on everyone's earnings, not only on wages. It quickly rose to 2.4 percent of 95 percent of income and was joined by a similar tax, the *Contribution au remboursement de la dette sociale* (*CRDS*), at the rate of another 0.50 percent of 95 percent of income. See **RDS**

CUCS (m.) See **Contrat d'union civile et sociale**

cuisine (f.) **américaine** A kitchen which is part of the living room, instead of being a separate room. A recent feature of many city apartments, it is meant to convey a modern lifestyle although, oddly enough, it actually revives what used to be the standard feature of old farmhouses, where *la cheminée* and the rest of the kitchen were in the same room as the table, in a room that was often simply called *la salle.*

culte (m.) Worship. *Tous les lieux de culte méritent respect, quelle* *que soit la religion en cause;* "All places of worship should be respected, regardless to which religions they belong." *Dans un temple protestant, le culte se dit aussi pour l'office;* "In a Protestant church, *le culte* is another name for the service."

In a landmark 1997 ruling, the difference between *une secte* and *une religion* was said to depend on whether the movement involved had *un caractère cultuel;* see **Scientologie.**

cumul (m.) **des mandats** One of the most controversial features of the current French political scene. It is possible to *cumuler les mandats,* "hold two or more posts simultaneously"; generally one is on the local level and the other(s) on the national level. Chirac, for instance, who was already *Maire de Paris,* was also *Premier ministre* from 1986 to 1988. His own first *Premier ministre,* Alain Juppé, appointed in 1995, was also elected *Maire de Bordeaux* at the same time.

In 1997, Lionel Jospin, Juppé's successor, declared that he was *pour le non-cumul, c'est-à-dire il voulait interdire le cumul des mandats.*

cuvée (f.) Vintage or year, as applied to wines and, by extension, when used figuratively. *"Les écolos cuvée 1996,"* "'1996-Style Environmentalists,'" was the headline in one newspaper.

CV (m.) *Curriculum vitae,* or résumé. In France, it commonly indicates the applicant's age and marital status and often includes the applicant's photograph. *Mettre à jour son CV,* to update your résumé. *En envoyant son CV il faut joindre une lettre de motivation, généralement manuscrite;* "You have to send a personal letter, usually a handwritten one, with your résumé."

D

Daewoo Korean firm to which the French government decided to sell **Thomson S.A.,** a money-losing communications firm, for *un franc symbolique* in 1996. There had been strong lobbying to sell it to Matra, a French firm. Thomson employees in Alsace protested strongly at the government's choice, although Daewoo promised to create five thousand jobs in Alsace. The European Commission later challenged the sale and Daewoo withdrew.

Dallas The American TV serial that was a major hit on French television and spawned French-made imitations.

Dame de Fer The Iron Lady—Margaret Thatcher, British prime minister for over eleven years until late 1990. *En tant que Premier ministre de la perfide **Albion** (q.v.), et en outre la première*

femme Premier ministre en Europe, elle a fortement impres-
sionné les Français; "As the prime minister of England, and
indeed the first woman prime minister in Europe, she made a
strong impression on the French." France's first woman prime
minister, Edith Cresson, was not appointed until 1991.

La dame de fer was also "the iron maiden," a medieval torture instrument (a hollow metal statue, with spikes inside in
it, in which the victim was enclosed). Did French journalists
adopt this term to designate the British PM because they
found her personality imposing?

dangerosité (f.) A relatively recent coinage, meaning dangerous-
ness. *Le Monde,* in April 1996, talked about *la dangerosité des
répliques d'armes,* "dummy weapons."

DATAR (f.) *Délégation à l'aménagement du territoire. Territoire*
here refers to France itself and not to the *DOM-TOM.* It is a
government agency to foster the development of the various
regions of France—for example, by attracting foreign and
other investment.

date (f.) **butoir** *Date limite* is still a perfectly good expression, but
date butoir has largely supplanted it in recent years. It is derived from *un butoir,* "a buffer," as at the end of a track in a
train station. *La date butoir pour achever la deuxième étape de
ce projet est l'an 2005;* "The deadline for completing the second phase of this project is 2005."

daube (f.) This word has long existed in the culinary sense but is
now becoming a popular colloquial way of saying that someone or something is flimsy or not creditworthy: *Les promesses
des hommes politiques, disait un des grévistes, c'est de la daube!*
The related verb *dauber,* "to denigrate or criticize," is not
much used anymore.

DDASS (f.) *Direction départementale de l'action sociale et sani-
taire.* The health and social services agency, best known to the
public as the official foster parent. When a child is orphaned
or abandoned, or when the courts decide to separate parent(s)
and child, in the interests of the child, the child will come under the authority of the *DDASS. Etre un enfant de la DDASS,*
therefore, carries the connotation of an underprivileged
childhood, of coming from a broken home, and, from then on,
of being looked after in an impersonal, institutionalized
setting.

Deauville Nearest beach to Paris, launched as a fashionable resort
during the Second Empire. Known today for its horse races
and other equestrian events and auctions and for its annual
festival du cinéma américain.

débâcle (f.) A ruinous defeat, such as that in 1870 by the Prussians
or that of 1940 by the Germans. By extension, *la débâcle sociale* is a term used by some economists, harshly criticizing the

result of economic policies applied by recent French governments.

Débarquement (m.) The D-day landing in Normandy on June 6, 1944. Another *débarquement* by Allied forces occurred on August 15 of the same year, in Provence, but is little commemorated now.

débordement (m.) Overflow; by extension, an excess, the fact of evading discipline, getting out of control. *Au cours du défilé des grévistes, il s'est produit quelques débordements;* "While the strikers were marching, things got out of hand here and there."

débrayage (m.) A work stoppage, generally briefer or more limited or symbolic than *une grève*, as in *Des débrayages ont eu lieu dans toutes les usines Renault en Europe après l'annonce de la décision de fermer* **Vilvoorde.**

Debré See **hébergement; loi Debré**

décalage (m.) **horaire** Jet lag. *Je sens encore le décalage horaire/Je ne me suis pas encore remis(e) du décalage horaire;* "I can still feel/haven't yet got over the jet lag." All of France is in a single *fuseau* (m.) *horaire,* "time zone."

de ceux/de celles Term often used by a speaker or writer to convey a personal opinion and at the same time to suggest that he or she is not the only one to hold that opinion, as in *Moi, je suis de ceux/de celles qui estiment/préconisent/mettent en garde contre/croient/souhaitent/condamnent,* etc.; "Personally, I am one of those people who consider/advise/warn against/believe/would like/are against, etc." Or "I am the kind of person who . . ."

déchets (m. pl.) Waste, especially industrial. *Les ordures* (f. pl.), garbage. *Décharge* (f.) *publique,* rubbish or garbage dump. *Une poubelle,* garbage can. *Les éboueurs,* garbage collectors. *Déchetterie®* (f.), garbage collection site. *Incinération* (f.), incineration. *Le volume des déchets/ordures a augmenté de façon spectaculaire avec l'introduction des bouteilles en plastique et des emballages tout faits pour les produits surgelés et les plats à emporter;* "The volume of waste has increased to a spectacular extent with the introduction of plastic bottles and ready-made packaging for frozen foods and carry-out foods."

décideur(euse) (m. or f.) Decision maker. *Les jeunes chefs d'entreprise sont les vrais décideurs de demain;* "Young business leaders are the real decision makers of the future."

décliner In addition to the more obvious meanings (*être sur le déclin* and *décliner une invitation*), *décliner* also means "to run through or exemplify all of the various categories or variations of something," just as with *des déclinaisons* (f. pl.) *de noms,* "noun declensions." *Notre nouvelle gamme de robinets* *se décline dans toutes les couleurs;* "Our new line of bathroom and kitchen taps comes in all colors."

Décliner son identité, to state one's name, address, and so on, when asked.

décloisonner *Une cloison* is "a partition or separation"; so *décloisonner le secteur public et le secteur privé,* for instance, means "to remove the barriers between the public and the private sectors."

découpler To consider separately. *Il faudrait découpler la crise du Golfe et la question palestinienne;* "The Gulf crisis should not be linked to the Palestinian question."

décrispation (f.) Relaxation on the political or diplomatic scene. *Il faut tout mettre en oeuvre pour arriver à une décrispation des tensions internationales;* "All efforts must be made to relax international tensions."

dédramatiser To stop considering (something) as *dramatique* (i.e., tragic). *Si on veut avancer dans ce dossier sur l'implantation du nouveau stade, il faut dédramatiser les conséquences du choix;* "If we're to make any headway on choosing a site for the new stadium, we must stop overdramatizing the results that our choice will have."

défavorisé(e) Underprivileged, tough (individuals, neighborhoods). *Quand on grandit dans des quartiers défavorisés, on risque forcément d'être marginalisé, disent les sociologues;* "Sociologists warn that people who grow up in underprivileged neighborhoods are likely to remain on the fringes of society." *Il faut faire davantage d'efforts en direction des défavorisés;* "More has to be done to reach out to people from underprivileged backgrounds."

Défense, La The business district on the western edge of Paris with a Manhattan-style skyline, built in the late 1960s and the 1970s; its towering office buildings and the *Grande Arche de la Défense* (1989) are visible from the *Place de la Concorde* through the *Arc de Triomphe.*

défense (f.) **d'afficher** Post no bills (i.e., it is forbidden to put up posters, ads, etc.). The words are still written in large black capital letters on countless walls and always followed by *"Loi du 29 juillet 1881."* See **afficher**

défense (f.) **de la monnaie** A major preoccupation of France's financial leaders is to protect *la monnaie,* "the national currency," against speculation and excessive fluctuation. *La politique du franc fort* has been the watchword. The official position in the mid-1990s was that *le dollar américain est sous-évalué depuis quelques années, ce qui fait du tort au franc,* "the U.S. dollar has been undervalued for several years, which is detrimental to the franc." Then, early in 1997, when the dollar had risen about 20 percent, several governments gathered together and agreed that its rise should be halted at approximately 5.60 French francs. A few months later the dollar was at about 6.30 francs.

déféré(e) *Etre déféré(e) au parquet. Dans cette affaire de corruption, le PDG de la société a été déféré au parquet;* "As part of this corruption investigation, the company's CEO was ordered to appear in court." *Dans le cadre des enquêtes sur les réseaux nationalistes en* **Corse,** *plusieurs suspects ont été déférés devant le juge;* "In connection with the investigation of nationalist networks in Corsica, several suspects were handed over to the law." See **parquet**

déferlante (f.) Figuratively, a tidal wave, an irresistible force for change. *Une déferlante est en train d'arriver avec l'émergence de la Chine.*

déficit (m.) A deficit can be literal or figurative. The best known of the **critères de convergence** under the Maastricht Treaty and perhaps one of the hardest criteria to meet concerns the size of each country's budget deficit in relation to its GDP. See **Traité de Maastricht**

In a radio interview early in 1997, Jacques Santer, head of the European Commission, spoke about *le déficit social de l'Europe actuelle,* meaning that employment protection measures were lagging behind other considerations in Europe today; see *pensée unique.*

défilé (m.) **du 14 juillet** The traditional Bastille Day parade in Paris from the *Arc de Triomphe* to the *Place de la Concorde.* It is an occasion for displaying every aspect of the armed forces, including the *sapeurs-pompiers* (m. pl.), the firefighters. A controversial innovation, introduced by President Mitterrand in 1994, was the inclusion of troops from a joint Franco-German regiment, created in an attempt to foster peace in Europe and emphasize the **couple franco-allemand.**

dégraisser One of the nastier images associated with *la suppression d'emplois;* it means that a firm pares away the fat, slims down, streamlines, sheds employees. A common term, although the official phrase might be *réduire les effectifs. La direction va procéder à un sérieux dégraissage.* When the new Socialist *Ministre de l'Education nationale* took up his functions in 1997, he looked at his unwieldy charge and said that he hoped to *dégraisser le mammouth,* "make the monster slim down."

dégriffé Said of clothing sold at very reduced prices because *la griffe,* "the manufacturer's or designer's label," has been removed.

délai (m.) Not a delay, which is *un retard,* but a period of time, or an extension thereof. *Le gouvernement a un délai très court* *pour répondre aux dernières propositions syndicales;* "The government does not have much time to react to the unions' latest proposals." *Les responsables du tunnel sous la Manche ont demandé aux banquiers de leur accorder un délai supplémentaire pour rembourser leurs créances;* "The heads of the consortium that built the Channel Tunnel asked the banks to extend the deadline for paying back their loans."

délégué(e) du personnel Nonunion employees' delegate or staff delegate, in dealings with management. *Délégué(e) syndical(e),* labor union delegate, shop steward.

délit (m.) **d'initiés** Insider trading or dealing, of which some of President Mitterrand's *proches collaborateurs* were accused during his second term. *Un délit* is "a misdemeanor" or "a criminal offense"; it is less serious than *un crime.*

délocaliser A verb that burst on the scene early in 1992, when it was announced that the sacrosanct *Ecole nationale d'administration (ENA), the grande école* which produces so many future top government officials, was going to leave *la rue de l'Université* in Paris and move to . . . Strasbourg! One reason, it was said, was that this would bring the ENA nearer the European Parliament, which is located in Strasbourg. In fact, this was a new term for the hitherto chimerical notion of *décentralisation,* which would be needed to overcome the immense amount of political power wielded by Paris in relation to all the rest of the country. See **province.** Since 1992, bits and pieces of other government functions or apparatus have also been moved from Paris to other cities.

The business world too has embraced the notion of *délocalisation,* "outsourcing." Hoover caused *un tollé général,* "a general outcry," in 1993 when it announced that it was closing its plant in Dijon and moving operations to Scotland. Moulinex household appliances announced plans in 1996 to use Mexican labor and lay off a significant portion of its workers in France.

Delors, Jacques The Frenchman who was president of the European Commission from 1985 to 1994; *un fervent partisan de la construction de l'Europe,* "an ardent supporter of the creation of Europe." As the end of his presidency neared, there was feverish speculation as to the role he could play thereafter in French political life. *Le PS espérait qu'il se présenterait comme candidat à la présidence de la République en 1995;* "The Socialist Party hoped that he would be its candidate for president in the 1995 elections." But Delors declined to run; Lionel Jospin became the Socialist candidate instead, and Jacques Chirac was elected.

delta plane (m.) Hang glider.

demandeur(euse) (m. or f.) **d'emploi** The official term for an unemployed person; literally, a job seeker. The unofficial but common term is *chômeur(euse)*. *Le nombre de demandeurs d'emploi a augmenté de 0,9% au cours du mois de mars, annonce le porte-parole du gouvernement,* The number of job-seekers increased by 0.9 percent in March, the government spokesman has announced.

démanteler Commonly heard in *démanteler un réseau de pédophilie/un réseau de trafic de drogues/un réseau nationaliste,* to break up a child abuse/drug dealing/nationalist network.

démission (f.) This usually means "resignation," as in *donner sa démission,* "to hand in one's resignation." But in talking about problems of violence and crime *chez les jeunes,* one cause often mentioned is *la démission des parents,* "the fact that parents abdicate their responsibilities."

dépénaliser To decriminalize; in other words, to legalize. *Il y a une grande controverse: faut-il ou non dépénaliser les drogues dites douces,* "so-called soft drugs"?

dépendance (f.) Dependency; *la dépendance des personnes âgées;* or addiction: *la dépendance des drogué(e)s.*

dépenses (f. pl.) **actives** See **revendications sociales des chômeurs**

dépistage (m.) Detection by following *une piste,* "a trail." *Arrivera-t-on un jour au dépistage systématique du virus du Sida?* "Will it be possible one day to track down the AIDS virus systematically?"

déplacement (m.) The fact of traveling about for business or professional reasons. *Les déplacements du Premier ministre sont toujours suivis de près par les journalistes. La directrice des ventes ne peut pas vous recevoir aujourd'hui, elle est en déplacement.*

Se déplacer, to move about within any given space. *Le PDG s'est déplacé personnellement pour lui serrer la main;* "The company's chairman came over in person to shake his (or her) hand." See **PDG**

dépôt (m.) **de bilan** Declaring bankruptcy: *déposer son bilan. Le nombre de dépôts de bilan chez les PME est en hausse cette année de 5% par rapport à l'année dernière;* "The number of small and medium-sized firms that have declared bankruptcy has gone up 5 percent over last year's figure." *La défaillance d'entreprise* is a synonym for *le dépôt de bilan.* See **PME**

dépôt-vente (m.) A second-hand or thrift shop. It has become increasingly widespread for women's clothing in recent decades but less so for men's and children's. You leave the clothes on deposit with the shop, which pays you 50 percent of the asking price if it succeeds in selling them. Often called *troc* (m.), but that term is something of a misnomer because *le troc* means barter. *La formule du dépôt-vente* now seems to be spreading, to some extent, to household goods and furniture as well. A sign of the times? *Les temps sont difficiles.*

dépoussiérer To update, dust off, freshen up *une loi, une image de marque, une position syndicale . . . ,* "a law, a brand image, a labor union position, etc."; *le depoussiérage.* Like *toiletter,* **toilettage.**)

déprime (f.) *Faire une déprime, être en pleine déprime,* and *déprimer* are colloquial ways of saying "to feel low, blue" and can extend to mean *faire une dépression,* "to have a nervous breakdown." *Une déprime* can apply to people or sectors of activity: *la Bourse est en pleine déprime;* "The stock market is having a major slump."

dérapage (m.) Skidding, getting out of control. *Le dérapage de la situation; le dérapage des accords de paix. Le déficit de la Sécu pourrait connaître un nouveau dérapage;* "The deficit in the Social Security budget could get out of hand again." *Certains propos de Monsieur Le Pen constituent un dérapage plus ou moins contrôlé* (see **détail; Durafour crématoire**).

déréglementer To deregulate. *Le transport aérien* en Europe est *déréglementé depuis le 1er janvier 1997;* "Air transport in Europe has been deregulated since January 1, 1997."

dérive (f.) Drifting off course. *La dérive mafieuse s'est-elle installée en* **Corse?** "Is Corsica drifting into a Mafia-type situation?" *Produits dérivés,* derivatives.

désaffection (f.) Disenchantment; falling out of love. Also called *le désamour. La désaffection du public avec tout ce qui touche de près ou de loin à la politique est palpable;* "The public's disenchantment with anything even remotely related to politics is blindingly obvious." *Le désamour des Français à l'égard d'Alain Juppé, premier Premier ministre de Jacques Chirac.* See **discrédit**

désamianter To remove *l'amiante* (m.), "asbestos," that was installed earlier. *Le désamiantage de la Faculté de Jussieu devait être achevé en 1997;* "They were supposed to finish stripping the asbestos from the building at *Jussieu* (*Université de Paris*) by 1997."

désamorcer To defuse a situation (*une crise, un conflit*) or prevent a thing (*une bombe*) from exploding.

descendre dans l'arène Said figuratively of a political candidate who campaigns actively; the image is that of a bullfighter. Bullfights are popular in certain towns in southwestern France, *mais souvent les combats sont du type dit corrida portuguaise, c'est-a-dire sans mise à mort,* "but they are often in the so-called Portuguese style (i.e., the bull is not killed in the arena)."

descendre dans la rue To go out and demonstrate in the streets; *manifester. Les étudiants ne sont pas encore descendus dans la rue cette année;* "Students have not yet staged demonstrations this year." *Les syndicats appellent leurs adhérents à descendre massivement dans la rue;* "The unions are urging their members to turn out in great numbers for a demonstration."

désenclaver Rural regions which no longer have any public transport—*la gare SNCF est fermée, et il n'y a aucun service de cars;* "the railway station is closed, and there is no bus service"— become *enclavées,* "land-locked," and *isolées,* "isolated." They wish to be *désenclavées.*

déséquilibré(e) (m. or f.) A person who is mentally unbalanced. *En 1997 le Ministre de la Culture, lors d'une cérémonie en public, s'est fait poignarder par un déséquilibré; heureusement ses blessures étaient légères.* "During a public appearance in 1997, the minister of culture was stabbed by a mentally unbalanced man; luckily he was only lightly wounded."

désertification (f.) The transformation—by drought, wind, overgrazing, and so on—of formerly fertile or semiarid land into desert.

A further meaning, applying specifically to France itself is the gradual abandonment of rural regions as farmers and shepherds move away to urban regions or die out. *Ces mesures fiscales sont destinées à aider la lutte contre la désertification;* "These tax measures are intended to help combat the abandonment of rural regions."

désincitation (f.) A neologism meaning "disincentive." *Si on baissait le SMIC cela désinciterait les gens à travailler puisqu'il se rapprocherait du RMI;* "If the minimum wage were lowered, that would discourage people from working because it would not be far above the minimum income allowance." See **RMI; SMIC**

désinformation (f.) The practice of distorting facts, often for propaganda purposes. *Les actualités cinématographiques pendant la guerre ont souvent pratiqué la désinformation;* "News reels during the war frequently distorted the truth."

Désir, Harlem First head of **SOS Racisme,** a prominent civil rights organization created in 1984 as the influx of immigrants, chiefly from former French colonies in Africa and North Africa, began giving rise to an anti-immigration reaction among part of the French population in France. See also **pote**

désistement (m.) An important electoral maneuver. *Après le premier tour de scrutin, un ou plusieurs candidats ou parties se désistent afin que les électeurs, lors du deuxième tour, puissent concentrer leurs voix sur le/la candidat(e) ou le parti le mieux placé;* "One or more candidates or parties withdraw, after the first round of voting, so that during the second round, voters will not scatter their votes and instead will be able to concentrate them on the person or party with the best chance."

dessous des cartes What the public is never told; the real explanation of what transpires in public. Each week, on *Arte,* a brief but dense TV program called *Le dessous des cartes* strives to provide the geopolitical background of a given historical situation or development.

destitution (f.) Impeachment. A word very rarely used in France, but in the autumn of 1998 the media asked, *Une procédure de destitution sera-t-elle engagée contre le Président Clinton?*

détail (m.) An ordinary enough word, but one that has become famous because in an interview in 1987, Jean-Marie Le Pen, the *Front national* leader, stated casually that *les chambres à gaz,* "the gas chambers," in which Jews were killed in World War II were *"un point de détail de l'histoire."* Ten years later, in Germany, Le Pen reiterated the statement while on a visit to a former Waffen SS member.

détenteur(trice) du record Record holder. *Est-ce que l'ukrainien, détenteur du record de saut à la perche, pourra encore gagner cette année?* "Will the Ukrainian, who holds the pole vault record, be able to win again this year?"

détourner To distract or deflect from the rightful or usual goal or path. *Un détournement d'avion,* a hijacking, committed by *un pirate de l'air. L'annonce de ces mesures risque de détourner des électeurs du Parti socialiste;* "The news of these measures is likely to make some voters turn away from the Socialist Party." *Un détournement de fonds,* embezzlement.

détraquer To make something (or someone) malfunction, go off the tracks, go haywire: *Le système politique (s')est détraqué. Un(e) détraqué(e),* a person who is not right in the head; a word that is much more *familier* than **déséquilibré.**

DEUG (m.) The first university degree, the *Diplôme d'études universitaires générales.* It is a two-year course of study, and students are allowed three years in which to complete it; that is, they may repeat either the first or the second year but not both. *Faire son DEUG* or *être en DEUG, obtenir son DEUG, rater son DEUG.* The next step after *le DEUG* is *la* **licence.**

deux vitesses Literally, two different speeds or gears. *Par manque de cohésion et de solidarité, notre société est devenue une société à deux vitesses; la France est maintenant un pays à deux vitesses.* "Because there is not enough equality or closeness in the society we live in, it has become a two-tier society; France is now a two-tier country." A variation on this theme is *plusieurs vitesses: Puisque tous les pays n'ont pas pu satisfaire en même temps aux critères de **Maastricht,** nous risquons d'avoir une Europe à plusieurs vitesses.*

développement (m.) **durable** A leading buzzword among environmentalists and economists; it means "sustainable development." *Le développement durable des ressources naturelles doit être notre objectif, au nom des générations futures;* "The sustainable development of natural resources must be our goal, for the sake of the generations to come."

DGCCRF (f.) *Direction générale de la concurrence, de la consommation et de la répression des fraudes,* the Directorate-General for Competition, Consumer Affairs, and Product Safety/Quality, a government agency with trust-busting and fraud-fighting functions. It investigates practices such as cartels and abuse of dominant position.

diaboliser To assimilate to the devil. *Le Front national accuse les autres partis et les médias de le diaboliser; il voudrait être dédiabolisé.* "The *Front national* accuses the media and the other parties of portraying it in diabolical terms; it wants to be given a clean slate."

dialogue (m.) **social** Contacts on the labor relations scene. *Le dialogue social fait des progrès ces temps-ci;* "Labor and management seem to be coming closer together lately."

Diana *La princesse Diana d'Angleterre est morte à Paris en août 1997, suite à un accident de voiture.* Among the very abundant comments in the media: *"La fin d'un roman-photo" (Le Point);* "'The end of a photo-romance.'" (A *roman-photo* is a sentimental love story laid out like a comic book but using photographs of actors instead of drawings; it is usually in black and white, and the characters speak in bubbles like comic book characters.) The magazine *Elle* talked about *"une femme libre,"* about *"ce don de lumière qui touche l'âme,"* and said that her life had quickly turned from *un conte de fées,* "a fairy tale," into *un compte de faits,* "a tale of hard facts." *Le Monde* called her *"Diana, princesse de la planète"* and noted that *"La Princesse de Galles était sans doute l'image par excellence"* but that *"à l'heure de la mort (les paparazzi) proposent l'image de la fin d'une image."* Another *Monde* article (September 9, 1997) talked about *"Drame en quinze ans et trois figures: la femme heureuse, la femme trahie, la femme moderne";* the commentator concluded, after watching Diana's funeral, *"Le foule endolorie chantait devant Westminster . . . et je me demandai . . . si nous ne venions pas d'assister, en Mondovision, au premier cours magistral de socialisme réaliste."*

dictée (f.) What could be duller, you may say, than this old pedagogical tool, to which generations of pupils have been subjected? Yet it is an annual event on a nationwide scale, publicized extensively, televised, held at the Sorbonne, master-of-ceremonied by Bernard Pivot (see **Apostrophes**). Participants, all adults and all volunteers, perspire over a dictation of diabolical subtlety and difficulty; *les accords des participes passés* *des verbes réfléchis* are only the beginning of the torture. Winners are often non-French individuals who apparently take French grammar and spelling even more seriously than the French do themselves. See **orthographe**

Dien Bien Phu Site of the final defeat inflicted on French forces in Indochina, in 1954. The trauma paved the way for international peace negotiations, led by then Prime Minister Pierre Mendès France, later that year.

"Dieu" What Mitterrand was often called by the satirical media, just as de Gaulle, in his day, was dubbed *Qui Nous Savons* or *Qui Vous Savez.* See also **Mongénéral**

différé, en When a radio or TV program is broadcast *en différé,* it has been recorded; it is not live. See **direct, en**

dimanche (m.) Controversial day of the week because a 1923 law requires commercial establishments (except those relating to food) to close on Sundays, except where specific features of society may compel them to do otherwise; unions were proud that their workers did not have to toil on Sundays. Today, however, with the prevalence of cars and two-salary households in which neither parent has much time to go shopping during the week, and with unemployed people often willing to work on Sunday rather than not work at all, the public's priorities have changed. In 1993, a prominent CD and video store on the *Champs-Elysées,* the **Virgin Mégastore,** *contestait la fermeture le dimanche,* "challenged the ban," *et réclamait le droit d'ouvrir le dimanche.* Ikea, the large Swedish home furnishings company with outlets throughout Europe, *a également demandé le droit à l'ouverture dominicale en France,* "also applied to keep its French stores open on Sundays." Court decisions in such cases have sometimes been contradictory. The European Court of Justice leaves it up to national governments to decide on the basis of specific sociocultural features at the national or regional level. See **ouverture dominicale**

diplôme (m.) *Un diplôme* is not just the piece of paper on which a university degree is officially certified; it is the degree itself. *Avoir beaucoup de diplômes. Ce qui manque ce sont des passerelles entre les diplômes et les emplois;* "What is lacking is some way to connect your degrees with getting a job." *Sur un curriculum vitae on indique ses diplômes;* "On your résumé you list your degrees."

direct, en "Live," in radio and TV terms. *Ce concert vous est diffusé en direct;* "This concert is brought to you live." *Avec CNN tous les téléspectateurs ont vécu la guerre du Golfe en direct;* "CNN brought the Gulf War live to television audiences everywhere." See **différé**

discours (m.) This is often used to mean not only a specific speech delivered at a specific time but, more generally, "discourse," "the content of what someone says over a period of time." *Le discours de Monsieur Untel est toujours aussi flou;* "Mr. So-and-So's statements are as vague as ever."

discrédit (m.) *On constate le discrédit croissant de la classe politique;* "Politicians as a whole are more and more discredited." See **crédible**

discrimination (f.) **positive** Translation of the American term "affirmative action" used on *Le téléphone sonne,* a radio talk show, on November 5, 1996, the night of the U.S. presidential elections; the program was devoted to the elections and to American society as a whole.

disjoncter Very common in *le langage familier* to mean "to disconnect, lose self-control suddenly."

disparaître Not only to disappear but also to die, to pass away. *Vingt ans déjà depuis la disparition d'Elvis Presley!* "Can it be twenty years already since Elvis died!"

dispositif (m.) Device, equipment, apparatus, system. *Malgré un dispositif anti-incendie ultramoderne, il a fallu plusieurs jours pour maîtriser l'incendie de forêt entre Marseille et Aubagne;* "Despite a state-of-the-art firefighting system, it took several days to bring the forest fire between Marseilles and Aubagne under control."

disque (m.) **d'or** A singer's or other performer's record that has sold one million copies.

disque (m.) **dur** Computer hard disk.

disque (m.) **noir** Or *disque vinyle,* or *33 tours* (m.), a long-play or 33⅓ rpm record; also referred to by its diameter: *un 30 cm.*

disquette (f.) Computer diskette.

dissolution (f.) The fact of dissolving the parliament and thus bringing about *des élections législatives anticipées.* President Chirac did not dissolve the parliament when he was elected in 1995, and in 1997 his party, the *RPR,* still had a very comfortable majority there, which it would have safely kept until 1998, when elections would have taken place. *Par conséquent son annonce de la dissolution au printemps 1997 et que des élections auraient lieu à peine quelques semaines plus tard a surpris (presque) tout le monde;* "Therefore, when he announced in the spring of 1997 that he was dissolving the parliament and that elections would take place barely a few weeks later, (almost) everyone was taken by surprise." It was widely criticized as a blatant electoral maneuver, since it was assumed that *l'opposition socialiste* would be caught off balance and that their women candidates in particular, who were new to politics, would be unprepared. In an upset victory, the Socialists won the elections by a handsome margin, and bitter infighting ensued within the ranks of the *RPR* and the *UDF.* See **con(ne); perspective**

distributeur (m.) **automatique de billets** Automatic teller machine.

divers gauche (m. pl.) A political term, referring to various small parties on the Left. *La voix d'un divers gauche s'est élevée contre le projet de loi;* "One *Député* from among the small leftist parties expressed opposition to the bill." *Divers droite,* same thing on the Right.

doctorat (m.) The highest university degree. There used to be *le doctorat d'université* and *le doctorat du 3e cycle,* which required two or three years, and *le doctorat d'Etat,* which often took ten or twelve or more. But by the end of the 1980s, they were replaced by *le doctorat nouveau régime* (*NR*), which requires between two and four years of research after *le DEA, diplôme* (m.) *d'études approfondies* (the *DEA* has replaced the old *doctorat du 3e cycle*). Hence, the present sequence of degrees is first *le DEUG;* then *la licence, la maîtrise,* and *le DEA;* and, finally, *le doctorat nouveau régime.* See **DEUG; licence**

DOM-TOM (m. pl.) *Départements d'Outre-mer et Territoires d'Outre-mer,* overseas former colonies that have become territories. The four "DOM" include *la Guadeloupe, la Martinique, la Guyane,* and *la Réunion;* each of these is also considered a region. The "TOM" are *les Iles Kerguelen, la Nouvelle Calédonie, la Polynésie française, Wallis-et-Futuna,* and *les Terres australes et antarctiques;* plus *St-Pierre et Miquelon* and *Mayotte.* See **outre-**

(se) doper To take performance-enhancing drugs. Much talked about during *les Jeux olympiques (les J.O.) et le Tour de France 1998: Le dopage des athlètes est devenu un problème majeur. Est-ce que les athlètes se surdopent?*

    Doper something, to strengthen it. *La baisse des taux d'intérêt va-t-elle doper la consommation?* "Will the lowering of interest rates give consumption a shot in the arm?"

doté(e) de Equipped with. *La France s'est dotée d'un réseau de chemin de fer extrêmement dense;* "France is equipped with (literally, built itself) an extremely dense railway network." *La France s'est dotée d'une bombe atomique dès 1960;* "France had built an atomic bomb by 1960."

double circulation (f.) In 1998 it was announced that for a period of three years after the euro was introduced on January 1, 1999, the **euro** and the franc would be in use simultaneously although euro coins and bills would not actually appear until January 1, 2002. By the end of 1997 many shopkeepers and restaurants began *le double affichage,* showing prices in both francs and euros (converting at a rate of between 6.5 and 7 francs to the euro), and special pocket calculators were put on sale. See **écu**

DPLG *Diplômé par le gouvernement;* the initials are used by architects, nurses, and other professional people to indicate that they are legally certified to practice.

Drancy A suburb north of Paris. During the Vichy years, it was the site of *un camp de détention* (or *camp d'internement*) where political prisoners, including Jews, were interned and from which most of them were deported to *des camps d'extermination,* "concentration camps," in Germany and elsewhere. Therefore, when *l'Eglise de France,* "the French Catholic Church," issued its **déclaration de repentance** in September 1997, it chose to do so at Drancy. See **Gurs; Vél d'hiv**

drapeau (m.) *Servir sous les drapeaux,* to do your military service. *Etre appelé sous les drapeaux,* to be drafted.

Dreux A small city about a hundred kilometers west of Paris, where Jean-Marie Le Pen's *Front national* party first came to nationwide attention when *FN* candidates won local elections in 1983. See **Toulon; Vitrolles**

DRH (m. or f.) *Directeur(trice) des ressources humaines,* a term that in the 1990s has replaced *chef du personnel.* A key word in these days of *chômage massif.*

drogue (f.) *Drogue dure,* hard drug; *drogue douce,* soft drug. *La cocaïne; la coke; le crack; le hash; l'héroïne* (f.); *la marijuana. La came,* junk; *se camer. La neige,* coke, snow. *Une syringue,* a needle. *Renifler, sniffer,* to snort; *une prise,* a snort. *La désintoxication,* treatment, detoxification; *faire une cure de désintoxication; être en cure. Etre en manque,* to have withdrawal symptoms. *Un(e) drogué(e), un(e) toxicomane,* addict. *Etre un(e) drogué(e)* or *un(e) toxicomane,* to be addicted. *Un dealer,* dealer. *Se piquer, se shooter,* to shoot up. *Planer,* to be high, stoned. *Mourir d'une overdose.*

droit (m.) A word that has arisen again and again with each new accusation of corruption in high places and each controversy over immigration and the status of undocumented immigrants: *Nous sommes un pays de droit/un état de droit;* "France is a law-abiding country/a country ruled by law. *Nous sommes un pays de droit, donc les élus impliqués dans les affaires de corruption doivent être mis en examen pour corruption passive,* ". . . therefore elected officials who are implicated in corruption scandals should be placed under investigation." *Nous sommes un pays de droit, donc il faut appliquer la loi à tous les immigrés,* ". . . therefore the law should apply to all immigrants."

droit (m.) **d'asile** Right of sanctuary or asylum. *Demander l'asile* (m.) *politique,* to request political asylum. *Le nombre de demandeurs d'asile augmente.*

droit (m.) **du sol** In July 1997, *le rapport Weil,* a report submitted to the newly elected Socialist government and containing recommendations on immigration policy and the assimilation of immigrants (*l'intégration des immigrés*), suggested *"un retour partiel à la loi antérieure: tout enfant né en France de parents étrangers serait un Français de plein droit à 18 ans"* (*Le Monde,* July 31, 1997); that is, the fact of being born on French soil would confer French nationality (*le droit du sol*). This contrasts with the **code de la nationalité,** whereby a person born in France of foreign parents can only acquire French nationality by applying for it.

droitiser To move to the (political) Right; analogous to *gauchiser,* to move to the (political) Left. *Etatiser,* to place under state control.

droits (m. pl.) **de l'homme** Human rights. These are considered to be a French invention because the French Revolution produced the *Déclaration des droits de l'homme et du citoyen* in August 1789. The preamble refers to *"les droits naturels, inaliénables et sacrés de l'homme."* Article 1 declares, *"Les hommes naissent libres et égaux en droits. . . ."* Article 2 states that *"les . . . droits naturels et imprescriptibles de l'homme . . . sont la liberté, la propriété, la sûreté et la résistance à l'oppression."*

   Plusieurs associations ont été fondées pour défendre les droits de l'homme et combattre le racisme; "Several associations have been founded to defend human rights and fight race discrimination." See **Désir, Harlem; SOS Racisme**

drôle de guerre (f.) The period between the Nazi invasion of Poland, in September 1939, and May 1940, when German tanks advanced southward through the forest of Ardennes from Belgium into France.

Drugstore® (m.) Burst on the scene in Paris in the early 1970s as a sort of glamorous neon-lit soda fountain/snack bar/restaurant selling novelty items and being the all-round place to see and be seen, at the top of the *Champs-Elysées* and at *Saint Germain des Prés.* The brainchild of Marcel Bleustein-Blanchet, it set the marketing trend in France for years thereafter. Now it is somewhat rivaled, though in a different register, by the fast-food chains, which are the sign, or the catalyst, of a different lifestyle, along with various "pubs," *galeries commerciales,* and the like.

dumping (m.) **social** *Faire du dumping social,* to adopt or follow an economic system that does not ensure a minimum (monthly) wage, pays a low hourly rate, and/or provides little or no safety net for workers. *Les Français, envieux du taux de chômage en Angleterre, qui est moins de la moitié du taux en France, oublient que ce pays pratique le dumping social,* note certain French economists; "The French, who envy the English their low unemployment rate (less than half the French rate), forget that England practices social dumping."

Durafour crématoire A pun by Jean-Marie Le Pen in 1988 in a verbal attack on Michel Durafour, the then *Ministre de la Fonction publique. Les fours crématoires,* the crematoriums in the Nazi concentration camps.

durcir *Durcir ses positions,* to take a tougher stance. *Dans ce conflit salarial, un durcissement sur toute la ligne est à craindre de la part des ouvriers;* "In this conflict over pay, it is to be feared that the workers will not budge an inch on any point."

dysfonctionnement (m.) *Des réformes sont nécessaires pour remédier à un dysfonctionnement des prisons qui risque d'engendrer chez les détenus des mutineries;* "Prison reform is necessary because the system is dysfunctional and is likely to lead prisoners to mutiny."

E

éboueur (m.) A garbage collector. Once a job category occupied chiefly by African immigrants but now, with the increase in *le chômage,* attracting native-born Frenchmen as well.

échéance (f.) The known and ineluctable date of something. *Avec l'échéance des élections législatives en perspective,* "with a view to the upcoming legislative elections." *Face aux échéances européennes, le gouvernement doit faire des choix très durs entre la convergence d'une part, et la croissance et l'emploi, d'autre part;* "Because of the deadlines for the launching of the European single currency, the government has to make some very tough choices between meeting the criteria for being included in that currency and fostering growth and employment.

échographie (f.) An ultrasound or CAT scan. One of the most widely prescribed types of medical examination.

(s')éclater To have a ball, a great time. *"Nous musiciens, on a besoin de danser pour s'éclater";* "'Dancing is the way we musicians have a ball,'" said one musician in a radio interview.

écologie (f.) Ecology; also environmentalism. *Ecologiste* (m. or f.), environmentalist, in both the political and the scientific senses; often shortened to *écolo* (m. or f.). *Les partis des écologistes,* the green parties. In fact, several rival environmentalist political parties exist in France (*Mouvement écologiste indépendant, Génération écologie, Les Verts . . .) L'environnement* (m.) is "the environment," but the word *environnementaliste* is virtually never used. *Ecologisme* (m.), environmentalism. *Ecosystème* (m.), ecosystem. *Protéger l'environnement* or *ne pas porter atteinte à l'environnement,* to be environment-friendly.

écomusée (m.) An open-air museum intended to demonstrate or bring to life some past or present feature of the local environment, often in relation to a once-prevailing local industry or activity.

économie (f.) **en surchauffe** An overheated economy.

économiquement faibles (m. or f. pl.) *Un terme politiquement correct,* "a politically correct term," for *les pauvres et les personnes âgées,* "the poor and the elderly."

écoutes (f. pl.) *Etre sur écoutes* (*téléphoniques*), to have your phone tapped, be subjected to wiretapping; *mettre sur écoutes,* to tap someone's phone.

But *être à l'écoute de la France profonde* is what politicians claim they are: "tuned in to the real France, the grassroots France." *Etre un homme/une femme d'écoute,* to be someone who knows how to listen to other people. *On dit que si Juppé n'avait pas la cote c'est parce qu'il ne donnait pas l'impression d'être à l'écoute des Français;* "They say Juppé was unpopular because he didn't give the French people the impression he was listening to them."

écran (m.) *Le grand écran,* movie screen. *Le petit écran,* television. *L'écran d'ordinateur,* computer screen.

Another kind of screen is, of course, the opaque kind, through which nothing is intended to be visible or audible. *Une société écran,* a shell company for laundering money. *Un écran antibruit,* antinoise barrier built, as an afterthought, alongside a congested highway (or along parts of *le boulevard périphérique* around Paris) to shield the inhabitants of nearby apartment buildings and houses from the traffic noise.

écu (m.) The original name of *la monnaie commune,* "the common currency," of the European Union, *l'Union européenne.* The name, however, was changed to *l'euro* (m.). But euro coins and banknotes remain an abstraction; they are not actually in circulation, as each country continues to use its own currency, *sa propre monnaie.* Attempts were made in the media and on billboards to familiarize people with the euro. *La monnaie unique,* "the single currency" was not a reality until January 1, 1999. See **double circulation**

Ecureuil (m.) A squirrel, the symbol and unofficial name of a nationwide savings institution, the *Caisse d'épargne et de prévoyance.* It is distinct from the *Caisse nationale d'épargne,* run by *la Poste* which, as in many other European countries, performs certain banking functions.

Edit (m.) **de Nantes** In 1598 Henri IV issued this edict to end the wars of religion between French Catholics and French Protestants; the bloodiest episode had been *la Saint-Barthélémy,* a massacre of Protestants in Paris in 1572, during the reign of Charles IX. *L'Édit de Nantes* granted French Protestants *la liberté du culte*, "freedom of religion." In 1998 its four hundredth anniversary was abundantly commemorated in France; President Chirac addressed Unesco, whose headquarters are in Paris.

In 1685, however, Louis XIV revoked *l'Edit de Nantes;* as a result of this *révocation* (f.), hundreds of thousands of Protestants emigrated from France. See **protestant(e)**

édito (m.) An editorial or a lead article *dans une revue ou un journal.*

Education (f.) **nationale** The *ministère* in charge of schooling at all levels, from *la maternelle* to *l'université,* throughout the ninety-six *départements* of France, as well as the **DOM-TOM.** It determines curricula and vacation dates, accredits and pays teachers, organizes nationwide competitive exams for their recruitment at certain levels, and so forth.

édulcorant (m.) **de synthèse** Artificial sweetener. *Les édulcorants de synthèse sont utilisés non seulement par des diabétiques mais sont aussi plébiscités par les personnes qui suivent un régime d'amaigrissement;* "They are used not only by diabetics but also, to a massive extent, by people on slimming diets." *De plus en plus de produits, même des comprimés de vitamines, sont marqués "sans sucre";* "More and more products, even vitamin tablets, are marked 'sugar-free.'"

effet (m.) **de serre** The greenhouse effect. *Réchauffement* (m.) *de la planète,* global warming.

effusion (f.) **de sang** Bloodbath. *Avec les agissements des intégristes terroristes, l'Algérie connaît une effroyable effusion de sang;* "Algeria is going through an appalling bloodbath because of the fundamentalists' terrorist attacks."

égalité (f.) **des chances** Giving everyone equal opportunity through schooling. This is the argument against **la sélection** and against the notion of *une* **élite** and *des élites.*

Eglise (f.) **Saint-Bernard** A church in the eighteenth *arrondissement* of Paris where, in July 1996, a group of undocumented immigrants, *des immigrés illégaux* or *immigrés sans papiers,* chiefly from Mali and other former French colonies in Africa, took refuge after having been expelled from other shelters. A number of them had children born on French soil; a number had been living and working in France for several years. They requested residence papers that would allow them to stay in France legally. They reminded the French authorities that their grandfathers or great-grandfathers had fought for France in World Wars I and II. A number of the **sans-papiers** went on a hunger strike that was to last seven weeks. Their cause was taken up by several human rights associations and film stars, who urged the government to negotiate with the *sans-papiers.* The government provided emergency medical treatment for the hunger strikers but said it could not make an exception to the law for an entire category of people, sent the police on a dawn raid to expel the immigrants from the church, and announced that it would review each case individually, *au cas par cas.* The case of the *sans-papiers* aroused intense debate throughout France. See **hébergement; loi Debré**

The police forcibly remove hunger strikers from the church, saying, "Come and get it!" (*A table,* in a police context, also means "OK, time to confess.")

by Ghertman in *Le Canard enchaîné,*
August 14, 1996

élan (m.) A leap forward or surge of vitality. When President Chirac decided to dissolve the parliament (see **dissolution**) in April 1997, he explained that the purpose was to give the country *un nouvel élan partagé.* Since *un élan* is also "an elk" or "a moose," cartoonists were delighted.

élections (f. pl.) **anticipées** Elections which occur earlier than scheduled, as when a **dissolution** takes place. See also **élan**

élections (f. pl.) **présidentielles** Under the **Cinquième République,** presidential elections take place every seven years; elected by direct universal suffrage, the president is the candidate who receives an absolute majority of the votes. *Si aucun candidat n'obtient la majorité absolue, un deuxième tour de scrutin a lieu 15 jours plus tard;* "If no candidate wins an absolute majority, a second round of elections takes place two weeks later." *Les élections doivent avoir lieu au moins 20 jours mais pas plus de 35 jours avant que le mandat du Président en exercice n'expire;* "The elections must take place at least twenty days but no more than thirty-five days before the incumbent's term of office expires."

éléments (m. pl.) **incontrôlés** These are individuals or groups or *les **groupuscules,*** "small groups," that get out of hand during *une manif,* "a demonstration," or *un meeting,* "a rally," or who are not really there to support the cause but are simply looking for some action. They are not necessarily **casseurs;** they may simply be noisy and rowdy, or they may carry disobedience or lawlessness to a murderous extent. See **muguet**

élite (f.) A group or category of individuals—especially *les diplômé(e)s des grandes écoles*—who are viewed by the great majority of people as wielding too much power and having too many privileges. *Les élites.* See **égalité des chances; sélection**

Eltsine, Boris The name of the Russian president, Boris Yeltsin, as transcribed into French.

élus (m. pl.) **locaux** Local officials; literally, those locally elected. *Le rôle des élus locaux dans cette campagne sera considérable;* "Local officials will play a significant role in this campaign." *La décision de permettre à **Eurodisney** d'acheter des terres agricoles et de s'installer à Marnes-la-Vallée a été prise sans que les élus locaux aient été consultés;* "Local officials were not consulted before it was decided to let Eurodisney buy up farmland around Marnes-la-Vallée and build on it."

Elysée (m.) The *Palais de l'Elysée* where French presidents have their offices and official residence. By extension, the presidency or presidential function itself.

E-mail (m.) See **courrier électronique**

embaucher To hire (someone). *Se faire embaucher,* to get (be) hired. *A l'embauche,* at the time of hiring. *Ils étaient trois cents ce matin à se présenter à l'embauche.* See **exojeunes**. It is logical, therefore, for *débaucher* to mean not only "to debauch" but also "to fire, lay off." See **congédier; licencier; suppression d'emploi.**

One way to combat unemployment, it has been suggested, is to offer older employees early retirement and hire younger ones to replace them; this is called *préretraite contre embauche. Le patronat prétend que cela coûte trop cher; certains syndicats rétorquent que cela coûte moins cher que les allocations chômage et le **RMI;*** "The employers' federation protests that that measure costs too much, but some of the unions retort that it costs less than paying out unemployment benefits and a minimum income allowance."

embryon (m.) **congelé** Frozen embryo. *Les embryons congelés portent une date de péremption, comme les aliments surgelés;* "Frozen embryos have an expiration date, just like frozen food."

emploi (m.) **de proximité** Often a euphemism for what used to be called *un petit boulot,* "an odd job." Also a neighborhood job, a work opportunity, as home help or in a convenience store or local business in one's own neighborhood as opposed to a job in *un supermarché* or *dans une zone d'activités* that requires a long commute. See **proximité**

énarque (m. or f.) A graduate of the *Ecole nationale d'administration* (*ENA*), *la plus grande des grandes écoles,* since its graduates, *les diplômé(e)s*, are automatically offered top positions in government, and, as they rise through the ranks and co-opt one another, they govern France at all levels; see **corporatisme.** They are often criticized (by *non-énarques*) for being remote from reality, too cerebral, with little or no hands-on experience of the daily nitty-gritty. A small percentage of graduates opt for top positions in business instead; see **pantoufler.** Admission to *l'ENA* is through a competitive exam, *un **concours.*** It has been said that France is neither *une monarchie* nor *une anarchie* but *une énarchie*. See **délocaliser.**

On a phone-in talk show one listener commented, *"Un énarque qui dirige mal une entreprise et lui fait perdre des milliards, il retrouve un poste dans la haute administration;"* "'If an ENA graduate makes such a mess of running a business that it loses billions (of francs), he'll be given a job as a top-level civil servant.'"

encadrement (m.) Supervision. *Lors de sorties scolaires, l'encadrement des élèves est parfois insuffisant à cause des restrictions budgétaires;* "On school outings, there aren't always enough people to supervise the pupils, because of budget restrictions."

enceinte (f.) *Enceinte* is not only the adjective that means "pregnant." It is also a noun meaning "a setting"; "a forum"; literally, "an enclosure." *"L'ONU est l'enceinte où on peut parler sérieusement de ces problèmes,"* said former President Valéry Giscard d'Estaing, about the Bosnian situation, on *Objection,* a radio talk show, in 1994.

Also, a baffle in a hi-fi system.

endettement (m.) Financial indebtedness; it applies to individuals as well as nations. *Les gens achètent trop facilement à tempérament ou avec leur carte de crédit et ensuite ne peuvent pas assumer leur endettement;* "People buy things too easily on the installment plan or with their credit cards and then cannot pay their debts." See **surendettement**

endogène (adj.) Endogenous, as in *la croissance endogène*, "growth determined by factors internal to the country," such as the development of telecommunications networks, the level of education, the setting in which people lead their daily lives, and so on.

énergie (f.) **renouvelable** Renewable (source of) energy. *Le nucléaire est une énergie renouvelable; le charbon et le pétrole ne le sont pas.* See **combustible; nucléaire**

engin (m.) *Un engin* is not actually an engine. A car engine is *un moteur.* The engine of a train is *une locomotive* or *une motrice.* An airplane's engines are *les moteurs;* a ship's engines are *les machines.*

Un engin is a nontechnical term for a device of any kind with working parts: *un engin explosif, un engin qui fait du bruit,* and so on. *La police a retrouvé caché sous un des sièges du troisième wagon un engin explosif;* "The police discovered an explosive device hidden beneath one of the seats of the third (train) car." A road sign may warn, *"Attention. Sortie d'engins";* "'Truck entrance'" (i.e., trucks, bulldozers and the like may emerge from a side road onto the main road).

engrenage (m.) The image is the meshing of gears and their implacable movement. *Un chômeur est vite pris dans l'engrenage des démarches à faire;* "An unemployed person soon gets bogged down in all the formalities he or she has to go through."

enjeu (m.) **électoral** An electoral issue, something that is at stake in an election. *La question de l'immigration va au-delà d'un enjeu électoral;* "The whole matter of immigration is not just an election issue."

enregistrement (m.) A recording in any sense of the term. *Le tout dernier enregistrement de Johnny Hallyday fait un malheur;* "Johnny Hallyday's latest record is up at the top of the charts."

Also, check-in, at the airport. *A l'enregistrement les agents de sécurité vous posent toutes sortes de questions. Faire enregistrer ses bagages,* to have one's baggage checked.

enseignement (m.) **libre** Private schools—that is, Catholic schools, as distinct from *l'enseignement laïc,* public schools, that is, nondenominational schools. The clash between them, *la querelle scolaire,* has not quite died away; see **Clovis; loi Falloux**

en temps (m.) **réel** In real time. A bureaucratic buzzword. *Je veux que ce rapport soit traduit en temps réel, c'est-à-dire pendant que la réunion se déroule;* "I want this report to be translated in real time—that is, while the meeting is taking place." The radio will announce, *"Les résultats de la Bourse en temps réel";* "'Stock market quotations as they happen.'"

entraîneur (m.) **sportif** Athletics coach. *Une entraîneuse* is the female equivalent; also, "a bar hostess."

entre-deux-tours (m.) The period between two rounds of an election, *le premier tour et le deuxième tour du scrutin.*

L'entre-deux-guerres always refers to the period between the end of World War I, *la grande guerre,* and the beginning of World War II, *la guerre de 39–45.*

L'entre-deux-mers is, of course, part of *le bordelais,* the Bordeaux wine-producing region.

enveloppe (f.) In budgetary terms, this is the total amount set aside for any given item. *A l'intérieur du budget global de l'Education nationale, il y a l'enveloppe de la maternelle, l'enveloppe du lycée, l'enveloppe de l'enseignement supérieur, etc.;* "The overall education budget includes funding for nursery schools, funding for high schools, and funding for higher education, and so on."

épingler To catch someone red-handed; a colloquial way of saying *prendre quelqu'un sur le fait. Se faire épingler,* to be caught in the act. *"Air France épinglée par l'administration américaine,"* said a headline in *Le Monde* on July 31, 1997; the Federal Aviation Administration (FAA) accused Air France of having unwittingly carried tanks of oxygen among the freight loaded on board two passenger flights. An Air France spokesman said it was up to the forwarder of a shipment to declare what the shipment contained.

épreuve (f.) **de force** Showdown: *C'est une épreuve de force entre Boris Eltsine et le parlement russe.*

Since *une épreuve* is "an ordeal or test," *une épreuve olympique* is "an Olympic event." *Le 100 mètres haies féminin est une des épreuves les plus attendues du public français;* "The women's 100-meter hurdles is one of the events most eagerly awaited by French fans."

équipement (m.) **sportif** Sports facility, such as *gymnase* (m.), *stade* (m.), *mur* (m.) *d'escalade . . . ,* gymnasiums, stadiums, rock-climbing walls, and so forth. *Après la deuxième guerre mondiale, la France a fait un énorme effort pour améliorer et augmenter les équipements sportifs, y compris les piscines municipales;* "After World War II, France went to tremendous lengths to improve and increase sports facilities, including public swimming pools."

équivalence (f.) Concerns the recognition of *diplômes* (m. pl.), "degrees," delivered by institutions of higher learning. *En principe, l'équivalence des diplômes universitaires entre les différents pays membres de l'Union européenne existe; en fait, c'est parfois un casse-tête.* "Theoretically, each member country of the European Union recognizes the university degrees conferred in the other member countries; in fact, it is sometimes a headache."

escalade (f.) The escalation or worsening of a situation. *Ce nouvel attentat à Alger représente un nouveau pas dans l'escalade de la violence en Algérie;* "This latest bomb attack in Algiers is a further step toward increased violence in Algeria."

escrime (f.) Fencing. *La France peut toujours compter sur plusieurs médaillé(e)s en escrime aux J.O.;* "France can always count on seeing several of its fencers win medals at the Olympics."

esprit (m.) **cartésien** A logical mind, something the French have long prided themselves on having. (The word *cartésien* derives from the name of the seventeenth-century philosopher René Descartes, best known for his *Discours de la méthode* and his famous phrase *"Je pense donc je suis,"* "'I think, therefore I am.'") It has its practical applications; *les plaques* (f. pl.) *d'immatriculation,* "automobile license plates," are a simple example. They are generally all the same size, shape and color throughout France but you can always tell where a car is from because the last two digits indicate the *département* in which the car is registered (14, *le Calvados;* 33, *la Gironde;* 43, *la Haute-Loire;* 75, *Paris;* and so forth).

ETA (f.) Pronounced euh-tay-ah. Basque separatist movement, Euzkadi Ta Askatasuna, "Basque Country and Freedom," in both France and Spain, founded in 1959. Has had a history of violent clashes with police, kidnappings (industrialists, foreign diplomats and local officials), and assassinations. The majority of the Basque population distances itself from the violence. See also **Euzkadi; Iparretarrak**

étaler les vacances To stagger vacation periods so that not all businesses or school districts are on vacation at the same time. *Arrivera-t-on un jour à un véritable étalement des vacances?*

Etat (m.) **de droit** *La France est un état de droit;* "France is a law-abiding country, a country ruled by law." For the context, see **droit.** *"La Corse s'enfonce dans un état de non-droit,"* wrote *Le Point,* March 16, 1996; "'Corsica is sinking into lawlessness.'"

Etat-patron (m.) The State as employer, another way of saying that in France *le secteur public* is huge. But many economists urge that a less interventionist government is needed to stimulate growth and therefore employment. *"Il faut oublier l'Etat-patron pour en revenir à l'Etat-arbitre,"* wrote *le Nouvel Observateur,* June 19–25, 1997; "'We must discard the concept of the State as employer and revive the idea of the State as arbiter.'"

état (m.) **des lieux** A phrase used in the real estate sector: *faire l'état des lieux,* to examine the property and determine what condition it is in. By extension, *le Parti socialiste devra faire l'état des lieux de l'économie;* "The *PS* will have to take inventory of the economy" (after its unexpected victory in the early legislative elections of 1997).

état-providence (m.) Welfare state.

Etats-Unis (m. pl.) Always conjugated with a plural verb in French: *Les Etats-Unis dominent la diplomatie occidentale. Les Etats-Unis attirent de plus en plus de touristes français. Les Etats-Unis ont imposé leur cinéma et leur **fast food** au monde entier;* "The United States dominates Western diplomacy. The United States attracts more and more French tourists. The United States has imposed its movies and its fast food on the entire world."

étranger(ère) en situation irrégulière Official term for undocumented immigrant. See **charter; Eglise Saint-Bernard; expulser du territoire; sans-papiers.** *Etre en règle,* to have all your official papers, to have gone through all of the required administrative formalities.

être au rendez-vous To be there on the appointed day, to avoid being left out. *Est-ce que la France sera au rendez-vous de **Maastricht?***

euphorisant (m.) Antidepressant medication.

euro (m.) **Jacques Delors,** discussing what is at stake in the creation of the euro, the projected single currency of the European Union, stated, *"Il faut que l'euro s'impose comme monnaie de réserve pour les banques centrales du monde entier, comme monnaie de placement pour les épargnants et comme importante monnaie de transaction dans les échanges mondiaux"* (*Nouvel Observateur,* August 7–13, 1997); "'The euro will have to gain acceptance as a reserve currency for central banks throughout the world, as an investment currency for individuals wishing to build up savings, and as a major transaction currency in world trade.'"

eurochômage (m.) Related to the idea of **eurogrève.**

eurocompatible One of the countless adjectives coined from the word *Europe* both before and since adoption of the **Traité de Maastricht** in 1992. *Est-ce que la solution adoptée en matière fiscale est eurocompatible?* "Is the solution that has been adopted with regard to taxes compatible with the requirements of the European Union?"

Eurocorps (m.) The combined Franco-German armored unit which took part, in 1994, in *le défilé du 14 juillet,* the traditional Bastille Day parade of French armed forces down the *Champs-Elysées.* It was President Mitterrand's decision, in an attempt to overcome lingering French animosity toward Germany, to include German soldiers in the parade. When interviewed, a number of older French people, who remembered the occupation of France or had had relatives deported or taken prisoner during World War II, disapproved of the German soldiers' participation in this *défilé.* Younger French people did not seem to mind.

    Eurocorps units of combined nationalities were first set up in 1992.

eurocrate (m. or f.) Pejorative, like *technocrate;* both are modeled on the word *aristocrate.*

eurodéputé (m. or f.) Member of *le Parlement européen, qui siège à Strasbourg et à Bruxelles,* the European Parliament which is based in Strasbourg and Brussels.

Eurodisney The first European incarnation of Disneyland. Its opening in **Marnes-la-Vallée,** east of Paris, in 1992, was hotly contested, and the appropriateness of its existence on French soil is still challenged in some quarters (see **élus locaux**). On the verge of bankruptcy by 1994, it succeeded—partly on the grounds that it created employment in the region—in convincing banks to keep it afloat. The name was changed to *Disneyland Paris* and the financial tide began to turn in 1995.

eurogrève (f.) In 1997, Renault, a French car manufacturer, abruptly announced that it was going to close down its plant at **Vilvoorde,** in Belgium; Renault had not consulted or informed Belgian authorities or the Vilvoorde workers beforehand. A solidarity movement sprang up among Renault workers in France and other auto workers in Europe, who went on strike to protest at what they considered a clear indication of sinister things to come, in the form of *eurochômage,* the creation of unemployment in one European country because of decisions reached by firms in another. Their strike was dubbed *la première eurogrève,* "the first Europewide strike."

Europe (f.) **à plusieurs vitesses** A split-level or multitier Europe. Those who questioned whether all the member countries of the *Union européenne* would be able to meet the **critères de convergence** by 1999 warned that, if not, the danger would be *une Europe à plusieurs vitesses,* in which—so to speak—all member countries would be created equal but some would be more equal than others. It was generally assumed that France and Germany would be in top gear (*vitesse*) or at the top level, along with England and some of the Scandinavian countries, but that Greece and Portugal, and perhaps others, would be in lower gear or at a lower level. See **deux vitesses.** Ultimately, in May 1998, Greece was the only one of the fifteen member countries that was made ineligible to adopt the euro.

Europe (f.) **passoire** Eurocritics maintain that the **Traîte de Maastricht,** and specifically the *accords de Schengen,* have made the national boundaries between member countries too permeable, like *une passoire,* "a sieve," facilitating both legal and illegal immigration.

Europe (f.) **sociale** The European Union from the standpoint of labor legislation, and particularly measures to foster or protect employment.

Eurostar (m.) The fast train that runs through the Channel Tunnel, linking London to Paris, Brussels, and Lille. The train went into operation late in 1994. See **Eurotunnel; tunnel sous la Manche**

Eurotunnel (m.) *Pour la première fois depuis 8000 ans environ, les îles britanniques sont reliées au continent par la terre ferme;* "For the first time in about eight thousand years the British Isles and the Continent are linked via dry land." The tunnel accommodates train traffic (see **Eurostar**) and carries motor vehicles on *les navettes,* "rail shuttles," thus offering at last two more options to travelers, whose only choice until then had been the ferry or the plane. See **tunnel sous la Manche**

Euzkadi The Basque word for *Basque.* The Basque country extends on both sides of the Pyrenees; about a quarter million Basques live in France, and about ten times that number reside in Spain. See **ETA; Iparretarrak**

évacuer *Evacuer le problème,* to avoid looking a problem in the face, to shun it. *S'agissant de l'immigration, il ne faut ni faire un amalgame ni évacuer le problème;* "Where immigration is concerned, it's no good either making false analogies or trying to dodge the issue."

événements (m. pl.) **d'Algérie** The official way of referring to the Algerian war for independence, ended in 1962 by the **accords d'Evian** (signed at Evian, on the shore of Lake Geneva); they recognized Algerian independence, declared *un cessez-le-feu,* "a ceasefire," and called for a referendum on *l'auto-détermination,* "self-determination," which accordingly took place in Algeria in July of that year.

événements (m. pl.) **de mai 68** The student riots and sit-ins that occurred in May 1968, one year before de Gaulle resigned as president. They grew out of student protests that originated in the sociology department of the *Université de Paris X* at Nanterre, just beyond La Défense on the western edge of Paris, and spread to the *Quartier Latin.* Similar movements took place *en province* at the same time. They caused a major and lasting social upheaval. People old enough to remember *mai 68* still divide history into two eras: *avant 68 et après 68.* See **Cohn-Bendit, Daniel; crèche; CRS; gaz lacrymogène; soixante-huit**

exception (f.) **française** The distinctively (or even uniquely) French way of doing things. In the conflict with Hollywood over film distribution rights, France has insisted on the unique-ness of French culture, *"l'exception française,"* as a reason for limiting the proportion of U.S. films distributed in France. *L'identité française* is a similar term.

   Concerning the controversy, beginning in about 1997, over the possible introduction of **fonds de pension** in France, *l'ex-ception française* refers to *le modèle social français qui insis-terait sur l'égalite, à la différence du modèle social américain, qui insisterait sur la liberté,* "the French vision of society, which the French believe to be more egalitarian, as distinct from the American vision, which is believed to place greater emphasis on individual freedom."

excès (m.) **de vitesse** Speeding, when driving a car. See **permis à points**

exclu(e) (m. or f.) See **exclusion**

exclusion (f.) One of the most prevalent words in France today. It means the fact of not being included in the labor market and/or in mainstream society. *Les **SDF** et tous les **nouveaux pau-vres** sont victimes de l'exclusion. Les immigrés sont souvent des exclus;* "Immigrants are often social outcasts/on the fringes of society." *Les chômeurs en fin de droits deviennent des exclus;* "A jobless person with no more benefits falls through the so-cial security safety net and becomes locked out of mainstream society." The **banlieues** are often called *des nids d'exclusion,* "breeding grounds of social marginalization." *Divers mouvements des droits de l'homme luttent contre l'exclusion;* "Various human rights movements try to combat the exclusion of certain categories of individuals from mainstream society whether on economic, social or racial grounds."

exercer des pressions (f. pl.) To bring pressure to bear. *Lors des dernières négociations salariales, les leaders syndicaux ont exercé d'énormes pressions sur les représentants du gouvernement.*

exode (m.) Any exodus, of course, but particularly *l'exode de Paris en juin 1940,* when civilians fled Paris and other northern cities as German troops and aviation approached. Immortalized in *Jeux interdits,* the film by René Clément, and countless other films and books.

L'exode rural, the tendency of young people, especially, to renounce farming and move to cities to seek employment. See **désertification**

exojeunes The name given to a measure to foster employment. *L'exonération des charges salariales pour l'embauche de jeunes non-qualifiés dans les entreprises de moins de 500 salariés;* "Employers whose firms had fewer than five hundred employees would be exempted from having to pay *des charges salariales* if they hired unskilled young people."

exploitant(e) (m. or f.) **agricole** A farmer; see **agriculteur.**

expulser du territoire A noneuphemism. *"Il faut expulser du territoire les étrangers en situation irrégulière,"* say people who take a hard line against undocumented immigrants; "'Foreigners who don't have the right papers must be expelled.'" The official euphemism is *reconduire à la frontière,* to accompany (foreigners) back to the border. See **charter; Eglise Saint-Bernard; sans-papiers**

extraterrestre (m. or f.) An extraterrestrial being, an alien. See **OVNI**

F

fac (f.) Short for *la faculté*—that is, college, university. *Ça fait trois ans que je suis en fac;* "I've been in college for three years." *Aller à la fac,* to go to college. *S'inscrire en fac,* to register in college. *Payer ses droits d'inscription en fac,* to pay the college tuition fees. *L'inscription, y compris la couverture Sécurité sociale, coûte environ 1000F par an;* "Tuition, including student medical coverage, costs about 1000F a year."

facile Used in certain phrases, to mean "to be too quick on. . . ." *Avoir la gachette facile,* to be trigger-happy. Two urologists in southern France were accused of having performed unnecessary operations. *Ils avaient le bistouri facile;* "They were scalpel-happy," said their unhappy patients.

faire la manche To panhandle, to beg. *En principe il est interdit de faire la manche dans le Métro, mais il y en a beaucoup qui la font;* "Theoretically, it's against the law to beg in the Metro, but a lot of people do it."

famille (f.) **nombreuse** A family of three children or more. *Les allocations familiales sont beaucoup plus intéressantes à partir du moment où on est famille nombreuse;* "Family allowances get much bigger starting with the third child." *Les allocations familiales* were launched by the French government in 1932, in an effort to bring the French population back up to its pre–World War I level, *afin de ramener la population à son niveau d'avant la guerre de 14–18.*

fantasmer To fantasize—*avoir des fantasmes* (m. pl.)—about sex, power, speed, whatever. *Une bagnole comme ça fait fantasmer tous les mecs;* "A car like that gets every man fantasizing." *Le candidat de la droite fantasme sur une victoire écrasante aux prochaines législatives;* "The candidate from the Right is daydreaming about a sweeping victory in the next legislative elections."

FAO (f.) The acronym of the United Nations Food and Agriculture Organization is the same in French as it is in English. Compare, for instance, with **ONU.** See **affamer**

farines (f. pl.) **animales** The animal-based meal, or cattle feed, at the root of *la crise de la vache folle,* the panic about mad cow disease, which originated in England in the late winter and spring of 1996. The meal was said to contain animal protein in the form of marrow from the bones of sheep, some of which carried a disease called scrapie. French butchers rushed to place signs in their windows assuring customers that they sold only *boeuf d'origine française* and that *"nous acceptons les contrôles,"* "'We will be happy to be inspected.'" *Certains hommes politiques français ont prétendu que la France, sous le gouvernement socialiste, aurait continué d'acheter ces farines de l'Angleterre pour nourrir des porcs et des poulets en France;* "Some French politicians alleged that under the Socialist government, France had continued to buy such meal from England to feed to French hogs and chickens." See **vache folle**

fast food (m.) *Le fast food fait partie désormais du paysage gastronomique et socio-économique de la France;* "Fast food has become part of the gastronomic and socioeconomic scene in France." The proper French term for it is *la restauration rapide.* People who are against the fast-food concept call it *le néfaste food,* "harmful food."

fausses factures (f. pl.) *L'affaire des fausses factures,* "the fake invoices scandal," is one of the numerous **affaires** that came to light early in the 1990s.

Favart, la salle Although it is less talked about than *l'Opéra Bastille* or *le Palais Garnier, la salle Favart* is the Paris theater reserved chiefly for *l'opéra comique;* most of its funding comes from the government.

fécondation (f.) **in vitro** In vitro fertilization. *La fécondation in vitro est devenue une pratique courante dans la médecine reproductive moderne;* "In vitro fertilization is now commonly used by modern reproductive science."

fellagha (m.) Algerian freedom fighter or rebel, during the **événements d'Algérie.** Compare with **harki.**

féminisme (m.) The feminist movement. (Note that the noun itself is masculine; see, however, **Ministre.**) It is not nearly so visible or audible as the feminist movement in the United States, although progress remains to be achieved on certain fronts. *Le salaire des femmes, par exemple, est souvent inférieur à celui de l'homme, à travail égal;* "Women's salaries, for instance, are often lower than men's for the same job." See **MLF**

femme (f.) **active** A woman who works outside the home, who is part of *la population active,* "the labor force." *Une femme au foyer,* a woman who is a housewife and/or mother but who does not work outside the home.

fer (m.) Railways, in professional parlance. *Pour ce qui est du transport des marchandises, le fer perd du terrain au profit de la route;* "When it comes to carrying freight, the railways are losing business to trucks."

fermeté (f.) Firmness; what the government claims that it seeks whenever its mediators sit around a bargaining table with strikers. *Dans les négociations avec les routiers, le gouvernement a joué l'apaisement dans la fermeté, disait un porte-parole;* "In the talks with the striking truck drivers (December 1996), the government tried to be firm and conciliatory at the same time, said one spokesman." See **transports routiers**

fermeture (f.) **annuelle** An inescapable feature of summer in France; see **août.** Because employers are required to give their employees five weeks of paid vacation per year, many small shops and services, and even factories, simply shut down for a month, *parfois le mois de juillet, parfois à cheval sur juillet et août, mais généralement tout le mois d'août,* "sometimes July, sometimes partly July partly August, but usually all of August."

Fête (f.) **de l'Huma** An annual fair-cum-celebration sponsored by *L'Humanité,* the Communist Party daily newspaper. It takes place every autumn at La Courneuve, a working-class suburb of Paris. It is popular, and people who attend are not necessarily party members or readers of *l'Huma.*

Fête (f.) **des Mères** Mother's Day, created in France about a decade before World War II, then relaunched by the Vichy government in 1941 as part of its overall program promoting
three major values, *Travail, Famille, Patrie*, Work, Family, Fa-
therland. Today the ideological origins of *la Fête des Mères*
have fallen largely by the wayside, but the commercial aspect
is still going strong. Like *la Fête des Pères*, it seldom falls on
the same day as the corresponding day in the United States.

Fête (f.) **du travail** Labor Day, which falls on May 1, *le premier
mai*. It is *un jour férié*, "a legal holiday." *Des délégations syndicales défilent dans la rue et les dirigeants syndicaux prononcent
des discours;* "Labor union delegations parade through the
streets, and union leaders make speeches." See **muguet**

feu (m.) **tricolore** Traffic light (*feu rouge, feu orange, feu vert*).
Brûler un feu, to drive through a red light. *Feu clignotant*,
flashing light. See **clignotants**

feuilleton (m.) **télévisé** TV serial or soap opera. *Hélène et les garçons* was a famous one, in a teenage setting.

FFF (f.) *La Fédération française de football*, the French soccer federation. *FIFA, Fédération internationale de football association. Le foot*, as it is called, is as cherished a sport in France
as baseball is in the United States.

FIAC (f.) *Foire internationale de l'art contemporain*, held annually
in Paris.

fief (m.) Pronounced to rhyme with *chef*. A stronghold, especially
in electoral terms. *Dans la couronne de Paris, Saint-Denis,
Bobigny, La Courneuve font traditionellement partie du fief du
PCF;* "In the greater Paris region, Saint-Denis, Bobigny, and
La Courneuve have always been part of the Communist Par-
ty's stronghold."

filière (f.) One of the key words in *le monde estudiantin*, "the student world." *Des tas de diplômes c'est très bien, mais il faut
trouver une filière qui débouche sur quelque chose de concret,
qui permette de trouver un emploi;* "It's all well and good to
have a lot of degrees, but you have to find a study program/
a sequence of degrees that leads to something practical, that
enables you to find a job."

The basic idea of *une filière* in any context is a trail or a
path leading somewhere, a series of connections. *La police essaie de remonter la filière de la drogue jusqu'au numéro un;*
"The police are trying to follow leads in the drug-dealing
world until they reach the brains of the operation."

*Un détective privé est chargé de filer l'épouse de cet homme
politique, qui est très en vue;* "A private eye is being paid to
shadow the wife of that very prominent politician." *Une fila-
ture*, the fact of shadowing or tailing someone.

fin (f.) **de non-recevoir** A legal term meaning "an objection," and
almost always used with the verb *opposer. La direction a op-*

posé à sa requête une fin de non-recevoir; "Management objected to/rejected his or her request."

FIS (m.) *Le Front islamique du salut,* Islamic Salvation Front, an Algerian political movement founded in 1989 urging adoption of the Sharia. In the early 1990s it almost won the Algerian elections, but they were then canceled by the Algerian army. Since then there have been recurrent terrorist actions by Islamic extremists throughout Algeria, targeting both foreigners and Algerians. See **effusion de sang; GIA; voiture piégée**

fisc (m.) The tax authorities; the equivalent of the IRS. *Il a déjà eu à plusieurs reprises des démêlés avec le fisc;* "He has already tangled with the tax authorities several times." See **percepteur-(trice); tiers provisionnel.**

Tous les ans le fisc envoie à chaque contribuable le formulaire "Déclaration des revenus" à remplir pour le début mars, et la radio vous rappelle la date limite; "Every year the tax authorities send each taxpayer the 'Declaration of Income' form, to be filled out by early March, and the radio reminds you of the deadline."

flash-info (m.) A news flash, on radio or TV. *Au cours de l'émission il y a eu un flash-info;* "The program was interrupted by a news flash."

FLE (m.) *Français langue étrangère.* A person with *un diplôme de FLE* can teach French as a foreign language in France or abroad, just as a person from the United States and other English-speaking countries who has a TEFL degree can teach English as a foreign language.

fléau (m.) A scourge or plague. Jacques Santer, chairman of the European Commission, noted on a radio talk show in 1997, *"La mondialisation est perçue par certains comme le fléau de notre époque";* "'In some quarters it is felt that the globalization of the economy is the scourge of modern times.'"

flexibilité (f.) A recent buzzword, a euphemism for the willingness to accept *un CDD, la précarité, le besoin éventuellement de déménager pour trouver // garder // accepter un emploi,* "a nonrenewable contract, the idea of relocating if need be in order to find/keep/accept a job." *Autrement dit, notent les cyniques, la fin de la sécurité d'emploi;* "In other words, say the cynics, the end of job security."

FLN (m.) *Le Front de libération nationale,* a movement founded by Algerian independence fighters in 1954, during the **événements d'Algérie.** Name of the ruling political party for many years after independence.

FLNC (m.) *Front de libération nationale de la Corse,* a Corsican independence movement. See **Corse.** There is also a branch called the *FLNC canal historique,* initially in favor of armed conflict.

fluide Smooth, when talking about traffic. *Jusqu'ici la circulation est fluide—les bouchons attendus ne se sont pas produits;* "So far traffic is smooth—the bottlenecks that were expected have not occurred." *Notre but est de fluidifier la circulation en créant une route à quatre voies;* "Our aim is to improve traffic flow by creating a four-lane highway."

flux (m.) **migratoire** The flow of emigration/immigration; often used to mean the influx of immigrants into France. *Une des grandes préoccupations des dirigeants politiques c'est de trouver des moyens de réduire le flux migratoire;* "One of the politicians' major concerns is to find ways to stem the tide of immigration."

flux (m. pl.) **tendus** *La gestion des stocks à flux tendus,* just-in-time management of stocks. *Le principe c'est de travailler en adaptant la production à la demande, en éliminant les stocks;* "The principle is to adapt supply to demand by not holding anything in stock." *Les flux tendus ont été très gênés par la grève des routiers en novembre 1996;* "The truck drivers' strike in November 1996 made things very touch and go for just-in-time management."

FNAC (f.) *Fédération nationale des cadres,* a purchasing cooperative founded in 1954 and since renamed *Fédération nationale d'achat.* Originally it was concerned only with photography and motion picture equipment; then it branched out into records and cassettes, TV and household appliances, video, hi-fi, books, computers, and sporting goods. *La FNAC* now has dozens of stores and service outlets throughout France and in several other European countries.

FNSEA (f.) *Fédération nationale des syndicats d'exploitants agricoles,* the federation *qui coiffe,* "which covers," the farmers' unions. See **agriculteur**

focaliser To focus. *Les journalistes ont tendance à focaliser sur l'aspect potentiellement scandaleux de cette transaction, alors qu'il faudrait focaliser sur l'aspect purement financier;* "The journalists tend to focus on the potentially scandalous aspect of this transaction, whereas they should focus on the strictly financial aspect."

Focéa (m.) Bernard Tapie's yacht, which he was accused of not having declared at its true value to *le fisc;* named for Marseilles, *la ville phocéenne.* See **OM**

foire (f.) **d'empoigne** A free-for-all. An old expression but still in use.

Foire (f.) **du Trône** A popular funfair held every year at the *Porte Dorée* on the southeastern edge of Paris, near the *Bois de Vincennes.*

fonctionnaire (m. or f.) A civil servant, *une personne qui travaille dans le secteur public.* Since *le secteur public* in France is so extensive—embracing *Air France,* the **SNCF,** the *EDF,* the **GDF,** *l'Education nationale,* and more—a very high proportion of French *salariés* are *des fonctionnaires. Le fonctionnariat,* all *fonctionnaires* as a whole. *Un haut fonctionnaire,* a high-level civil servant. *Les personnes qui travaillent dans le secteur privé ont tendance à envier les fonctionnaires parce qu'en principe ils ne risquent pas de perdre leur emploi, mais les fonctionnaires rétorquent que les salaires dans le secteur privé sont plus élevés;* "People who work in the private sector tend to envy civil servants because they are not in danger of losing their jobs, but government employees point out that private sector employees are better paid." In the envious (and colloquial) view, *un fonctionnaire c'est un planqué—il a trouvé la bonne planque,* "a civil servant has it soft—he's found a cushy job." But see **pantoufler.** See also **secteur public**

fonds (m.) **de pension** Retirement pensions are funded by two sources, *la Sécu* and *les caisses de retraites complémentaires. Dans les deux cas l'employeur cotise aussi bien que l'employé(e);* "In both cases, the employer as well as the employee pays into the system." *Les fonds de pension* would be along the lines of American pension funds; *seul l'employé(e) cotiserait,* only the employee would contribute. Critics of this potential *troisième pilier des retraites* in France say that only those individuals who do not really need the additional retirement pension will be able to afford it; hence, the system would be inegalitarian and might even lead the government to reduce state pensions. They find, therefore, that it runs counter to *le côté égalitaire de l'exception française* and is typical of *la liberté accentuée par le système américain.*

football (m.) **américain** Term used to distinguish this game from *le foot* or *le football tout court*—that is, soccer. See **Coupe du monde, Mondial, pluriel(le), Stade de France**

forçat (m.) A convict or a galley slave. When the truck drivers went on strike at the end of 1996, they called themselves *"les forçats de la route,"* a term traditionally used for *les coureurs du Tour de France.*

force (f.) **de frappe** Strike force. *Force de frappe nucléaire,* nuclear weapons strike force; also termed, by de Gaulle, *force de dissuasion,* deterrent force.

forces (f. pl.) **de l'ordre** The police plus *les gendarmes* and the *Compagnie républicaine de sécurité* (**CRS**), riot squad. *Pour prévenir tout **dérapage** au cours de la manifestation, le gouvernement a fait appel aux forces de l'ordre;* "To prevent the demonstration from getting out of hand, the government called out the police." *Les organisateurs de la manif avaient leur propre service d'ordre;* "The demonstration's organizers had their own people who were in charge of maintaining order."

forces (f.) **vives de la nation** A phrase that recurs in virtually every speech by Jacques Chirac, both as presidential candidate in 1995 and since then as president; Alain Juppé, his first *Premier ministre,* was fond of it too. *Il faut mobiliser les forces vives de la nation;* "We must call upon this country's vital energies/ mobilize this country's living strength." *On asphyxie les forces vives de la nation.*

formation (f.) **continue** Adult (continuing) education. *Tout employé qui a plus d'un an d'ancienneté peut bénéficier de la formation continue, aux frais de l'employeur,* "Any salaried person who has been on the payroll for over a year is entitled to some adult education or vocational (re)training, at the employer's expense."

formation (f.) **politique** Another term for *un parti politique.*

formule un (f.) Formula One racing car. See **coureur**

Fort (m.) **de Brégançon** The president's summer residence, near Bormes-les-Mimosas, between St. Tropez and Toulon.

fossé (m.) **des générations** The generation gap.

foulard (m.) A scarf, you may say. Quite right. But in today's media, *le foulard* instantly means *le foulard islamique, le **chador** or **tchador**. Le port du foulard s'est produit pour la première fois au collège de Creil en 1989;* "The first time a Muslim pupil wore the headscarf to school was in 1989, at a junior high school in Creil." *"Le port du foulard est une atteinte au 'pacte de la nation,'"* said François Bayrou, *Ministre de l'Education nationale,* in October 1993; "When Muslim girls wear the Islamic head scarf to school in France, that is an attack on the "nation's pact"/with all of its citizens." *Le foulard* is also sometimes called *le voile.* See **Clovis; laïcité; tchador; voile à l'école**

fourches (f. pl.) **caudines** *Passer sous les fourches caudines* is a phrase harking back to ancient Rome. When in 321 B.C.E. the Romans were defeated in a narrow gorge near Caudium, they had to bow and pass under the victors' yoke. Today the phrase still means "to capitulate," "to accept drastic and demeaning conditions," in political or other contexts. Thus, in an article on the stranglehold that retail giants can have over small firms, *"Sous les fourches caudines des hypermarchés, les PMI—qui réalisent parfois jusqu'à 50% de leur chiffre d'affaires avec une seule enseigne—acceptent tout, jusqu'à l'étranglement: délais de paiement qui s'allongent, marges bénéficiaires sur les produits qui rétrécissent implacablement (Marianne,* August 14– 20, 1997). " 'The huge supermarkets leave small and medium-sized suppliers—who sometimes count on a single supermarket for as much as 50 percent of their turnover—no choice; even if it strangles them, they put up with waiting longer and longer to get paid and seeing their profit margins shrink mercilessly.' "

fourchette (f.) A bracket or range. *Ils sont donnés gagnants dans* *une fourchette de 40 à 45 sièges,* "They are expected to win by a margin of forty to forty-five seats more than their opponents."

fracture (f.) **sociale** The gaping separation between rich and poor, between the employed and the unemployed, between *l'immigré* and *le Français de souche,* "the native-born French person." Like **forces vives,** *il faut réduire la fracture sociale* is a phrase much used by Jacques Chirac. (It is also a pun because *réduire une fracture* is the standard medical term for setting a broken limb or rib.)

The opposite of *la fracture sociale* is *la cohésion sociale* or *la solidarité. Pour arriver à davantage de cohésion sociale, il faudra entre autres réduire l'écart des revenus;* "To arrive at a more unified society, we must narrow the income gap, among other things."

fragilisé(e) An adjective that has come into very common use in recent years, to signify "vulnerable, in a precarious situation." *"La magistrature est fragilisée,"* said one radio commentator in July 1996, when it was being asked whether *les juges* investigating corruption charges in numerous **affaires** were sufficiently independent of the government or were instead subject to pressure. *L'Etat-nation et le service public sont aujourd'hui fragilisés;* "The concepts of nation-state and public service are in a weakened position today."

From the adjective to the noun is only one short step, and it is frequently taken; *"On observe une fragilisation du paysage du chômage,"* said a 1993 radio program; "'The unemployment situation is becoming more vulnerable.'" *Fragile* is often used to describe a particularly sensitive person or one who is potentially unstable, delicate, high-strung.

frais (m. pl.), **en faire les** To pay inadvertently and figuratively for something. *Suite à la décision de dissoudre l'Assemblée et tenir des élections anticipées, une centaine de Députés RPR-UDF ont perdu leur siège; ils ont fait les frais de la dissolution.* "Once it was decided to dissolve the parliament and hold early elections, approximately one hundred right and center-right *Députés* lost their seats; the dissolution took place at their expense."

France (f.) **profonde** Grassroots or heartland France, the authentic France you can only find far away from the capital. For some Parisians it carries condescending overtones of backwardness rather than authenticity.

France Télécom The telephone, fax, and Minitel company—a government monopoly. It was scheduled to be privatized in 1998, and its employees, worried at the prospect of losing their status as **fonctionnaires,** began protesting ahead of time. In fact, about 25 percent of its capital was put on the market (see **actionnaire**) in 1997; *L'Etat* kept control over the rest.

The post office, not so many years ago, was called *les PTT,* for *Poste, Téléphone, Télégraphe,* and those words are still engraved or painted over the doors of a few older post offices, especially in *la **France** profonde.* Then *les PTT* briefly became *P et T, Poste et Télécommunications.* The two functions were later split into *la Poste* and *France Télécom.*

Francilien,enne(s) Resident(s) of the Ile-de-France region around Paris.

franc-maçon (m.) Freemason. *La franc-maçonnerie est plus secrète et suspecte en France qu'aux Etats-Unis;* "Freemasonry is surrounded by more secrecy and suspicion in France than in the United States." *Sous le gouvernement de Vichy, un certain nombre de franc-maçons ont été déportés;* "Under Vichy, a number of Freemasons were deported." *Appartenir à une loge franc-maçonnique,* to be a member of a Masonic lodge.

franco-français(e) A term much in vogue to express the idea of disagreement between different political or ideological factions but within a typically French framework. *La controverse au sujet de **Clovis** en 1996 est le type même de désaccord franco-français;* "The debate over Clovis in 1996 is the perfect example of a purely French internal difference of opinion." *Dans la formation dispensée par les grandes écoles, il y a une vision franco-française;* "The type of teaching dispensed by the *grandes écoles* fosters a purely French vision of things." *Le Minitel est une invention purement franco-française puisqu'il ne s'est étendu à aucun autre pays;* "The Minitel is a purely French invention that has not been adopted by any other country."

francophonie (f.) A linguistic situation that has been elevated to the rank of a national policy. French is spoken in several European countries, Canada, and the **DOM-TOM,** and it is still spoken to some extent in former French colonies in Africa and North Africa. Official French policy is to maintain and foster the linguistic and historical ties, and therefore the influence of French language and culture; support by the French government is given in various forms. The heads of state of the Francophone countries are invited to an annual summit meeting in France.

fraude (f.) **fiscale** Tax fraud. *Le gouvernement fait de la lutte contre la fraude fiscale une de ses plus grandes priorités;* "One of the government's top priorities is the campaign against tax fraud."

friche (f.) *Laisser la terre en friche,* to let land lie fallow, especially as official Brussels policy, to avoid overproduction of certain crops. See **gel des terres; jachère; oléagineux; PAC; paysan**

friche (f.) **industrielle** Land zoned for occupation by industry but standing empty. *Le stade pour la Coupe du monde de football de 1998 s'est implanté dans une friche industrielle à*

Saint-Denis; "The stadium where the 1998 soccer World Cup took place was built on a vacant industrial site in Saint-Denis."

frileux(euse) In ordinary usage, this adjective applies to a person who feels cold very easily. *Plus frileuse que moi tu meurs (familier);* "Nobody but nobody feels cold easier than I do." By extension, it can apply to an atmosphere: *Les négociations se sont déroulées dans un climat frileux;* "The mood surrounding the negotiations was pretty chilly." By further extension, it can mean hesitant, reluctant: *Nous sommes frileux sur les services à développer aux personnes âgées, aux chômeurs, et ainsi de suite;* "We're not very bold when it comes to expanding services for elderly people, the jobless, and so on." *Les analystes soulignent la frilosité du marché aujourd'hui;* "Analysts point out that the market today is very hesitant."

frime (f.) *Frimer,* to show off. *Les années frime, les années fric*—years of showing off and making juicy deals, of hot air and big bucks—is a phrase used by some **politologues** in evaluating the years 1981–1995, corresponding to two Socialist **septennats** (including two periods of *cohabitation avec la droite,* 1986–1988 and 1993–1995) and the numerous **affaires** that came to light on both sides of the political spectrum during that time.

fringues (f. pl.) Rags—that is, clothes. A very casual and colloquial term; *se fringuer.* The styles, age groups, and attitudes that go with them are far removed from those traditionally related to *la haute couture.*

froid (m.) **industriel** Refrigeration.

Front (m.) **national** Extreme Right political party, founded by Jean-Marie Le Pen in 1972. First came to national prominence in 1983 when it won by-elections in Dreux, west of Paris. In 1995 the FN candidate was elected mayor in each of three southern cities, Marignane, Orange, and **Toulon** (the first city of over one hundred thousand inhabitants to "fall" to the FN); in 1997 the FN candidate was elected mayor of **Vitrolles,** again in southern France. The FN has an anti-immigration (and anti-immigrants) platform. See **préférence nationale.** See also **détail; Durafour crématoire; inégalités de race; Pucelle; récupérer.**

La classe politique s'agite beaucoup autour du FN: Comment le combattre? Est-ce un parti politique comme un autre? Faut-il inviter ses dirigeants à répondre aux questions des journalistes à la radio et sur le plateau des émissions télévisées? Faut-il l'interdire? Est-ce que cela ne ferait pas plutôt le jeu du FN? "Politicians are very bothered by the FN: What is the best way to combat it? Is it a party like any other? Should its leaders be invited to answer journalists' questions on radio and TV programs? Should the party be banned? Or would banning it play right into the FN's hands?"

frottis (m.) A Pap smear. *On conseille aux femmes de faire faire un frottis tous les deux ans;* "Women in France are advised to have a Pap smear done every two years."

Fun Radio One of the numerous small radio stations opened in the late 1980s and early 1990s; it is aimed chiefly at a teenage and young adult audience. More conservative media have been very critical of it; the magazine *Le Spectacle du monde,* for instance, headlined an April 1994 article on it *"Les porno-phones."*

Furiani In May 1992, a section of a stadium at Furiani, near Bastia, in Corsica, collapsed during a soccer match, killing fifteen and injuring over two thousand. An investigation revealed that the faulty section was temporary seating that had been hastily added on to the permanent structure.

fusée (f.) Rocket. See **Ariane; programme spatial**

G

galère (f.) An expression that is very colloquial but perfectly correct. *C'est la galère,* "It's very tough," "it's a tough situation." *Galérer,* to have a rough time of it. (*La galère* was "a galley ship, propelled by oars," and *les galériens,* "the oarsmen," were convicts sentenced to do a period at hard labor in this manner. The system of *galères* was abolished in 1791, during the French Revolution.) *Galérer* leads directly to *ramer,* "to row"—that is, to have a rough time of it; *Qu'est-ce qu'on rame!*

L'Itinérant, un journal des SDF, includes a section called *"Guide antigalère,"* providing names and addresses of places where meals, lodging, and a bath or shower can be found.

L'équipe du PSG a galéré pour s'imposer enfin dans les trois dernières minutes de jeu; "The Paris–St. Germain soccer team struggled throughout the match and only managed to take over in the last three minutes."

Galligrasseuil A satirical or cynical joke; the name of a fictitious publisher combining the first syllables of the names of the three real publishers—Gallimard, Grasset and Editions du Seuil—that tend, year after year, to win most of the major French literary prizes, *le Goncourt, le Renaudot, le Fémina, le Médicis,* and *l'Interallié.* It is often alleged that the awarding of these prizes every autumn is rigged so that Galligrasseuil will win; of course, the allegation is just as often denied.

galvauder To debase or overwork something, make it trite. *Alors qu'il avait un vrai talent au point de départ, il se contente d'écrire tout et n'importe quoi, et son talent est galvaudé à présent;* "He had a genuine talent to begin with, but he's just been writing any old thing, and by now his talent is worn thin."

Gardanne *Une circonscription,* electoral district, in the *Bouches du Rhône* in southern France, from which Bernard Tapie had been *le Député* (*socialiste*). In 1996, because Tapie was under investigation on corruption charges (see **OM**), his seat became vacant. Then Bernard Kouchner, a doctor who founded **Médecins sans frontières** and was later *Ministre de l'action humanitaire* in the Socialist government, ran for election to replace Tapie, but lost to *le candidat du PC,* the Communist candidate. Nonetheless, relief was felt in some quarters because it had been feared that the **Front national** candidate would win.

Garde (m.) **des Sceaux** Literally, Keeper of the Seals; in fact, the minister of justice. See **parquet.**

gardien(ne) The politically correct term for **concierge,** a term that has virtually vanished.

(se) gargariser *Se gargariser de mots,* to be taken in by one's own words. *Quand la France, avec une population de moins de soixante millions, prétend faire la leçon à la Chine, dont la population est vingt fois plus grande, elle se gargarise de mots creux;* "If France, with a population of less than sixty million, thinks it is in a position to lecture China, whose population is twenty times larger, France is just deluding itself."

Les Français aiment à dire et à se dire que la France est traditionnellement une terre d'asile mais quand on voit leur désarroi actuel devant le phénomène d'immigration on se demande s'ils ne se gargarisent pas de mots; "The French like to say, and to tell themselves, that France is a land of refuge, but today, when you see how dismayed they are by immigration, you can't help wondering whether they aren't just deluding themselves."

gaspi (m.) A short form of the word *gaspillage* (m.), waste (of time, money, etc.). *"Haro sur le gaspi!"* or *"Chasse au gaspi!"* (Down with waste! No mercy on waste!) is said to be the slogan of *la Sécurité sociale, soucieuse de combler son déficit,* anxious to fill in its financial "hole."

gauche (f.) *La gauche* in politics refers to the spectrum of relatively socialist-minded political parties. *L'extrême gauche* is the far Left, factions such as *les trotskistes, les maoistes, Lutte ouvrière, Gauche prolétarienne,* and so on. Then, moving away from the far Left, comes *le Parti communiste;* then, moving more toward the center, are *le Parti socialiste* and *le Mouvement des citoyens.* The terms *la gauche, la droite,* and *le centre* correspond quite simply to the way the *Députés* of the various parties are seated in the *Chambre des Députés,* or *Assemblée* *nationale,* as seen from the rostrum of *le Président de l'Assemblée.* The semicircular chamber itself is *l'hémicycle* (m.).

La France est/Les Français sont un peuple de gauche, goes the famous phrase: "France is/The French are a nation whose heart is on the Left."

"My left is too far left / And my right's gone slack, / My center's no better / And the Front's a fucking hack. / "Oh dear me, I surely / Do feel kind of poorly."

These words are a political parody of the lyrics to a famous *chansonette comique, Je n'suis pas bien portant* (I'm kind of poorly), © 1932 by E. Bousquet, Editeur, 61 Faubourg St-Denis, Paris Xe. The lyrics were by Géo Koger, the music by Vincent Scotto and Ouvrard. The song begins, *"J'ai la rat', qui se dilat', / J'ai le foi', qu'est pas droit"* and goes on for dozens of couplets about physical ailments, including *"Dans les yeux, c'est pas mieux. / J'ai le droit, qu'est pas droit / Et le gauche', Qu'est bien moch',"* etc. etc.

The cartoon appeared between the two rounds of the early legislative elections brought about by the dissolution on which President Chirac had decided. *Gauche* means both the left and, of course, clumsy. *Le Front* means both the forehead and the Front National.

by Loup in *Marianne,* May 19–25, 1997

gauche (f.) **caviar** The derisive term used by opponents of the Socialists, claiming that they spout leftist statements but cleave to a comfortable or even luxurious bourgeois lifestyle, sending their children to posh private schools and so on.

Gaullisme (m.) The philosophy of statesmanship faithful to or inspired by the actions of Charles de Gaulle. See **Appel du 18 juin.** Today *le Rassemblement pour la République (RPR*—the political party headed by Jacques Chirac, Philippe Seguin, and others) *et d'autres formations de droite et de centre-droite se réclament du Gaullisme,* "and other right and center-right groups consider themselves as de Gaulle's spiritual heirs."

gay (m. and adj.) Gay, homosexual. *Les gays.* Contrast with *gai(e),* an adjective meaning "gay, bright, cheerful."

gaz (m.) **lacrymogène** Tear gas. For anyone fifteen to twenty-five years old in May 1968, it brings back memories of pitched battles between student demonstrators and the **CRS** in Paris (chiefly *le Quartier latin*) and in cities *en **province.***

GDF/EDF *Le GDF* is *le Gaz de France,* the state monopoly on the production and distribution of gas as a source of energy. *L'EDF* (f.) does the same for electricity. The employees of both monopolies are **fonctionnaires.** See also **grogne**

gel (m.) **des terres** The fact of "freezing" farmland, taking it out of use. See also **Beauvilliers; friche; jachère; PAC**

gémonies (f. pl.), **vouer aux** Like **fourches caudines,** this expression harks back to ancient Rome. The *scalae Gemoniae* were steps on the Aventine Hill in Rome; criminals' bodies, before being thrown into the Tiber, were dragged to these steps and there exposed to the public, who could heap scorn and blame on them. Found today in such phrases as *Le pouvoir politique est voué aux gémonies,* "Political power is the target of general scorn."

Génération (f.) **Ecologie** One of the more prominent environmentalist parties, created in 1990. See **Verts**

géométrie (f.) **variable** Said of an airplane wing that can change shape to adapt to the wind. By extension, said of anything that adapts to opinion or circumstances: *Certains hommes politiques ont des principes à géométrie variable. La politique économique du gouvernement est à géométrie variable.*

gérer A verb used so widely that it has almost become a sort of verbal crutch. *Gérer son temps,* to manage your time. *Une situation difficile à gérer,* a hard situation to handle. *Avoir du mal à gérer ses émotions,* to have trouble keeping your feelings under control. *Un grand sportif doit être capable de tout gérer,* a real athlete must be able to handle anything.

    Le/La gérant(e) d'un magasin is, of course, "the manager of a store"; its management is *la gérance. La gestion* is "the science of business management" and is also called *le manage-*

ment. C'est un piètre vendeur mais un formidable gestionnaire;
"He is a very poor salesman but an expert manager." In the
1980s and early 1990s numerous *écoles de gestion ou instituts
de gestion,* "business schools," flourished in France. *On con-
sidérait que pour parfaire son parcours il fallait en plus faire
des études aux Etats-Unis en vue d'obtenir son MBA;* "It was
commonly considered that to polish off your degree, you had
to go to an American university as well, to earn an MBA."

GIA (m.) *Groupe islamique armé* in Algeria; extremist terrorist
organization that in 1993 began urging foreigners to leave the
country. Held responsible for the kidnapping and deaths of
seven French Trappist monks in Algeria in 1996 and for the
death of many Algerian civilians, often by means of *une voiture* (f.) *piégée,* "car bomb," or by *égorgement* (m.), "the slit-
ting of throats." See **FIS**

GIGN (m.) *Groupement d'intervention de la gendarmerie nationale,* specialized crisis unit police. For instance, in 1994, when
a gunman entered *une école maternelle,* "a nursery school," in
affluent Neuilly, just outside Paris, and took a schoolteacher
and her pupils hostage, *prenant en otage une maîtresse et ses
élèves,* it was the *GIGN* that succeeded in entering the building, encircling the classroom and shooting the gunman without wounding the teacher or the children.

giratoire, sens (m.) A rotary intersection or traffic circle. Also
called *un rond point.* A considerable number of these were
built throughout the French countryside in the 1990s, replacing the previous *carrefours* (m. pl.) *à angle droit non munis de
feux,* "right-angle intersections with no traffic lights." *Dans un
sens giratoire les voitures déjà engagées ont priorité sur celles
qui cherchent à y entrer;* "In a rotary intersection cars that
have already entered it have the right of way over cars seeking
to enter it."

Girondins (m. pl.) The Bordeaux soccer team, *l'équipe de foot de
la ville de Bordeaux, située dans le département de la Gironde.*
(During the French Revolution, *les Girondins* was the name
of a political group, many of whose members were from the
Gironde.)

gisement (m.) **d'emploi** *Un gisement* is usually "a lode or deposit
of some raw material"—*un gisement de pétrole,* for example.
Un gisement d'emploi is "a source or pool of employment, of
potential jobs": *Il faut trouver de nouveaux gisements d'em-
ploi/des gisements d'emploi européens.* Conversely, *un bassin d'emploi* is "a labor catchment area," in the economists'
parlance—in other words, an area where (wo)manpower is
available.

globalement This adverb is another verbal crutch (see **gérer**).
"Globalement on fume moins aujourd'hui"; "'By and large

people are smoking less,'" said one participant in a July 1996 radio talk show on the theme *"20 ans après la première loi antitabac."* But it does not necessarily mean "globally" (i.e., "worldwide"); this speaker was talking about France only.

GO (m. or f.) *Gentil(le) Organisateur(trice) au Club Méditerranée. Les Gentils Membres (GM) sont encadrés par les GO;* "the Friendly Organizers take charge of the Friendly Members and organize activities for them."

goncourable Said of a book or author that or who seems to stand a good chance of winning *le prix Goncourt.* See **Galligrasseuil**

gourou (m.) A guru, of course. *Nous vivons une époque où, à défaut de croyance religieuse profonde, les gens se cherchent un gourou;* "We live in an age where people lack profound religious faith and are looking for a guru." (See **Ordre du Temple solaire**.) *Tel professeur de Harvard est le dernier gourou à la mode chez les adeptes du management;* "A certain Harvard professor is the latest guru for people who are really into business management."

graffiti (m. pl.) Graffiti. They flourished in the very early 1990s, although the density of graffiti *sur les wagons du Métro parisien* never quite achieved the density of those on the New York subway cars. *Un tagueur,* graffiti artist. *Taguer, faire des graffiti. Un tag,* graffiti logo or signature.

grand(e) admissible A candidate who has attempted a **concours,** especially *l'Agrégation,* several times and has succeeded in the written part and therefore been *admissible à l'oral,* "allowed to take the oral," but has then failed it.

grand âge (m.) Whereas *le troisième âge* refers to senior citizens or elderly people in general, *le grand âge* means "very very elderly," as in *résidence pour les personnes du grand âge.* A recent arrival in the French language, reflecting *l'allongement de l'espérance de vie,* "the lengthening of life expectancy."

Grand bleu (m.) A film by Luc Besson about the marvels of the underwater world. It was a cult film among the younger generation in the early 1990s. *La grande bleue* is a traditional name for *la mer Méditerranée,* particularly along the French coast.

For another cult film, see *le Cercle des poètes disparus.*

grande guerre (f.) Also called *la guerre de 14–18* and *la première guerre mondiale. Tous les ans à l'occasion du 11 novembre on constate qu'il y a de moins en moins d'anciens combattants de la grande guerre encore en vie;* "Every year on Armistice Day we find that there are fewer and fewer surviving World War I veterans."

grand-messe (f.) **médiatique** *Les infos de 20h à la télévision,* "the 8 P.M. TV news," has been called the media version of high mass: *Tous les spectateurs participent à la grand-messe mé-*

diatique. Vingt heures c'est l'heure de grande écoute, "In France 8 P.M. is prime time."

grandes écoles (f. pl.) University-level institutions but outside the university as such. Very sought after. Admission to any of the *grandes écoles* is only through competitive exams called *des concours,* and prospective applicants often spend a year or two after *le Bac* preparing for them or try them only after getting an undergraduate degree (e.g., *une licence de droit*) at the university. See **sélection; X**

grande surface (f.) A supermarket or hypermarket, or *un grand magasin,* department store. Among the best-known names are *Atac, Auchan, Carrefour, Casino, Champion, Continent, Intermarché, Leclerc, Mammouth,* and *Sodiprix. Les petits commerçants se plaignent que les grandes surfaces sont pour eux la mort;* "Small retailers complain that supermarkets are killing them off." See **fourches caudines**

Grand Orient (m.) *Le Grand Orient de France* is one of the most prominent Masonic lodges in the country. Among others are *la Grande Loge féminine* and several lodges that are for both men and women: *la Grande Loge mixte de France, la Grande Loge mixte universelle,* and *la Grande Loge traditionnelle.* See **franc-maçon**

grand rabbin (m.) The grand rabbi of France. In 1987, for the first time, *un juif séphardique* was chosen, reflecting the influx of North African Jews (along with other **pieds-noirs**) that began in 1962, at the end of the Algerian war and the beginning of Algerian independence, and the relative decline in numbers of *juifs ashkenazes* in France.

Grand Satan (m.) Used in the French media when reporting on the name given in Iran and Iraq to the United States.

grands corps (m. pl.) *Les grands corps de l'Etat* refers to the highest echelons of the civil service. In September 1993, *Histoire parallèle,* a television program which shows and comments on news reels from fifty years earlier, discussed the decisions made after the liberation of France in 1944 and 1945 *concernant l'épuration des fonctionnaires sous Vichy,* "concerning the purge of government officials and civil servants under the Vichy government"; Stanley Hoffman, the American historian, commented on *"le respect de de Gaulle pour les grands corps après la Libération."* See **Papon, Maurice**

grands programmes (m. pl.) **sociaux** Entitlements. See **acquis sociaux; minima sociaux; protection sociale**

Grand Timonnier (m.) China's Great Helmsman—that is, the late Mao Zedong.

Greenpeace A thorn in President Chirac's side when he announced, a few weeks after his election in 1995, that France would resume nuclear testing in the Pacific, *des essais nucléaires dans le Pacifique.* In protest, Greenpeace sent a boat, the *Rainbow Warrior II.* For an earlier conflict between Greenpeace and the French government, see **Rainbow Warrior.**

greffe (f.) **d'organes** The medical technique that consists of replacing a diseased or incapacitated organ by a healthy one. *Cet hôpital est spécialisé dans la greffe du rein;* "This hospital specializes in kidney transplants." *Le Dr. Barnard, en Afrique du Sud, a été le premier à réussir une greffe du coeur humain;* "Dr. Christian Barnard, in South Africa, was the first doctor to carry out a human heart transplant successfully."

grenouiller To maneuver, using dubious means if necessary. *Parmi tous les dauphins qui grenouillaient autour de l'actuel PDG, c'est X qui a été choisi pour lui succéder;* "X was chosen to take over from the current CEO, from among all of the heirs apparent who were jockeying for position."

grève (f.) Strike—one of the most visible features on the French scene. *Faire grève,* to go on strike. *Gréviste* (m. or f.), striker. *Revendiquer le droit de faire grève,* to demand/defend the right to go on strike. See **grogne; syndicat**

grogne (f.) Discontent, particularly as expressed through strikes (see **grève**) and demonstrations, *des manifestations.* In June 1996 one Paris daily published *"un calendrier de la grogne"* for the next four days, along with a city map to show which routes the different *cortèges* (m. pl.), "processions," would follow and which unions were calling the workers out on strike. It read as follows: *"Lundi 3 juin, manifestation SNCF à l'appel de Sud Cheminots; grève sur la ligne D du RER à Paris et sur le réseau banlieue gare de Lyon. Mardi 4 juin, France Télécom à l'appel de la CGT, la CFDT, la CFTC, FO,"* etc. *"Mercredi 5 juin, EDF à l'appel de la CGT, la CFDT, la FO; journée de grève contre la déréglementation du service public et de l'électricité. Jeudi 6 juin SNCF, EDF, France Télécom. Postes et RATP."* "'Monday June 3, demonstration by SNCF workers, called out by the Sud Cheminots union, plus strike on D trains of the Paris commuter train network and on suburban trains to and from the Lyon station in Paris'"; etc. etc.

gros porteur (m.) Jumbo jet aircraft. *Air France vient de commander douze gros porteurs à l'Aérospatiale;* "Air France has just ordered twelve jumbo jets from Aérospatiale." But see **petit porteur**

groupuscule (m.) A very small group or splinter group. The word came into common use during and as a result of the *événements de mai 68. Tout le problème c'est de regrouper tous les groupuscules pour créer une grande formation politique;* "The whole problem lies in bringing all the minifactions together to form a single large political party."

guerre (f.) **du Golfe** The brief war against Iraq, the Gulf War, in 1991. France sent approximately twenty thousand men, plus tanks, armored vehicles, helicopters, fighter planes, and warships. *Le Ministre de la défense à l'époque,* "the French defense minister at the time," resigned from his post because he was opposed to French participation in the war; see **MDC.**

guerre (f.) **des étoiles** Star Wars, in the days of *le Président Reagan.*

guerre (f.) **de 39–45** World War II, also called *la seconde guerre mondiale* or *la deuxième guerre mondiale.* See **drôle de guerre; grande guerre**

Guignols (m. pl.) *de l'Info* Like the ***Bébête Show,*** a fiercely satirical TV show (but using cartoonlike human masks instead of animal puppets), pretending to be *les informations,* "a news broadcast." No politician or TV personality is spared. *Faire le guignol,* to goof off, do goofy things.

    The old-fashioned Guignol show, still given in some *jardins publics,* is a puppet show for children, in which Guignol is the good guy, up against *le méchant,* who may be *un gendarme* or *le grand méchant loup,* "the big bad wolf."; *Guignol lui donne des coups de bâton;* "Guignol hits him or it with a big stick."

Gurs In southwestern France, north of the Pyrenees. Site of a *camp de détention* that has now vanished but where, as a huge sign reminds people driving past, some sixty thousand people were interned between 1939 and 1945: *"23.000 républicains espagnols, 7.000 volontaires des Brigades internationales et 30.000 juifs dont 12.000 arrêtés par Vichy."* See **Drancy**

halte-garderie (f.) A day care center with a flexible approach: for instance, you may leave your child there only three and a half days a week so that you do not need to pay for full-time care.

harcèlement (m.) **sexuel** Sexual harassment. Not nearly so much of an issue in France as in the United States. In 1993 the *Nouvel Observateur,* a weekly, devoted eight pages in its April 15–21 issue to an article titled *"Menace sur les Femmes. Aux Etats-Unis leur condition régresse. Et en France?"* "'Women in danger. In the United States their situation is getting worse. What about their situation in France?'" (See **féminisme.**)

    Il est vrai qu'en France, à travail égal, les salaires féminins ont tendance à être inférieurs aux salaires masculins dans des proportions qui varient selon la catégorie d'emploi; "It is true that in France, for the same job, women's salaries tend to be lower than men's to an extent that varies from one job category to another." *Beaucoup déplorent, en outre, qu'il y ait relativement peu de femmes dans la vie politique française, comparé à d'autres pays européens, et estiment qu'il faudrait instaurer un quota pour réserver par exemple 30% des sièges de Député à des femmes;* "Many people deplore the fact that there are fewer women in politics in France than in other European countries and believe that a quota system should be created so as to set aside, say, 30 percent of the seats in the *Assemblée nationale* for women." The Jospin government, which began in 1997, even proposed *la **parité** à cet égard entre hommes et femmes.*

Gender differentiation even of inanimate objects is built into the French language, as into other Latin-derived languages. For example, the words *table, chaise,* and *porte* are feminine; *fauteuil, plancher,* and *plafond* are masculine. The words *médecin, conservateur* (in the sense of curator), *professeur, ministre, secrétaire d'état,* and *juge,* are masculine; therefore, until 1997 women who held such functions were officially addressed as *Madame le conservateur, Madame le ministre, Madame le secrétaire d'état,* and so forth. But see **Ministre.**

Parts of the female body with the most overt sexual functions are designated by masculine words: *un utérus, un sein, un vagin, un ovaire* (uterus, breast, vagina, ovary). A Fallopian tube, however, is female: *une trompe.* Conversely, many male attributes are designated by feminine words: *une moustache, une barbe, une verge, les bourses* (moustache, beard, penis, scrotum); *pénis* and *testicule* are, however, masculine. Is this merely strange? Or is it significant? If so, how?

harki (m.) *Les harkis* were Algerian soldiers who fought on behalf of the French colonial power and thus against their fellow Algerians during the Algerian war for independence that ended in 1962. Former *harkis* now living in France, and their children, feel caught in the middle, claiming that the French government is not as grateful to them as it should be and that the Algerian authorities reject them. See **fellagha**

harmoniser To harmonize—that is, standardize, make uniform—be it regulations or units of measurement.

Haut Conseil (m.) **de la francophonie** Government body that promotes the use of the French language, strives to prevent it from being contaminated by linguistic imports, and maintains ties with French-speaking populations around the world, said to total approximately 160 million people. See **francophonie**

hébergement (m.) The fact of providing accommodations, lodgings, shelter. In 1997, in an attempt to track down illegal immigrants, a bill called *la **loi Debré** (after the then *Ministre de*

l'Intérieur) was introduced, requiring anyone who had provided accommodations to a foreigner to report the fact after
his or her departure and sign *un certificat d'hébergement.* This
caused an uproar chiefly by *la gauche,* which said the law was
uncomfortably reminiscent of practices under the Vichy government and was *une invitation à la délation* (i.e., would incite
people to denounce their neighbors). Well-publicized petitions against the law were signed by numerous intellectuals
and others. *Est-ce que les certificats devraient être établis au
niveau local, par les maires? ou au niveau national, par les préfets, nommés par Paris? Si c'était au niveau local, n'y avait-il
pas un danger particulier dans les communes où le maire était
Front national?* "Should the certificates be issued locally, by
mayors, or at the national level, by *préfets* appointed from
Paris? If it was done at the local level, wasn't there a special
danger in the towns whose mayor belonged to the *Front National?*" The bill was altered so as to shift the onus to *les préfets* rather than *les maires.*

hectare (m.) The standard unit of land surface measurement in
Europe; ten thousand square meters, or approximately two
and a half acres (2.47 acres). Small land surfaces may be measured in *ares; un are* is one one-hundredth of *un hectare,* or
one hundred square meters.

Hélène et les garçons One of the most successful *feuilletons télévisés,* aimed at *un public adolescent,* "a teenage audience."

helvétique Swiss, because the official name for Switzerland is *la
Confédération helvétique* or, more rarely, *l'Helvétie.* Cars registered in Switzerland are recognizable as such by a sticker
saying *CH* on the rear of the car.

hémicycle (m.) The fan-shaped or semicircular chamber in which
the *Chambre des Députés* (*l'Assemblée nationale*) holds its
sessions, in *le Palais Bourbon.*

héraut (m.) Herald, or leading proponent. *Untel, héraut du néolibéralisme,* "so-and-so, leading advocate of neoliberalism."

heure (f.) **d'été** The summer version of daylight saving time, which
generally begins during the last weekend in March or the first
one in April. The radio reminds you, *"La France va passer à
l'heure d'été dimanche prochain à 3 heures du matin; n'oubliez
pas d'avancer votre réveil d'une heure."* "'France will go on to
daylight saving time next Sunday at 3 A.M.; remember to put
your clock one hour ahead.'" *L'heure d'hiver* begins at the end
of September or early in October. *Il faut retarder sa montre //
son réveil d'une heure; vous allez gagner une heure de sommeil.*
"You have to set your watch or clock back an hour; you get
an extra hour's sleep."

*Tous les ans il y a des protestations en France contre le
changement d'heure, sous prétexte qu'il perturbe le rythme biologique du bétail, des jeunes enfants et des personnes âgées. En*

1997 la France aurait voulu ne pas changer d'heure mais il lui a été répondu par Bruxelles qu'il lui fallait faire comme tous ses partenaires européens; "Every year some people object to the practice of changing time, saying that it confuses the cattle as well as very young children and elderly people. In 1997 France would have liked to stop switching hours but was told by the Brussels authorities that it had to follow the same practice as the other member countries of the European Union."

hexagone (m.) France, because on the map it is a vaguely six-sided figure, if you do not count either *le Cotentin,* the Normandy peninsula culminating in Cherbourg, or the island of Corsica. *Les hexagonaux,* the French, or French chauvinists. *Une attitude bien hexagonale,* a typically French (or French chauvinist) attitude.

histoire (f.) **belge** A joke that makes fun of the Belgians; a very special form of French humor. See **Belgique**

homéopathie (f.) Homeopathic medicine; far more widespread than in the United States. *Les remèdes homéopathiques sont remboursés par la Sécurité sociale comme les autres médicaments;* "Homeopathic medicines are reimbursed by the Social Security just like any other medicine." See **allopathie**

homo (m. or f. and adj.) A shortened form of *homosexuel(le).*

hooligan (m.) A troublemaker at a sports event, generally *un match de football,* a soccer game. The word entered French usage after a certain number of incidents in England and others involving *des supporters anglais,* "English fans," at games played on the Continent.

hôpital (m.) **de jour** Out-patient care; often mentioned in connection with the treatment of *les sidéens* or *les malades du Sida,* "AIDS patients" (see **Sida**).

horodateur (m.) A parking machine in which you insert coins or a magnetic card so as to obtain a ticket stating the time of your arrival (day, hour, minutes) and the time at which you must depart.

horoscope (m.) The horoscope is taken more seriously in France than in the United States; virtually every magazine and newspaper devotes a column to it. *De quel signe du zodiaque êtes-vous? Quel était l'ascendant le jour de votre naissance?* "What sign of the zodiac were you born under? What was the ascendant on the day of your birth?" *L'astrologie,* astrology; *un(e) astrologue* (m. or f.), an astrologist.

Hôtel (m.) **Matignon** The offices of *le Premier ministre,* on the *rue de Varenne* in the seventh *arrondissement* in Paris, a district where there are also a number of other *Ministères.*

HT *Hors taxe.* When a price is marked *HT,* it means plus tax (i.e., not including tax). When it is marked *TTC,* it includes tax: *toutes taxes comprises. 200F HT* becomes *241,20F TTC* when it includes the *TVA, la Taxe à la valeur ajoutée,* "the value-added tax," at 20.6 percent, which is the rate that applies to many goods and services.

(French decimal figures use a comma where in English they use a point; and conversely, a point is used in French to separate hundreds, thousands, millions, etc., where in English a comma is used; e.g., 123.456.789,12 francs, *cent vingt-trois million quatre cent cinquante-six mille sept cent quatre-vingt-neuf francs et douze centimes.*)

huit mai (m.) *Le 8 mai est un jour férié parce que c'est l'anniversaire de la capitulation allemande en 45;* "May 8 is a holiday because it is the anniversary of the German surrender in 1945."

hypermarché (m.) A superbig *supermarché.* See **grande surface**

hystérisation (f.) An overreaction or hysterical reaction. Concerning the **NTM** incident in 1996, some commentators used the term *hystérisation de la situation.*

I

IAD (f.) *Insémination artificielle avec donneur,* artificial insemination by donor.

IFOP (m.) *Institut français d'opinion publique,* a public opinion research institute. *D'après un sondage IFOP . . . ,* "According to an IFOP poll. . . ." See also **IPSOS; sondage**

Ile (f.) **de Beauté** Corsica; see *Corse.*

Ile (f.) **d'Yeu** Small island off the Atlantic coast of France. In 1945, when *le Maréchal Pétain,* aged eighty-nine, was tried for his activity as head of the Vichy government, he was first sentenced to death. But, because of his age, the sentence was not carried out, and **Pétain** lived the rest of his life on *l'Ile d'Yeu,* where he died in 1951.

After François Mitterrand became president, in 1981, he went to *l'Ile d'Yeu* every year to lay a wreath on Pétain's grave; in 1993, however, after strong protests from former World War II *résistants* and relatives of Jewish deportees, he ceased to do so.

îlotage (m.) This is akin to the idea of **proximité,** in that it focuses on neighborhood policing, whereby a relatively small urban district, *un îlot* (literally, "a small island"), is patrolled by police officers (*îlotiers, îlotières*) who come to be known and trusted by its inhabitants.

image (f.) **cathodique** TV image. See **cathodique; signalétique**

imam (m.) An imam, a Muslim religious leader or person officiating in a mosque. See **mosquée**

immigration (f.) One of the words looming largest over the French mental landscape in the 1990s. *L'immigration suscite une polémique acharnée;* "Immigration arouses fierce debate." The extreme Right has hastened to equate immigration with unemployment for native-born French men and women or to claim that immigration is the single greatest cause of such unemployment. Immigration is immediately associated with many words, both for and against, such as *abus du système d'allocations familiales, Arabe, banlieue, chador, charter, chômage, cité, clandestin, code de la nationalité, droit au logement, droit du sol, droits de l'homme, Eglise Saint-Bernard, exclusion, expulser, foulard, foyer, intégration, intolérance, Islam, Maghreb, mosquée, quartier difficile/sensible, racisme, reconduire à la frontière, respect de l'autre, sans-papiers, situation irrégulière, tchador, tolérance, voile à l'école.*

immobilier (m.) *L'immobilier* is the sector of economic activity dealing with *les biens immeubles,* "unmoveable property" (i.e., real estate). *La crise de l'immobilier* began in about 1992; prices that had risen to giddy heights, especially for city apartments, suddenly sagged.

immunité (f.) **parlementaire** A privilege (going back to June 1789) to which members of the French parliament (*l'Assemblée nationale* and *le Sénat*) are entitled, as are members of *le Parlement européen,* which sits in Strasbourg: they are exempt from criminal prosecution or legal liability or prosecution for the duration of their term.

Much discussed in 1995 and 1996 in connection with Bernard Tapie, a businessman and owner of the *Olympique de Marseille* (**OM**) soccer team; he was also a *Député* elected on the Socialist ticket from **Gardanne,** a district in southeastern France, as well as a member of the European Parliament. Tapie was accused, with others, of having bribed players from the *Valenciennes* team to throw soccer matches, of tax fraud, and of having received unduly large loans from the *Crédit Lyonnais.* The question was whether he should be stripped of his parliamentary immunity: *fallait-il lever son immunité parlementaire? Son immunité a été levée.*

impérialisme (m.) **américain** An accusation often leveled at U.S. foreign policy.

implantation (f.) Settlement, as in *les implantations israéliennes,* "Israëli settlements."

impulser To generate, as in *impulser des projets économiques.*

inaugurer les chrysanthèmes The traditional way of defining the role of French presidents under the *Troisième République,* 1870–1940, and the *Quatrième République,* 1946–1958. In other words, they were essentially figureheads. See **chrysanthèmes**

incinérer To incinerate refuse; also to cremate. *Préferer l'incinération à l'enterrement,* to prefer cremation to burial. Cremation is practiced less widely in France than in the United States.

incitatif(ive) Incentive. *Une mesure incitative,* incentive.

incitation (f.) **à la haine raciale** A punishable offense under French law. *Les discours/propos de certaines personnalités politiques constituent une incitation à la haine raciale;* "The speeches/remarks made by certain politicians are an incitement to hatred on racial grounds." See **inégalités de race**

incompressible Cannot be reduced or diminished. *L'accusé a été condamné à une peine incompressible de trente ans;* "The defendant was given a thirty-year sentence that cannot be reduced on any grounds."

indemnité (f.) **de licenciement** Severance pay. *Indemnité de départ* may be the same thing or may mean compensation or a golden handshake for (having accepted) early retirement. *Indemnisation* (f.), the fact of making or receiving such payment: *être indemnisé(e).*

indexation (f.) **des prix** The indexation of prices—that is, their adjustment in relation to the cost of living index or some other economic indicator. *Il y a aussi l'indexation des salaires, des retraites, et ainsi de suite.*

indicatif (m.) Theme song or music or sounds announcing a radio or TV program.

indice (m.) **CAC 40** See **CAC 40**

indice (m.) **du prix de la construction** Cost of building index. See also **Insee**

industrie (f.) **du cinéma** The motion picture industry. *Les cinéastes français reprochent à Hollywood d'exercer un monopole écrasant;* "French filmmakers accuse Hollywood of being a monopoly that crushes them."

inégalités (f. pl.) **de race** One of the most famous of the many provocative remarks by Jean-Marie Le Pen, leader of the *Front national.* In September 1996, he stated, *"Il est indéniable qu'il existe des inégalités de race."* The *Garde des Sceaux* decided, after some hesitation, that the government could not bring charges against him because Le Pen had not stated which race was superior and therefore, as the law stood at that time, the government would not have been certain of winning its case against him.

Commentators and political figures nonetheless exclaimed that his remarks were *une **incitation à la haine raciale*** and urged the government to *renforcer la législation anti-raciste.* Debate in the media was intense. *Est-ce que ses propos tombent sous le coup de la législation antiraciste? Ils suscitent une prise de conscience collective. Est-ce que le gouvernement devrait prononcer la dissolution de son parti politique, en vertu* *de la loi de 1936?* "Do his remarks fall under the legislation making racism a punishable offense? They force everyone into awareness. Should the government dissolve his political party, under the terms of the 1936 law?"

inféoder *Etre inféodé,* to be pledged to; hence, by extension, to be subservient to, unable to free oneself from the control of. In discussing the employment situation in France, one writer, Viviane Forrester, in a controversial 1996 book entitled *L'horreur économique,* stated that *"la société demeure inféodée au système périmé fondé sur le travail,"* "'society is still in thrall to an outdated system based on work.'"

In his **appel de Cochin** issued in 1978, Jacques Chirac, who at that time was mayor of Paris and had been *Premier ministre* under President Giscard d'Estaing, protested against the proposed creation of a European entity in which France would be absorbed, claiming, *"On prépare l'inféodation de la France: on consent à son abaissement."*

info (f.) **ou intox** (f.) A succinct summing up of the ongoing debate over the quality, or not, of today's mass media: *sont-ils source d'information ou d'intoxication? Est-ce de l'info ou de l'intox?* "Do they inform or deform?"

informations (f. pl.) The news, often abbreviated as *les infos. Regarder les informations; écouter les informations. Qu'est-ce qu'ils ont dit aux informations?* "What did they say on the news?" *Une information* (sing.) *toute récente,* a last-minute news item, a piece of news hot off the press.

informatique (f.) Data processing; computer science; the fact of using computers. *L'informatique a complètement bouleversé les mentalités;* "Computers have completely altered people's way of thinking." *Aujourd'hui tout est informatisé;* "Everything is computerized today."

Infotélé (f.) Informal coined word for TV news, as in *Parmi les stars féminines de l'infotélé sont Claire Chazal, Christine Ockrent, Anne Sinclair . . .*

ingéniérie (f.) **sociale** Social engineering. *L'ingéniérie sociale par la voie fiscale,* social engineering through tax measures.

ingérable Impossible to manage (*gérer*). *Mon nouvel emploi du temps est absolument ingérable!* "My new schedule is just impossible."

ingérence (f.) Interference. *Le principe bien établi veut que chaque pays se garde bien de s'ingérer dans les affaires d'un autre pays;* "It is a well established principle that each country shall refrain from interfering in the affairs of another country." Nonetheless, the phrase *ingérence humanitaire* came to the forefront during the war *en ex-Yougoslavie,* 1992–96; Bernard Kouchner, then *Ministre de l'action humanitaire, réclamait pour la France un droit d'ingérence humanitaire,* "urged that

France should have the right to intervene for humanitarian purposes." See **convoi**

inné (m.) That which is inborn, natural, as opposed to *l'acquis* (m.), that which is acquired; nature as opposed to nurture. Hence, in an article on recent genetic research: *"Traditionnellement gagnés à l'acquis (le capital socio-culturel), les Français voient l'inné (le capital génétique) regagner du terrain"* (*Le Point,* July 5, 1997); "Whereas the French have always believed in the supremacy of education and other cultural influences, the importance of genetic influences on human behavior is gaining new ground."

inquiétude (f.) **identitaire** Phrase used in *Libération,* March 25, 1997, in describing the anxiety that French people are prone to feel at this time as to their national identity. See **exception française**

s'inscrire en faux contre To challenge a view or to express a viewpoint that is contrary to another; a legal phrase often used outside the context of legal proceedings. *Je m'inscris en faux contre les propos de Monsieur le Ministre au logement;* "I object to the remarks by the minister of housing."

Insee (m.) *Institut national de la statistique et des études économiques*—an institute that takes the nation's pulse in all aspects of economic activity, assigns Social Security numbers, and establishes indices that are used as references nationwide. For example, *l'indice Insee du coût de la construction,* building cost index, is used as the basis on which to determine rent increases, insurance premiums, and so forth.

insertion (f.) This does not involve inserting a coin or a card into a machine; the verb for that is *introduire: Introduisez votre carte. Insertion* today means bringing jobseekers into mainstream society through employment. *Il faut oeuvrer aujourd'-hui pour l'insertion des jeunes et la réinsertion des chômeurs de longue durée; sinon ce seront des exclus.* "Every effort must be made today to help young people and the long-term jobless fit into society; otherwise they will be marginalized." This is close to the concept of workfare or welfare-to-work.

instit (m. or f.) Short for *instituteur* or *institutrice,* grade school teacher. A popular TV series was called *l'Instit.*

insupporter *Insupportable* means "unbearable" and *supporter* means "to bear, to put up with." *Nous supportons l'odeur tant bien que mal;* "We put up with the smell as best we can." But the verb is a more recent back-formation, in which the former subject (we, you, etc.) becomes the direct object. *L'image de ces atrocités nous insupporte;* "We find the sight of these atrocities unbearable."

intégrale (m.) Someone's complete works, as in *Trois maisons de disque différentes rivalisent pour sortir l'intégrale des sym-*

phonies de Mozart dirigées par trois chefs d'orchestre différents; "Three record companies are competing with one another to bring out Mozart's complete symphonies conducted by three different conductors."

The word can have commercial applications as well. *Par les temps qui courent, où il est difficile d'attirer le consommateur, il faut repenser l'intégrale de ses produits;* "Nowadays, what with consumers being hard to attract, you have to rethink your complete product line."

intégration (f.) Today the word refers essentially to the integration of immigrants into French society. *Quelles sont les mesures que le gouvernement devrait prendre pour faciliter l'intégration de la population maghrébine?* "What steps should the government take to facilitate the integration of people from the Maghreb living in France?" See **code de la nationalité**

intégrisme (m.) Fundamentalism. *L'intégrisme parmi les catholiques de France* was led or embodied by **Monseigneur Lefebvre.** *L'intégrisme* in France, first considered a conservative tendency, has now come to be associated with *l'extrême droite* and hence has been accused of intolerance, racial and otherwise; the Paris church best known for its fundamentalist leanings is *St Nicolas du Chardonnet.*

L'intégrisme parmi les musulmans is associated, in France, chiefly with *l'Algérie et certains pays du Moyen orient.* The French authorities are concerned that it may take hold (*trouver des adeptes*) among the Muslim population in France. That is why, when Charles Pasqua, then *Ministre de l'Intérieur,* spoke at the inauguration of the first mosque in Lyons, *la première mosquée à Lyon,* in September 1994, he urged, *"Il faut un Islam de France,"* as distinct from *Islam en France.*

interdit(e) *Etre interdit(e) de chèquier,* to be deprived of the right to write checks because of past trouble with *des chèques sans provision,* "checks that have bounced."

No-nonsense signs in French public parks and gardens used to warn, *"Pelouse interdite,"* which meant "Keep off the grass." But then attempts were made to translate these signs for the benefit of foreign tourists, and the result has been "Forbidden lawn" or "No walking."

intérimaire (m. or f.) A temp, a person hired on a temporary basis. *Faire de l'intérimaire,* to temp. *Engager un(e) intérimaire. Une agence d'intérimaire.*

Internet (m.) Internet. *Surfer sur l'Internet,* to surf/navigate/ browse on the Net. *Internaute* (m. or f.), Net surfer, Web surfer. *Adresse* (f.) *Web,* Web address. *Site* (m.) *Web,* Web site. *Se brancher* or *se connecter sur Internet,* to log on the Internet; *connecté(e),* on-line. */Début (m.) de/ connexion* (f.), log-in, logging on. *Fin* (f.) *de connexion,* log-off, log-out, logging off. *Ac-*

céder à, to access; *accès* (m.), access. *Adresse* (f.) *URL,* URL address. *Afficher,* to display; *affichage* (m.), display. *Coder,* to encrypt; *décoder,* to decrypt; *décryptage* (m.), decryption. *Chercher,* to search; *moteur* (m.) *de recherche,* search engine. *Consulter,* to consult. *Courrier* (m.) *électronique,* E-mail; *courrier vocal,* voice mail. *Dossier* (m.), directory, folder. *En ligne,* on-line. *FAQS* (*la Foire aux questions*), FAQS (frequently asked questions). *Fichier* (m.), file. *Fournisseur* (m.) *d'accès,* access provider; *fournisseur de services,* service provider. *Fonction* (f.), capability, feature, function. *Héberger/loger,* to house. *HTML,* HTML, hypertext mark-up language. *Image* (f.) *numérisée/digitalisée,* scanned image. *Imprimer,* to print out; *imprimante* (f.) *à jet d'encre,* ink jet printer; *imprimante couleur,* color printer, *imprimante laser,* laser printer; *imprimante matricielle,* dot matrix printer. *Modem* (m.), modem. *Mot* (m.) *clé,* keyword. *Netiquette* (f.), netiquette. *Nom* (m.) *de domaine,* domain name. *Page* (f.) *perso/nnelle/* or *page d'accueil,* home page. *Protocole* (m.), *HTTP,* HTTP, hypertext transport protocol. *Télécharger* (*à partir d'un site ou d'un serveur*) *vers votre ordinateur,* to download; *télécharger vers le/un serveur* (*à partir de votre ordinateur*), to upload. *Toile* (f.), Web. *Webmestre* (m.), Webmaster. *WWW,* WWW, World Wide Web.

Courrier (m.) *postal,* snail mail.

See also **courrier électronique; E-mail; Minitel; piraterie**

intoxication (f.) See **info ou intox**

interroger son répondeur à distance To call in to your answering machine to pick up messages.

Iparretarrak A pro-independence movement in the French Basque country. Outlawed by the French government in 1987, it uses terrorist means. See **ETA; Euzkadi**

IPSOS (m.) Named after a place in ancient Phrygia, this institute carries out *études par enquêtes et sondages d'opinion,* "surveys and opinion polls."

ISF (m.) *Impôt de solidarité sur la fortune.* It has replaced the *impôt sur la grande fortune.* It is a special income tax levied on individuals "worth" 4.6 million francs (approximately seven hundred fifty thousand dollars) or more.

Islam (m.) *La deuxième religion de France*—which does not mean the second, in chronological order, to be adopted but the one with the second largest number of faithful today after Catholicism. See **intégrisme**

isoloir (m.) Voting booth. *Ce qui compte en fin de compte ce n'est pas les réponses aux sondages—c'est ce qui se passe dans l'isoloir;* "In the end, what counts is not how people answer opinion polls—it's how they actually vote."

IUT (m.) *Institut universitaire de technologie.* These institutes of higher education (*enseignement supérieur*) were created in 1966. They may be considered less prestigious than *les facultés elles-mêmes* but are more pragmatic, offering courses that lead more directly to job opportunities. Their two-year program—termed *l'enseignement supérieur court,* as opposed to *l'enseignement supérieur long* dispensed by *les facultés*—leads to a degree called the *Diplôme universitaire de technologie* (*DUT*).

IVG (f.) *Interruption volontaire de grossesse,* deliberate interruption of pregnancy, the legal term for *un avortement,* an abortion. An *IVG* was made legal by the *loi Veil* in 1974. See **avortement**

J

jachère (f.) *Laisser les terres/les champs en jachère,* to let land lie fallow. This is what many French farmers have been instructed to do since it was decided during *les négociations du GATT* that there was a glut of *oléagineux,* "oilseed-bearing plants," chiefly *les tournesols* (pl.), "sunflowers." In exchange for doing so the farmers were to receive *des subventions* (f. pl.), "subsidies." The farmers have protested that they do not wish to be idle or to become *des assistés,* "people receiving government handouts." See **friche; gel de terres; oléagineux; PAC; paysan**

Jean Moulin A World War II resistance leader who has since become a national hero and the symbol of the resistance movement in occupied France. Betrayed, he was arrested and tortured by the Gestapo (see **Barbie, Klaus**) but refused to talk. He was then deported but is said to have died in Metz before reaching his destination. His ashes were transferred to the Pantheon in 1964. It has never been fully determined who betrayed him.

Jeanne d'Arc Joan of Arc, of course. Revered for generations as the national symbol of France, belonging neither to the Right nor to the Left. But since the beginning of the 1990s, she has been *récupérée,* "taken over," by the *Front national,* which every year on the *Fête Jeanne d'Arc* in early May rallies around her gilded equestrian statue on the *Place des Pyramides,* near the *Louvre,* and sets off from there in a procession. See **Pucelle; récupérer**

jetable Disposable, as in *mouchoirs jetables,* paper handkerchiefs, and *couches jetables,* disposable diapers. In the context of unemployment, one rallying cry is *"Pas de travail jetable!"* " 'No short-term nonrenewable contracts!' " See **CDD**

jeu (m.) **vidéo** Video game. *Jeu interactif,* interactive game. *Jeu multimédia,* multimedia game. *Arcade* (f.) *de jeux vidéo,* video arcade.

JMJ (f. pl.) *Les Journées mondiales de la jeunesse,* World Youth Day. *Les 12es JMJ ont eu lieu à Paris en 1997; elles ont attiré des centaines de milliers de jeunes catholiques du monde entier. Le Pape Jean-Paul II est venu dire la messe. En 1993 les JMJ avaient eu lieu à Denver; en 2000 c'est à Rome qu'elles auront lieu.* "The twelfth World Youth Day took place in Paris in 1997, attracting hundreds of thousands of young Catholics from all over the world. The pope came to say Mass. In 1993 the World Youth Day took place in Denver; in 2000 it will be in Rome."

joindre To reach someone. *Où peut-on vous joindre?* "Where can you be reached?" *Elle n'est pas joignable/Elle est injoignable;* "It's impossible to reach her."

jouer dans la cour des grands The image is borrowed from school days: little children yearning to be allowed to use the big kids' playground. *Le sous-secrétaire d'état a fait une déclaration qui dépasse ses compétences mais il a tellement envie de jouer dans la cour des grands!* "He is a junior official and made a statement that goes beyond what his job entitles him to say, but he's so eager to be up there in the big leagues!"

(se) jouer dans un mouchoir To be really close, a real cliffhanger. *Les élections se jouent dans un mouchoir;* "The outcome of this election hangs by a thread."

jour (m.) **férié** Public holiday. In France the list includes a number of religious holidays: *Noël, le lundi de Pâques* (Easter Monday), *le jeudi de l'Ascension* (some time in May), *le lundi de la Pentecôte* (Whitmonday, in late May or early June), *l'Assomption* (August 15), and *la Toussaint* (November 1). Nonreligious holidays are *le jour de l'An, le premier mai* (*la Fête du travail,* Labor Day); *le 8 mai* (*la Fête de la Victoire,* end of World War II in Europe, 1945); *le 14 juillet* (Bastille Day), and *le 11 novembre* (Armistice Day, 1918). *Quand un jour férié tombe un vendredi ou un lundi, ce long weekend s'appelle un pont. Quand un jour férié tombe un jeudi ou mardi, les salariés prennent souvent le vendredi ou le lundi en plus pour faire un pont de quatre jours.* "When a holiday falls on a Friday or a Monday, this creates a long weekend. When a holiday falls on a Thursday or a Tuesday, employees often take the Friday or the Monday off so as to have a four-day weekend."

jour J (m.) The great day, or D day, so to speak: the appointed day, whatever it may be. *Les préparatifs étaient très fatigants, mais ça valait la peine parce que le jour J tout était fin prêt;*

"The preparations were very tiring, but it was worth it because on the appointed day everything was ready down to the last detail."

journal (m.) **télévisé** TV news. *Le journal télévisé de 20 heures n'a pas soufflé mot de cette histoire;* "There wasn't a word about it on the 8 P.M. news on TV."

juge (m. or f.) **d'instruction** The examining judge who undertakes or orders an investigation into the facts of a case. Such judges have been much in the news in recent years because of the number of **affaires** *de corruption* in which political figures, both on the national scene and at the local level, have been alleged to be involved. *Est-ce que les juges d'instruction ont trop de pouvoir?* "Do examining judges have too much power?" *"Si les juges remplissent l'espace, c'est qu'il n'y a plus de contre-pouvoir en France,"* according to a former *Ministre* on *Objection,* a radio talk show, in October 1994; "'The judges are taking up all the room, because there are no more checks and balances in France.'" *Est-ce qu'au contraire ils sont soumis à des pressions venant du gouvernement?* "Or is it the opposite: are they pressured by the government?" See **mise en examen; présomption d'innocence; secret de l'instruction**

jumelage (m.) Twinning of cities in France with cities in Germany and/or England and other European countries, for the purpose of promoting peace and understanding through cultural exchanges, reciprocal school visits, and so on. *La ville de Sèvres à côté de Paris est jumelée avec Wolfenbüttel en Allemagne.*

juppette (f.) In 1996 the then prime minister, Alain Juppé, put a bonus into effect whereby anyone who owned a car that was ten years old or more could trade it in for a new one and get a ten thousand franc reduction on the price. *La juppette a dopé les ventes de voitures neuves alors que les ventes de voitures d'occasion ont fléchi;* "The bonus stimulated new car sales whereas used car sales drooped." *La juppette a permis de nettoyer le parc automobile;* "The bonus took the worst of the old cars out of circulation." See **doper; parc automobile.** Journalists derisively dubbed this incentive *la juppette* (*une jupette* is *une petite jupe,* "a small skirt.") Juppé's predecessor, Edouard Balladur, had introduced a similar *prime* (f.), which had been dubbed *la Balladurette.*

Jussieu, Faculté (f.) **de** See **désamianter**

juste à temps (m.) *Le juste à temps* is similar to **les flux tendus.**

justice (f.) The judicial system. *Un Comité de réflexion sur la justice fut créé en janvier 1997, avec pour mission de rendre un rapport au gouvernement en juillet de la même année sur des réformes à faire. Il s'agissait entre autres du lien entre **le parquet** et le **Garde des Sceaux,** ainsi que de la détention provisoire et de* *la **présomption d'innocence**. Pourrait-on créer une justice de proximité, pour que les Français fassent davantage confiance à la justice de leur pays?* "A commission on reform of the judicial system was set up in January 1997 and instructed to report to the government six months later. Among other points, it was to deal with the relation between the judges and the Ministry of Justice, as well as with the practice of remanding in custody and acceptance (by the public, despite the media) of the principle that a person is presumed innocent until legally proven guilty. Could the judicial system be brought closer to the people, so that they would have more confidence in it?"

justice (f.) **sociale** Social justice—that is, a fairer, more egalitarian society. *Tous les partis politiques prétendent lutter pour davantage de justice sociale;* "All political parties claim that they are fighting for a fairer society."

K

K One thousand. Job ads will often indicate salary as, for instance, 132K, meaning 132,000 francs a year or 11,000 francs a month.

K7 (f.) Shorthand for *cassette* (f.) *vidéo* or *audio.* An abbreviation very commonly used in ads, promotional material, and so on.

kinésithérapeute (m. or f.) Physical therapist. *Le médecin m'a prescrit dix séances de kiné(si) pour faire de la rééducation;* "My doctor has prescribed ten physiotherapy (rehab) sessions."

Kourou See **Ariane**

krach (m.) Pronounced "crock." Used only in *un krach boursier,* a stock market crash. *Krach larvé,* a crash that is waiting to happen. *Krach rampant,* a crash that is building up slowly. *Le krach d'octobre 1997 est parti de la Thaïlande, puis de Hong Kong.*

L

La Courneuve Paris suburb where *la Fête de l'Huma(nité)* takes place every year in the fall.

La Fontaine, Jean de Although he died in 1695, his *Fables,* with their moral endings, are still taught to French schoolchildren and are quoted from or alluded to every day, no doubt, in some part or other of the media, in contexts ranging from sports to music to economics. Has there ever been a French kindergarten class that did not act out *Le corbeau et le renard?* In May 1995, just before the *élections présidentielles,* each candidate was asked, on an hour-long television program, to say which was his or her favorite fable and why.

La Hague This is not The Hague in the Netherlands, which is *La Haye.* No, *La Hague* is the windblown, rocky point of land jutting out into *La Manche,* "the English Channel," west of *Cherbourg.* Famous in recent years for *une usine de retraitement de déchets radioactifs* that was built there. See **centrale nucléaire; nucléaire**

laïcité (f.) The secular spirit that is supposed to reign dans *les écoles de la République.* The notion of *laïcité* is at the root of both *la querelle entre l'école publique (l'école laïque) et l'école privée (l'école religieuse)*—which has raged since *la séparation de l'Eglise et de l'Etat* in 1905—and *la controverse au sujet du* **chador** *à l'école.* See **Clovis; loi Falloux**

lait (m.) **cru** Raw—that is, unpasteurized—milk; the basis of many of the best-known French cheeses. Early in the 1990s it was rumored that European Community authorities, headquartered in Brussels, were going to prohibit the making of cheese from unpasteurized milk, on the grounds that such cheeses were a health hazard. The anti-Maastricht segment of French public opinion condemned this as the ultimate interference by the **eurocrates.** See **Bruxelles; Maastricht**

langue (f.) **de bois** The opaque doubletalk spoken by politicians. *Est-ce que les femmes qui se lancent dans la politique pratiquent la langue de bois autant que les hommes politiques?* "Do women who go into politics utter as much doubletalk as men in politics?"

Latché Name of President Mitterrand's house in the *Landes,* in southwestern France, below Bordeaux. See **Bousquet, René; Solutré**

La Villette Former cattle market and slaughterhouse in northeastern Paris; the grounds and part of the buildings have been converted into an exhibition and science center, museum, theater, and experimental music and dance facility.

leader (m.) *Un leader politique* has become a very common phrase even though French has perfectly adequate phrases of its own: *un chef de file politique, une personnalité politique importante. Leader* is not confined to the political sphere: *Cette société est leader dans la vente de lunettes et de* **lentilles.** *Exercer le leadership. Le leadership de Yasser Arafat est parfois contesté par sa propre base;* "Arafat's position as leader is sometimes challenged by his own rank and file."

Leclerc Edouard Leclerc and his son challenged established marketing principles by opening their own supermarkets, *les centres Leclerc,* with systematically lower overheads and lower prices.

lecteur (m.) **de disques compacts** CD player. *Lecteur de cassettes,* cassette player, tape deck.

législateur (m.) An excellent example of a practice which is common in French: the word in the singular is taken to represent the plural or an entire category. *En interdisant le cumul des mandats le législateur voudrait éviter la concentration du pouvoir entre trop peu de mains;* "The purpose of the law which would prohibit the holding of more than one elective office at a time is to prevent power from being monopolized by too few individuals."

lentille (f.) A contact lens, also called *un verre de contact. Aujourd'hui il y a des lentilles souples, des lentilles jetables, des lentilles que l'on peut garder une semaine, des lentilles qui changent la couleur des yeux, . . .* "Today there are soft lenses, throwaway lenses, lenses you can keep in a week at a time, lenses that change the color of your eyes, and so on. Of course *une lentille* is also "a lentil."

lepénisme (m.) The doctrine espoused by Jean-Marie Le Pen; see *Front national. Lepéniste* (m. or f.), person adhering to this doctrine; member of the *FN. Lepénisation* (f.), the influence of Le Pen on *la scène politique.*

lettre (f.) **de motivation** The covering letter you must send with your **CV** when you apply for a job. *Souvent elle doit être manuscrite;* "It is often required to be handwritten."

levée (f.) **de boucliers** An extremely vigorous protest. In August 1995, for instance, Alain Madelin, then *Ministre de l'Economie et des Finances* in the first Juppé government, predicted *une véritable levée de boucliers de la part des syndicats,* "a real outcry on the part of the labor unions." (At the end of November the **cheminots** went on strike, and the movement spread rapidly to other unions, partially paralyzing the country for three weeks.)

libellule (f.) Dragonfly, but also an informal term for *un hélicoptère.*

libération (f.) Usually refers to the liberation of France, beginning with the June 6, 1944, D day landing (*le débarquement en Normandie*); then the French and Allied landing in Provence in August 1944; then the liberation of each town and region. *La libération de Paris* was achieved by August 25, 1944; that of Strasbourg, three months later.

    La libération de la femme, women's lib. See **féminisme; MLF**

libre-service (m.) Self-service, as in *un magasin à libre-service. Un restaurant à libre-service* is more commonly called *un self,* a truncated version of the English word *self-service.*

licence (f.) Roughly equivalent to a bachelor's degree. *Etre en licence,* to be working toward a *licence; avoir une licence; boucler (terminer) sa licence. Pour faire sa licence, il faut d'abord avoir réussi son* **DEUG.** *Etre licencié(e) en mathématiques,* to have a bachelor's in math; but see **licencier.**

licencier To dismiss, fire, lay off. *Etre licencié(e),* to be fired. *Le licenciement économique,* dismissal on economic grounds, layoff; *le licenciement sec,* dismissal for reasons other than economic.

Licra (f.) *Ligue internationale contre le racisme et l'antisémitisme,* founded in 1927. Frequently mentioned alongside the more recent **SOS Racisme.** See **droits de l'homme; exclusion**

lieu (m.) **de mémoire** A site that is singled out for protection and commemoration because it is linked to some event in French history or aspect of French daily life. For instance, the *pavés de Roubaix,* a stretch of road also called *l'enfer du nord,* known to *Tour de France* participants and other cyclists for its vertebrae-jangling paving stones. See **pavés du nord**

lifté(e) Something which is *lifté* has been revamped or rejuvenated—that is, given a face-lift (*un lifting*). See **chirurgie esthétique**

ligne (f.) **droite** *La dernière ligne droite avant quelque chose (avant les élections, avant la date fixée pour l'entrée en vigueur de la monnaie unique,* etc.) is the final phase prior to some event or

What is good for the company is good for employment.

"And what's good for the company?"

"Making profits."

"To do that, we've got to be competitive."

"And to be competitive, we've got to fire people."

"So, firing people is good for employment."

by Dominique Boll in *Marianne,* July 7–13, 1997

deadline. *On entre dans la dernière ligne droite;* "We are coming into the home stretch."

ligne (f.) **intérieure** Domestic airline. This used to mean only *Air Inter.* Then in the early 1990s came *Air Liberté, AOM,* and others, but by 1996 they were *en difficulté* because of *la déréglementation,* also called *la dérégulation.*

Lille The fourth largest city in France (after Lyon and Marseille-Aix-en-Provence), with a population of just under one million. Linked to London and Brussels by the **Eurostar.** *Lille était candidate pour être le site des J.O. de 2004 mais n'a pas été retenue par le Comité des jeux olympiques (CJO)*: Lille was in the running to be the site of the 2004 Olympics but was not chosen by the International Olympics Committee."

limogeage (m.) Dismissal of a high-ranking individual. *Le limogeage du PDG de la société est imminent;* "The company's chairman is going to be divested of his powers any day now."

lion (m.) The emblem of Peugeot cars, *la marque du lion.* Hence, one of Peugeot's slogans: *"Un fabricant sort ses griffes";* literally, "a manufacturer bares its claws (paws)." See **chevrons**

liposuccion (f.) See **chirurgie esthétique**

liste (f.) **rouge** *Etre sur liste rouge,* to have an unlisted telephone number.

livret (m.) **de caisse d'épargne** Savings account passbook. *Le Livret A de la Caisse nationale d'épargne (CNE),* administered by *La Poste,* provides tax-free interest on an amount up to one hundred thousand francs; in 1998 the rate was 3 percent. (Banks give an identical rate of tax-free interest on amounts up to thirty thousand francs placed on a savings account called *un Codévi*—i.e., *compte pour le développement industriel.*)

livret (m.) **de famille** A booklet that you are given at *la Mairie* when you get married and are expected to keep forever. It contains several pages to be filled in, as and when appropriate, by the proper officials. The first pertains to the wedding itself: date, place, exact names and dates of birth of the two spouses, and names of their parents. Another is provided for divorce. There is one page for each future child: date and place of birth, given names, names of parents, and date and place of death.

    Un extrait de naissance, "a birth certificate," is a separate document, as is *une fiche d'état civil,* literally, "a certificate of your civil status," combining a birth certificate with a marriage certificate if applicable.

LOA (f.) *Location avec option d'achat;* leasing.

location (f.) **saisonnière** The rental of accommodations on a seasonal basis; chiefly vacation rentals. A phone-in talk show in August 1997 discussed, *"Comment déjouer les pièges de la location saisonnière? Si les locaux que vous trouvez en arrivant* *ne correspondent pas à la description qu'on vous en a donnée, quels recours avez-vous? Vaut-il mieux passer par une agence ou louer directement auprès du propriétaire?*" "'How can you avoid being disappointed by your vacation rental? If you have rented sight unseen and the premises do not live up to the description you were given, what can you do about it? Is it better to rent through an agency or directly from the owner?'"

loge (f.) *Une loge maçonnique,* a Masonic lodge. Such lodges are far more secret, less visible than their counterparts in the United States. See **Grand Orient; franc-maçon**

logiciel (m.) Software. A specific branch of it is *le ludiciel,* "gameware." See **piratage**

logisticien(ne) (m. or f.) A logistics expert.

loi (f.) **antitabac** The first law limiting advertising for tobacco was passed in 1976 (*loi Veil*). The 1991 *loi Evin* forbade all advertising for cigarettes. The next step *dans la lutte contre le tabagisme* came in 1992: all restaurants and institutions open to the public were required to create *un espace non-fumeurs,* a nonsmoking section, and in the Paris Metro all corridors, platforms, and cars were declared *non-fumeurs.* The government derives revenue from the sale of tobacco; at the same time the cost of medical treatment for health problems attributable or related to the use of tobacco is blamed for a considerable portion of *le déficit de la Sécu(rité sociale).* Cigars, cigarettes, and tobacco are sold only *dans les tabacs* (and sometimes in cafés or restaurants), not *dans les supermarchés ou les stations d'essence;* the manager of *un tabac* is *un(e) buraliste.*

Un tabac is often *un bar-café* as well. Above each *tabac* hangs a large vertical reddish-orange sign, *la carotte,* since slices of raw carrot used to be put into shredded tobacco to keep it moist. *Un tabac* will sell lottery tickets (see **loto**) and a small selection of the most common postage stamps; there is always *une boîte aux lettres,* "a mailbox," outside *un tabac.* See **SEITA**

loi (f.) **Debré** See **hébergement**

loi (f.) **Falloux** Passed in 1850, at a time when Catholicism was still the State religion, it entrusted primary schools to the Church, but it was amended in the 1880s to affirm the nonreligious nature of public elementary schools. Each *commune* was authorized to pay no more than 10 percent of the maintenance expenses of private (i.e., Catholic) schools. The separation of Church and State came about in 1905. The *loi Falloux* remained on the books but was half-forgotten.

Decades later, in 1994, after a report showed that half of all independent school buildings were unsafe, the then *Ministre de l'Education nationale,* François Bayroux, announced plans for *une révision de la loi Falloux* to allow mayors to allocate funds derived from local taxes for such repairs in Catholic schools (i.e., to increase the 10 percent ceiling). This measure caused a **levée de boucliers** *chez les enseignants et les parents d'élèves de l'école laïque.* The *Conseil constitutionnel* overruled the government's bill.

loi (f.) **quinquennale** Five-year plan or law, as in *la loi quinquennale pour l'emploi* enacted by *le gouvernement Balladur* in 1994.

Longo, Jeannie *Championne cycliste,* bicycling champion. *Elle a décroché une médaille d'or aux J.O. de 96;* "She won a gold medal at the 1996 Olympics."

look (m.) This word is taken over directly from English, but the double *oo* is pronounced as in *moon* or *food. Avoir le look,* to have that "in" look, that fashionable look. *Le look grunge; le look jeune; le look new wave.*

loto (m.) A form of weekly national lottery, played on cards sold in *tabacs* (see **loi antitabac**). (Other popular lotteries include *Bingo, Tac O Tac,* and *Keno.*) In some cases the card must be scratched to reveal a number: *"Gratter—ça peut rapporter gros";* "'Just scratch—see how much you catch,'" goes the easily parodied slogan. Lotteries are run by a firm called *La française des jeux.* The old *Loterie nationale* was phased out in 1990.

loubard (m.) A thug, a tough. *Aujourd'hui on suppose automatiquement que les jeunes loubards viennent des banlieues/des cités;* "Today people immediately assume that young toughs come from the **banlieues.**" *La loubardisation.*

Louis Delluc This prize is to films what the *prix Goncourt* is to books (see **Galligrasseuil**). *Le prix Louis Delluc* has been awarded to the best French film of the year every year since 1937 (except from 1940 to 1944).

M

Maastricht The city in the Netherlands where the treaty, the **Traité de Maastricht,** formally creating *l'Union européenne,* was signed in September 1992. The name itself is used as shorthand for the treaty, as in *être pour ou contre Maastricht.* See **critères de convergence** *(critères de Maastricht).* The adjective is *Maastrichien,* as in *Est-ce que la nouvelle majorité est aussi Maastrichienne que l'ancienne?* "Is the new government as pro-Maastricht as the previous one?"

Madame Soleil A fortune-teller some years ago who called herself this. Still referred to today, always in the negative, as a way of denying that one has prophetic powers, as in *Sur le taux de croissance des 12 mois à venir, je ne suis pas Madame Soleil;* "I cannot predict what the growth rate over the next twelve months will be."

magasin (m.) **de proximité** Neighborhood shop; a convenience store to which you can walk, in town, as opposed to *une grande surface,* a supermarket, to which you drive, somewhere outside town. *Souvent un magasin de proximité restera ouvert très tard, jusqu'à 22 ou 23 heures.* See **proximité**

Maghrébin(e) Objectively, this is a person from *le Maghreb,* the region of northern Africa where from the early nineteenth century on, France had a colony, Algeria, and two protectorates, Morocco and Tunisia. (In 1955 the French protectorate over the sultanate of Morocco came to an end, and in 1957 Morocco became a kingdom; in 1956 Tunisia gained its independence, a year after agreements establishing Tunisian autonomy; and in 1962 Algeria became independent; see **accords d'Evian.**)

Less objectively, however, this is a person from *le Maghreb* who has become a more or less recent immigrant in France and is therefore accused by the extreme Right in France of causing several things: *le chômage parmi les Français de souche,* "unemployment among native-born French people"; *de l'instabilité par l'affaiblissement des valeurs morales traditionnelles* (*c'est-à-dire chrétiennes*), "instability through the weakening of traditional (i.e., Christian) moral values in French society"; *une croissance de la criminalité,* "an increase in crime"; *le trou de la Sécu,* "the Social Security deficit"; and *l'abaissement du niveau dans les écoles,* "the lowering of attainment levels in schools."

magnétoscope (m.) VCR. *Programmer son magnétoscope n'est pas toujours évident;* "It's not always easy to program your VCR."

magouille (f.) Like *une combine,* this term means "an illegal or potentially illegal or irregular trick or scheme to achieve something." *Beaucoup d'électeurs estiment que tous les partis politiques magouillent plus ou moins pour arriver à leurs fins;* "Many voters believe that all the political parties get around the law more or less in order to get what they want." *Un bon exemple de magouille c'est de changer la méthode d'élection législative à peine 18 mois avant les élections;* "One good example of a slippery political ploy is to change the method of voting for legislative candidates barely eighteen months ahead of the elections."

mai 68 The heady weeks when student strikes—supported by the labor unions although their members did not riot along with the students—brought France to a standstill and wrought far-reaching changes, ultimately breaking down certain class barriers in French society, demonstrating the clout wielded by adolescents and very young adults, and causing a vast influx of students into the universities. *Toute personne ayant participé aux événements de mai 68 ou les ayant observés s'en souvient encore et considère cette période comme une date charnière;* "Anyone who took part in or observed the events of May 1968 still remembers them and considers that date as a dividing line/watershed." *Pourtant le 25e anniversaire des évènements, en 1993, n'a pratiquement pas fait de vagues;* "Yet in 1993, the twenty-fifth anniversary of that period caused hardly a ripple." See **Cohn-Bendit, Daniel; crèche; CRS; événements de mai 68; gaz lacrymogène; soixante-huit**

maigrir To lose weight or to slim down. *Sur le marché il y a pléthore de produits qui sont censés vous faire maigrir sans danger;* "There is a superabundance of products available that they claim will make you lose weight safely." See also **minceur.** *Les années de vache maigre/grasse,* lean/fat years.

maillot (m.) **jaune** The yellow T-shirt that the winner of the Tour de France is entitled to wear. The wearer may change each day on the basis of accumulated points. *A la fin de l'étape d'aujourd'hui, c'est le coureur belge qui en principe endossera le maillot jaune;* "By the end of today's lap, it is expected that the Belgian cyclist will get to wear the yellow T-shirt."

mainmise (f.) Exclusive control over something. *Les salariés prétendent que c'est la mainmise des marchés, c'est-à-dire la Bourse et les actionnaires, qui dicte la politique de l'emploi des entreprises;* "Workers claim that companies' employment policies are dictated by what the financial markets—that is, the stock markets and shareholders—want." See **pensée unique; pognon**

Maison (f.) **blanche** Designates both the White House in Washington and the Russian parliament. In the latter context, the term was heard especially in 1991, when Gorbachev was ousted and Yeltsin came to power.

maison (f.) **de Molière** An unofficial but affectionate name for *la Comédie-Française,* because many of Molière's plays were written for one of the troupes from which it was created soon after he died in 1673. The plays by Molière, Racine, and Corneille are still the mainstay of the *Comédie-Française*'s repertoire, but the works of other authors, both classic and modern, both French and non-French, have been added. Actors and actresses at the *Comédie-Française* are first *pensionnaires* on one-year contracts, then may become *sociétaires,* who in fact are shareholders in it and are bound to it for ten or twenty years or more.

maîtriser les coûts de la santé The great aim of the *Sécurité sociale* authorities: to keep public health costs from getting out of control. Doctors are held largely responsible for spiraling costs because, it is alleged, they overprescribe costly treatments.

maladie (f.) **franco-française** A continuing and possibly morbid fascination with a given period of French history (*par exemple, la période Vichy*) or with a specifically French feature of daily life (*par exemple, la tendance à faire grève*).

maladie (f.) **sexuellement transmissible** Or *MST,* sexually transmitted disease (STD). *Les chercheurs dans le domaine des MST réclament davantage de fonds;* "Medical researchers in the field of STDs are clamoring for more funding."

Malik Oussekine See **bavure**

malfaiteur (m.) Literally, an evil-doer. In fact, a word commonly used by the media to mean (petty or would-be) criminal, thug. *Trois malfaiteurs ont tenté de braquer une banque à Vittel;* "Three thugs tried to hold up a bank in Vittel." The media also commonly use *gangster* (m.).

mammographie (f.) Mammogram. *On conseille à toutes les femmes de plus de trente-cinq ans de faire faire une mammographie tous les deux ans;* "All women over thirty-five are advised to have a breast X-ray every two years." *La mammographie fait partie des examens de routine prescrits aujourd'hui par les gynécologues;* "A mammogram is one of the tests that gynecologists routinely prescribe today." See **échographie; frottis**

manager This is both verb and noun. *Manager une entreprise* is simply a more modern, "in" way of saying *gérer une entreprise.* When the word is a noun—*être un bon manager*—you hear the final *r. Le management doit constamment s'adapter à la conjoncture;* "Business management methods must constantly adapt to changing circumstances."

Manche (f.) The English Channel. *L'ouverture en 1994 du tunnel sous la Manche, bien que saluée à l'époque comme un événement majeur, n'a pas vraiment rapproché davantage les deux peuples;* "Although the opening of the 'Chunnel' in 1994 was hailed at the time as an event of prime importance, it has not really brought Great Britain and France closer together." *Outre-Manche on continue à rouler à gauche;* "The British continue to drive on the left."

Les leaders politiques d'outre-Manche refusaient l'Europe sociale; "British political leaders did not accept the Maastricht provisions concerning labor legislation" (the number of hours in the standard workweek, the creation of a minimum wage, etc.). *Mais l'élection de Tony Blair en 1997, à la tête des travaillistes, ouvre de nouvelles perspectives sur l'Europe sociale;* "But since Labour, with Tony Blair at its head, was elected in 1997, the outlook for European labor legislation has changed."

See also **Eurotunnel; outre-; tunnel sous la Manche**

mandat (m.) A mission or term of office. *La Constitution de la Cinquième République prévoit un mandat présidentiel de sept ans;* "The Constitution of the Fifth Republic stipulates that the president's term of office is seven years." *Vers la fin du deuxième mandat du Président Mitterrand, réélu en 1988 mais atteint d'un cancer incurable, beaucoup de membres de l'opposition réclamaient un amendement à la Constitution pour réduire le durée du mandat présidentiel de sept ans à cinq seulement;* "Mitterrand was reelected in 1988; toward the end of his second term, when he was dying of cancer, many non-Socialist politicians urged that the Constitution be amended so as to reduce the president's seven-year term to five years." This was not done, however. See **quinquennat; septennat**

mandat (m.) **d'amener** An arrest warrant. *Il y a un mandat d'amener à l'égard de Monsieur X, ancien collaborateur du Maire;* "A warrant has been issued for the arrest of Mr. X, the mayor's former aide."

Mans, Le *Le Mans,* about two hours west of Paris, is famous for two annual races. *Les 24 heures du Mans, une course automobile, remontent à 1923;* "The twenty-four-hour automobile race began in 1923." *Une course de motos appelée les 24 heures du Mans-moto date de 1978;* "A motorcycle race was added in 1978." Accidents are not unknown; *La course du printemps 92 a été particulièrement meurtrière;* "The number of fatal accidents during the spring 1992 race was unusually high."

maquis (m.) Synonymous with the Resistance movement during World War II: *prendre le maquis* meant *entrer dans la Résistance,* whose members were *les maquisards* or *les résistants.* By extension, even half a century later, *prendre le maquis* can still have the connotation of being in the (underground) opposition. *Bon nombre d'indépendantistes corses ont pris le maquis;* "Many members of the Corsican independence movement have gone underground." See **milice**

marasme (m.) Like **morosité** and **sinistrose,** this word, meaning "slump" or "stagnation," is often used to describe the economic atmosphere or the pulse of the nation in the 1990s. *Comment sortir du marasme où on est?* "How can we get out of the slump?"

marché (m.) **des changes** The exchange rate market. *Le dollar est manifestement sous-évalué par rapport au franc sur le marché des changes, disait VGE à la fin 96;* "The U.S. dollar is clearly undervalued in relation to the franc on the exchange market, said former President Valéry Giscard d'Estaing at the end of 1996." *Puis, au cours de 1997, le dollar est monté à près de*

6F50, ce qui a dopé les exportations françaises; "Then, for a while in 1997, the dollar rose to nearly 6F50, which was good for French exports." Daily reports on the radio will note, for instance, *"aujourd'hui le dollar a cédé deux centimes (ou gagné deux centimes)."*

marée (f.) **noire** An oil spill. *L'accident survenu à l'*Amoco Cadiz *en 1978 a provoqué une marée noire sans précédent sur les côtes bretonnes;* "The *Amoco Cadiz* incident in 1978 caused an oil spill such as had never been seen before on the coast of Brittany."

marginal (adj. and n.) A word very commonly used in recent years to designate a person who appears to be a misfit or an outcast, voluntarily or involuntarily on the fringe of society. The verb is *se marginaliser. Son frère est devenu un marginal. Le plus grand danger pour un chômeur c'est de devenir un marginal/ c'est d'être marginalisé. La marginalisation, c'est ce qui guette tous ceux qui ne possèdent pas les techniques de l'informatique;* "Anyone who is not computer-literate is in danger of being left out in the cold." See **exclu(e); exclusion**

Marianne She is the symbol of *la république* and is always shown by cartoonists as wearing *un bonnet phrygien. On peut voir son buste dans toutes les Mairies de France;* "Her bust is displayed in every town hall in the country."

Brigitte Bardot was officially chosen in 1969 as the new model for her bust. Late in 1996, however, after she had married a man with a fairly high rank in the *Front national,* expressed admiration for Jean-Marie Le Pen, criticized the way Muslims in France slaughtered lambs or sheep for use in ritual meals, and was taken to court by human rights movements protesting her remarks, one French mayor decided to stop displaying Marianne in his town hall, explaining, *"On nous avait proposé Brigitte Bardot pour le buste de Marianne parce qu'elle avait des formes généreuses et pas d'idées, mais maintenant nous n'en voulons plus parce qu'elle a des idées qui ne sont pas généreuses";* "'Brigitte Bardot was chosen for the bust of Marianne because she had a generous figure and no ideas at all; but now we don't want her anymore because she has ideas that are not generous.'"

marin pêcheur (m.) Professional sea-going fisherman. *De temps à autre les marins pêcheurs espagnols sont accusés d'avoir pénétré dans les eaux territoriales françaises, et inversement;* "Now and again Spanish fishermen are accused of having entered French territorial waters, and vice versa."

Marnes-la-Vallée Just outside Paris, to the east, and accessible by the *Réseau Express Régional* RER (see **Port Royal**), this is the spot where **Eurodisney** opened to the public in April 1992.

marquer contre son propre camp To score points (inadvertently) against your own team. Said of a government official or party member who has put his or her foot in his or her mouth.

Marseille Was sometimes called *le Chicago français* because it had a reputation for gangland violence.

m'as-tu vu (n.) A show-off attitude (literally, did you see me?). *Il aurait mieux fait d'être plus modeste et moins m'as-tu vu, il aurait davantage de gens de son côté;* "If he'd been more modest and less of a showoff, he'd have more people on his side."

match (m.) **aller** In the sports world, this is "an away game"; *un match retour is "a home game." Un match amical* or *un match d'entraînement est un match qui n'a aucune incidence sur le classement de l'équipe,* "is a friendly or practice game that does not affect a team's ranking."

matière (f.) **grise** Gray matter; brains. *La course à l'emploi dans cette époque de haute technologie privilégie la matière grise;* "To find a job in this hi-tech day and age, brains are the key factor."

MATIF (m.) *Le marché à terme international de France,* French futures market.

Matignon *L'Hôtel Matignon,* where *le Premier ministre et ses chefs de cabinet,* "the prime minister and his staff," have their offices. It is on the *rue de Varenne,* in the seventh *arrondissement* of Paris.

mayonnaise (f.) *La mayonnaise ne prend pas,* "the mayonnaise is not thickening as it should," is a homey culinary metaphor for any scheme or maneuver, especially political, that does not work out as planned.

McDonald's Become a household word since the late 1980s; the most visible exponent of *le fast food,* also called *la restauration rapide. Maintenant on peut petit-déjeuner aussi chez McDo* (pronounced "Mac dough"); "Now you can have breakfast, too, at McDonald's." People never used to go out for breakfast—or else it was the traditional café breakfast of coffee with baguette, croissants, or *tartines* (buttered baguette).

  Dans les premiers temps, McDonald's en France ne proposait ni bière ni vin, mais très rapidement ils ont modifié cette politique en fonction des goûts des Français; "When McDonald's started out in France, it did not serve wine or beer, but it soon changed that policy to cater to French tastes."

MDC (m.) *Mouvement des citoyens,* a left-leaning political party founded in 1992 by Jean-Pierre Chevènement, former Socialist defense minister at the time of the **guerre du Golfe,** of which he disapproved. *Le MDC était également anti-Maastrichien, et c'était en 1992 que devait avoir lieu le référendum où les Français ont eu à dire si oui ou non ils étaient en* *faveur du traité de Maastricht; le oui l'a emporté par une marge très étroite (51%),* "The MDC is anti-Maastricht, and it was in 1992 that a referendum was to be held in which French voters had to say whether or not they were in favor of the Maastricht Treaty; the ayes defeated the nays by a very narrow margin (51 percent)." See **Maastricht; Traité de Maastricht**

mécénat (m.) The fact of sponsoring, providing funds. *Les banques rivalisent entre elles dans le domaine du mécénat culturel ou autre; l'une financera une série de concerts de musique classique, telle autre apportera son soutien à une équipe amateur de foot.* "Banks compete with each other as sponsors of cultural or other events; one provides support for a series of classical music concerts while another sponsors an amateur soccer team."

Médecin, Jacques Mayor of Nice for years until the early 1990s and son of the previous mayor; the dynasty lasted for decades, until a warrant was sworn out against the son on corruption charges. *Il est parti en Uruguay, et il y est resté plusieurs années jusqu'à son extradition vers la France, où il est passé devant les tribunaux;* "He vanished to Uruguay where he spent several years until he was extradited to France and put on trial." *Condamné, il a passé deux ans en prison en France; une fois libéré il est reparti en Amérique du Sud;* "He was sentenced and served two years in prison in France, then he left for South America again."

Médecins (m. pl.) **sans frontières** An international humanitarian organization originated by French doctors in 1971. *Médecins du monde, Vétérinaires sans frontières,* and *Pharmaciens du monde* are groups along similar lines.

médias (m. pl.) *Les médias ont acquis un pouvoir redoutable;* "The media have acquired a disturbing amount of power." *Aujourd'hui quand quelqu'un est mis en examen ou même simplement soupçonné, il n'échappe pas à un procès par les médias avant que la justice n'ait fait quoi que ce soit;* "Today, when someone is being investigated or even is simply suspected, he cannot avoid a trial by media before the legal system has even lifted a finger."

Médiatique: Cette candidate a une présence médiatique fantastique; "This woman candidate comes over fantastically well on the media."

Médiatisé(e): Le déroulement de la justice est devenu complètement médiatisé, ce qui fausse tout; "Justice cannot take its course without the media dogging every step, which distorts everything." *La médiatisation du résultat des sondages a des conséquences graves;* "Opinion poll results are given a lot of play in the media, which has serious effects."

mendicité (f.) Begging, being *un(e) mendiant(e). Avec l'augmenta-*

*tion du nombre de **SDF**, la mendicité s'est accrue également;* "With the growing numbers of homeless people, begging has also increased." *Le Maire de Nice a fait procéder à un référendum en 1996 pour interdire la mendicité dans le centre-ville; d'autres villes en France avaient déjà pris des décisions de même type.* "The Mayor of Nice had a referendum held on the question of forbidding begging in the central parts of the city; other French towns had already taken similar decisions." *La mendicité est interdite dans les wagons du Métro;* "Begging in Metro cars is forbidden." *Faire la manche,* to panhandle, an informal way of saying *mendier.*

mensualisation (f.) The fact of being paid on a regular monthly basis, twelve months of the year, *et non pas sur une base journalière, hebdomadaire, saisonnière, ou irrégulière. Les ouvriers du secteur portuaire réclament la mensualisation;* "Dockworkers want their pay to be spread out evenly on a monthly basis." It can also mean having pay for, say, ten months' work spread over twelve months.

Mensualisation can also apply to the payment of income tax, which is not withheld at source; instead, it is due in three installments during the year; see **tiers provisionnel.** *Puisque le fisc préférerait avoir des rentrées d'argent étalées à intervalles rapprochés tout au long de l'année, il invite les contribuables à opter pour la mensualisation;* "Since the tax authorities would rather receive payments at brief intervals throughout the year, they urge taxpayers to choose to have their tax payments deducted monthly from their bank account." *Mais la mensualisation est encore facultative et non pas obligatoire,* "But the monthly payment of taxes is still optional, not compulsory."

See also **annualisation de l'emploi**

mère (f.) **célibataire** Single mother—now a recognized (and very common) legal status. There is a world of difference, sociologically speaking, between this term and the damning phrase it has replaced, *fille-mère,* "unmarried mother," which was disdainfully used until a couple of generations ago. See **MLF**

Mère Denis (f.) The image used by a prominent brand of washing machines in its TV commercials in the 1970s and still referred to as an example of successful marketing and a sort of sociological landmark. She was a good old-fashioned, stout, gray-haired, blue-aproned farm wife, unglamorous but genuine, happily discovering *le confort moderne,* "modern conveniences."

mère (f.) **porteuse** Surrogate mother. Also called *mère accoucheuse. La législation concernant les mères porteuses est encore assez floue;* "The legal position concerning surrogate mothers is still quite vague." The biological mother is *"la mère génétique."*

Mère Veil (f.) Satirical nickname that journalists gave to Simone Veil, an *UDF* stalwart and *Ministre de la Santé et du Travail* in the Balladur government until 1995. *Mère Veil* sounds identical, of course, to *merveille* (f.), "marvel."

Simone Veil was also the first woman to be president of the European Parliament. See **avortement; loi antitabac**

mesures (f. pl.) **parcellaires** Piecemeal efforts to deal with a problem. One participant in a radio talk show on the theme of *Combattre l'exclusion* said, *"Le gouvernement ne fait qu'appliquer des mesures parcellaires pour nous bercer, au lieu d'adopter une vue d'ensemble";* "'All the government is doing is applying piecemeal measures to keep us quiet/to keep up an illusion, instead of standing back and taking an overall look at the question.'" See **exclusion; rustine**

météo (f.) Short for *météorologie* and *les prévisions* (f. pl.) *météorologiques;* the weather forecast. *Les présentateurs(trices) de la météo/Ceux/Celles qui font la météo à la télé sont devenu(e)s des vedettes à part entière;* "The commentators who do the weather forecast on TV have become celebrities in their own right."

Une vague de froid va descendre au cours de la nuit sur toute l'Europe depuis Moscou jusqu'à Lisbonne. A Tunis et à Alger par contre les températures seront au dessus de la normale saisonnière. "A cold wave is going to hit all of Europe tonight from Moscow to Lisbon. Meanwhile, in Tunis and Algiers the temperature will be milder than usual at this time of year."

Météo marine, weather bulletin for vessels at sea.

métèque (m. or f.) Very pejorative term for a foreigner or a person of mixed French and foreign blood. Georges Moustaki, a popular Franco-Greek singer and composer from the 1970s on, was fond of calling himself *un métèque.* The word did not contain the hysteria associated in more recent decades with *les **Arabes**, l'**immigration**,* and *les **Maghrébin(e)s**.*

mètre carré (m.) The unit used for measuring floor space or land surface. *Un mètre carré est l'équivalent de onze pieds carrés;* "One square meter is equal to about eleven square feet." Real estate prices are usually expressed as so much per square meter. *Un appartement de 80m2 que l'on doit payer 24.000F le m2 à Paris ne coûte souvent que 10.000 ou 12.000F le m2 en province;* "An apartment measuring about nine hundred square feet and costing 24,000F per eleven square feet in Paris often costs only half that much, or less, in other French cities."

Métro-boulot-dodo In the days of full employment, *le plein emploi,* this was the wryly comical way of summing up the average person's fate: commuting to work in the morning, putting in a day's work, and commuting home and going to bed. The routine was the subject of a book and then a film, *Elle court, elle court, la banlieue.*

métropole (f.) *La métropole*—or *la France métropolitaine*—is continental France plus Corsica; in other words, it does not include the **DOM-TOM.**

mettre un dossier à plat To take a completely fresh look at a question or issue, or even to start working on it again from scratch. *Pour répondre aux revendications des étudiants en médecine, le gouvernement va devoir mettre le dossier à plat;* "To deal with the demands of the students in medical school, the government is going to have to think through the whole question all over again from the very beginning."

Ne pas confondre avec, "not to be confused with," *mettre les pieds dans le plat,* to make a blunder.

Milice (f.) This was a vital aspect of *la guerre franco-française* during the Vichy period, since *la Milice* was a semimilitary police force made up entirely of French volunteers, established early in 1943 and led by Joseph Darnand. *Collaborant activement avec l'occupant allemand et même faisant une partie de la sale besogne à sa place, la Milice était le contraire du* **maquis;** "Collaborating actively with the German occupying forces and even doing part of the dirty work for them, *la Milice* was the opposite of *le maquis.*" Louis Malle's film, *Lacombe Lucien,* deals with the subject.

minceur (f.), **amincissement** (m.), **amincissant(e)** *La mode est à la minceur;* "Fashion insists on slimness." *Le marché des produits d'amincissement est énorme;* "Dieting products are very big business." The slogan for Contrexéville, a mineral water, was *"Contrex—mon contrat minceur."* See **maigrir**

mines (f. pl.) **antipersonnel** Land mines. *La campagne contre les mines antipersonnel a reçu le Prix Nobel de la paix en 1997, quelques mois avant la signature du Protocole d'Ottawa. Les efforts dans ce sens de la Princesse Diana et sa mort soudaine y ont été peut-être pour quelque chose.* "The campaign against land mines received the Nobel Peace Prize in 1997, a few months before the signing of the Ottawa Protocol. Princess Diana's efforts to have land mines banned and her own sudden death may have had something to do with it." *Le déminage,* removal of land mines. See also **Diana**

minima sociaux (m. pl.) Government minimum income allowances, in one form or another. A term which appeared at the end of 1997; see **revendications sociales des chômeurs.**

Ministre (m. or f.) A Cabinet member. Invariably a masculine word until the Jospin government appointed a substantial number of *femmes Ministres* in June 1997. They each insisted on being addressed as *Madame la Ministre* and no longer as *Madame le Ministre.*

Ministère (m.) **de la Ville et de l'intégration** Cabinet post created in the mid-1990s *dans le but de combattre l'**exclusion** et la **marginalisation** des habitants de la banlieue/des **banlieues** et des quartiers défavorisés dits quartiers à risque,* "in an attempt to bridge the gap between the mainstream French population and the immigrant or second-generation population."

Minitel® (m.) A nationwide computerized information network using telephone lines and accessible on a small computer-like home apparatus, with keyboard and screen, which is also called *le Minitel.* The system was first introduced by *la Poste* in the mid-1980s; cleverly, *la Poste* began by giving away the apparatus free of charge. Parents quickly discovered that their children had already discovered that they could play an array of games via the *Minitel* and had run up a hefty phone bill in the process.

It is widely used as a means of obtaining information more quickly and more extensively than via phone calls and the printed phone directory. *Si vous désirez vous renseigner sur un futur employeur, faites le 3614 code (. . .). Pour connaître l'horaire des trains de Paris à Toulouse, faites le 3615 code SNCF.* TV show hosts will say, *"Si vous voulez savoir les titres des livres que nous avons consultés en préparant cette émission, faites le 3615 code (machin chouette)";* "'If you want to know which books we used in putting this program together, just type in 3615 code (whatever).'" See **Ravel.** However, the *Minitel* has no international ramifications (i.e., is not connected to any other country).

The **Internet** arrived on the scene and swept most of the developed world but barely made a dent in France. Gradually it was felt, and the media began saying (e.g., *l'Express* in July 1997) that the *Minitel* was *"un phénomène purement **franco-français"*** that was actually isolating France from the rest of the world and preventing France from moving onto the Internet. In the summer of 1997, Lionel Jospin, the newly elected Socialist prime minister, issued a vigorous statement in favor of adoption of the Internet in France and adaptation of the *Minitel* so as to link it with the **Internet.**

mise (f.) **en cause** The fact of calling into question or pointing a finger at some person or some established practice. A *Front national* spokesman, on a radio talk show called *Le rendez-vous politique* in late 1996, claimed that *"le système des préférences nationales dans le service public était mis en cause,"* "'the principle of giving preference to French nationals in the civil service was being endangered.'"

mise (f.) **en examen** The fact of placing someone under judicial investigation. *Vers la fin de 1996, la trésorière du RPR a été mise en examen par un juge, et l'épouse du Maire de Paris, par un autre; du coup, le RPR s'est trouvé en mauvaise posture.*

"Toward the end of 1996 both the treasurer of the *RPR* and the wife of the mayor of Paris were placed under formal investigation by two different judges; because of these two cases, the *RPR* looked pretty bad." *La mise en examen ne vaut pas accusation mais aux yeux du public elle est néanmoins synonyme d'accusation et même de culpabilité;* "The fact of being placed under investigation is not synonymous with being accused, but in the public mind it does mean accusation nevertheless and, indeed, guilt." The procedure became common in the early 1990s especially with regard to political figures and prominent business figures accused of improper dealings. The opposite is *un non-lieu; bénéficier d'un non-lieu,* to have the case against you dismissed. See **abus; présomption d'innocence**

mise (f.) **sous condition de ressources** A measure which aroused strong reaction in 1997, when the newly elected Socialist government, seeking ways to reduce government expenditure, decided to make the granting of *les allocations familiales* subject to *les ressources,* "the income," of each family. *Les familles dont les ressources dépassaient un certain plafond n'y auraient plus droit;* "Families with incomes above a certain level would no longer be entitled to family allowances." The government withdrew the proposed measure in 1998. See **AGED**

mise (f.) **sur orbite** Placing on orbit (*d'un satellite* etc.). *La mise sur orbite de cette station spatiale est une réussite pour la société Ariane Espace.* See **Ariane; programme spatial**

mixte *Une société mixte* is one whose ownership is mixed public and private. *Un mariage mixte,* mixed marriage.

Mixte, when said of a school, means "co-ed"; *la mixité,* "the co-ed system itself." *Cette école n'a toujours pas d'élèves filles; c'est le dernier lycée privé à n'avoir pas opté pour la mixité.* "That school is still for boys only; it's the last private high school not to have gone co-ed." *La mixité a été introduite dans les établissements secondaires d'état à partir des années 70;* "Starting in the 1970s state-run high schools began to become co-ed."

MLF (m.) *Mouvement pour la libération de la femme,* founded in 1970. *Mais le mouvement féministe en France est nettement en retrait par rapport au féminisme aux Etats-Unis et dans les pays anglo-saxons en général;* "But the feminist movement in France is distinctly less prominent than its counterpart in the United States and in English-speaking countries in general."

Simone de Beauvoir was a precursor of the feminist movement in France, followed by Gisèle Halimi, Monique Wittig, Antoinette Fouque, and others. But none of them was in the public eye to the same extent or in the same ways as the most prominent feminist leaders in the United States.

Among feminist milestones in France: 1946: women granted

the vote. 1968: a married woman no longer needs her husband's permission to have a profession and open a bank account. 1968: the *loi Neuwirth* authorizes contraception. 1970: the *MLF* created. The *Code civil* acknowledges that the man is no longer head of the family; both spouses share parental authority. 1971: manifesto by 343 women publicly stating that they had had an abortion. 1972: *procès de Bobigny.* 1974: President Giscard d'Estaing appoints Françoise Giroud to head the first *Secrétariat d'Etat à la condition féminine.* 1974: the *loi Veil* legalizing abortion.

See **avortement; féminisme; harcèlement sexuel; libération**

mobilier (m.) **urbain** Covers all of the more or less permanent fixtures selected and installed by cities: *les arrêts d'autobus, les entrées du Métro, les corbeilles à papiers, les bancs des jardins publics, les lampadaires, les parcmètres, . . . ,* "bus stops, Metro station exits // entrances, wastebaskets, park benches, streetlamps, parking meters, and so on." *Le style sélectionné pour le mobilier urbain a une influence très durable sur le **look** (sic) de chaque ville;* "The style of urban fixtures that is selected has a long-lasting influence on each city's personality."

mobiliser To interest someone, get someone involved. *Sur cette question, les leaders syndicaux semblent avoir du mal à mobiliser leur base;* "The union leaders seem to be having trouble getting their rank and file to move on this issue."

mode (m.) **d'emploi** This means instructions for use, of course, as with a tool, an appliance, an item bought as a kit to be assembled, and the like. The media will use it facetiously, as in *CSG mode d'emploi* or *Impôt sur la Fortune mode d'emploi,* "how the *CSG* works" or "how the wealth tax works." See **CSG; ISF**

Molière (m.) *Les Molières* are prizes which have been awarded annually in the French theater world since 1985: *meilleur metteur en scène, meilleur acteur, meilleure actrice, meilleur décor,* and so on. See **César**

Mondial (m.) *See* **Coupe du monde; pluriel**

mondialisation (f.) The globalization of the economy. In some quarters it is held responsible for many evils. For instance, *Le mondialisation est la plus grande menace pour l'emploi en France; comment voulez-vous que les employeurs français, avec les charges sociales qu'ils sont obligés de payer, puissent concurrencer des employeurs du Tiers monde et vendre leurs produits à des prix compétitifs?* "Globalization is the greatest threat to employment in France. What with all of the health insurance, retirement, and other benefits that French employers have to pay for, on top of salaries, how can you expect French employers to compete with Third World employers and sell their products at competitive prices?" See **AMI**

monétique (f.) Umbrella word covering all means of payment aside from cash, such as *la carte de crédit, la carte bancaire,* and *la carte de paiement.*

Mongénéral A satirical way of referring to de Gaulle while he was president. *Le Canard enchaîné* was still using it on July 9, 1997. (*Mon général, mon capitaine,* and *mon lieutenant* are the standard forms of salute in the French military.)

monnaie (f.) **commune** The common currency of Europe, to be introduced on January 1, 1999; originally dubbed the *écu* but renamed the **euro.** But for some time before 1998 it was unclear whether it would be the **monnaie unique,** the single currency, or would exist concurrently with *le Deutschemark, le franc français, la livre sterling, la lire italienne,* and the rest. *Aux Etats-Unis le dollar est à la fois la monnaie commune et la monnaie unique;* "In the United States the dollar is both the common currency and the single currency." In late 1996, in an effort to prepare customers for the idea of the *euro, les centres Leclerc,* a nationwide chain of somewhat iconoclastic supermarkets, began producing a series of billboards showing *des articles de consommation courante,* "common consumer items," such as *une baguette de pain,* and a single question: *"Ça fait combien en euro?"* "'How much does it cost in euros?'"

monnaie (f.) **forte** Strong currency; specifically, a strong French franc. A cornerstone of official French monetary policy in the 1990s and therefore a sore point with certain economists and exporters. *Faudrait-il dévaluer légèrement le franc pour le rendre plus compétitif face au dollar U.S.?* "Should the franc be slightly devalued to enable it to compete better with the dollar?"

monnaie (f.) **unique** Single currency. This topic has been a major bone of contention; see **monnaie commune.**

Monseigneur Lefebvre French prelate who in 1974 issued a manifesto protesting against Vatican II. *Par exemple, il a continué de dire la messe en latin au lieu de la dire en français, et il a continué à ordonner des prêtres même après qu'il ait été suspendu;* "For instance, he continued to say Mass in Latin instead of in French, and he continued to ordain priests even after he had been suspended."

Monseigneur Lefebvre est mort en 1991 mais son mouvement traditionnaliste dans l'Eglise en France continue; en dehors de son mouvement certains l'appellent l'intégrisme. "Monsignor Lefebvre died in 1991 but his traditionalist movement within the French Church continues; in certain quarters outside the movement it is called *l'intégrisme,* 'fundamentalism.'" See **intégrisme; St. Nicolas du Chardonnet**

Monsieur (m.) **Bons Offices** Unofficial name given to a mediator or ombudsman; a troubleshooter. *Bill Clinton continue de jouer le Monsieur Bons Offices dans le conflit sur Jérusalem.*

monter au créneau (m.) A military phrase commonly used by the media: to go into attack mode, mount an attack, taking the risk of exposing oneself to enemy fire. *Pour défendre son projet de réforme de la Sécu, le Premier ministre n'hésite pas à monter au créneau.*

morosité (f.) The ailment from which France has been repeatedly said to suffer since the early 1990s. *Le gouvernement cherche à combattre le climat de morosité générale afin d'inciter les Français à consommer davantage;* "The government is trying to overcome the country's glum state of mind so as to induce the French to become bigger consumers." See also **marasme; sinistrose**

mosquée (f.) Mosque. Becoming a more common feature in the French landscape since massive immigration from *le Maghreb* began. *Quand le Roi du Maroc est venu en France en visite officielle en 1996, il a promis, entre autre choses, les fonds nécessaires à la construction d'une mosquée dans l'est de la France;* "When the king of Morocco came to France on an official visit in 1996, he promised among other things to provide the money for the building of a mosque in eastern France."

moto-crottes (f.) *Nom officieux donné à une tentative officielle de la Ville de Paris de résoudre le problème des crottes de chien sur le trottoir,* unofficial name given to an official attempt by the Paris authorities to solve the problem of removing the mess left by dogs on the sidewalks. *C'est une moto munie d'un long aspirateur;* "It is a motorbike equipped with a long suction tube." The person riding it is an employee of *la Ville de Paris.*

Only half-hearted attempts have been made to urge city dwellers to train their dogs: *"Apprenez-lui le caniveau";* "'Teach him to use the gutter,'" say the signs. *Mais les pénalités invoquées ne semblent pas être appliquées;* "But the penalties that were announced do not appear to be applied."

mouvance (f.) Sphere of influence. *Tous ceux dans la mouvance du Parti socialiste sont touchés par ces accusations;* "Everyone who is related in some way or other to the Socialist Party is affected by these accusations."

mouvement (m.) **de grève** Strike movement. *En 68, le mouvement de grève, qui était parti de Nanterre, prit rapidement une ampleur nationale;* "In 1968 the strike movement, which originated at *Université de Paris X* in Nanterre, rapidly became nationwide."

Un mouvement de grève est lancé—rien ne peut maintenant l'arrêter; "A strike movement is under way—nothing can stop it now." *C'est une semaine riche en événements sociaux qui commence avec des mouvements de grève dans les secteurs de la banque, du Métro, et ainsi de suite;* "This is a significant week on the labor front, beginning with strike movements in various sectors—the banks, the Metro, etc."

Mouvement (m.) *social* is an offshoot of this. As you wait on the platform for the next Metro, for instance, a loudspeaker may warn that service will be interrupted along part of your route; *"Suite à un mouvement social le service est perturbé entre La Motte-Picquet et la Concorde."*

Mouvement (m.) **pour la France** Conservative political party founded by Philippe de Villiers. Considered as definitely to the right of the *RPR* but not so far right as the *Front national.*

MRAP (m.) *Mouvement contre le racisme et pour l'amitié entre les peuples.* Founded in 1949, it is one of the groups in the forefront of antiracist demonstrations and protests. See **Licra; SOS Racisme**

muguet (m.) Lily of the valley, sold on every street corner on *le premier mai,* **Fête du travail;** the first of May, which is Labor Day; cakes and greeting cards are decorated with *muguet.* On May 1, 1995, *des éléments incontrôlés,* "unidentified youths," who were tailing a *Front national* procession in Paris caught a young **Maghrébin** on the banks of the Seine and pushed him into the river, where he drowned. In response to the outcry from *divers groupes contre le racisme et l'exclusion,* President Mitterrand made a symbolic gesture of solidarity that was widely approved: he tossed a bouquet of *muguet* into the Seine from the spot where the incident had taken place.

multimédia (m.) *Le multimédia c'est l'avenir. Cela implique un changement fondamental dans les mentalités.* "Multimedia is the wave of the future. It will revolutionize people's way of looking at the world."

multipropriété (f.) Time sharing in the real estate sector. *Le multipropriétaire achète une certaine tranche de temps dans l'année, normalement une ou plusieurs semaines, où il peut venir occuper le bien en question;* "A timesharer buys a certain amount of time per year, usually one or more weeks, when he or she can come and occupy the property he or she has bought into."

Mururoa An atoll in French Polynesia. *La première explosion atomique à Mururoa a eu lieu en 1966;* "The first atomic explosion at Mururoa occurred in 1966." *Les derniers essais nucléaires sousmarins français ont eu lieu ici en 1995;* "France's final underwater nuclear tests took place here in 1995." *Pour protester contre ces essais, Greenpeace a envoyé un bateau, le* Rainbow Warrior II, *qui a été **arraisonné** par les Français;* "In protest against the tests, Greenpeace sent a ship, the *Rainbow Warrior II,* which was boarded and inspected by French authorities." For the clash between France and Greenpeace one decade earlier, see ***Rainbow Warrior.***

musculation (f.) *La musculation est un des types les plus courants* *de mise en forme;* "Body-building is one of the most popular types of fitness activity." *Beaucoup de citadins vont en salle deux fois par semaine pour faire de la muscu/faire du body building;* "Many city dwellers go to a gym twice a week to do body-building." *Si on fait de la muscu de façon intensive, il est conseillé d'être suivi(e) par un médecin/de la faire sous contrôle médical;* "If you go in for intensive body-building, it is a good idea to have a doctor keep an eye on you." *Faire des poids* (m. pl.) *et haltères* (m. pl.), to lift weights.

N

narco (m.) Drugs pedlar. *Narcodollars* (m. pl.), money earned through the drugs trade. *Narcomarketing* (m.), drugs market- ing. *Narcotrafic* (m.), drugs dealing. *Narcotrafiquant* (m.), drugs dealer. *Brigade* (f.) *des narcotiques, des stupéfiants,* drugs squad of the police.

nationalité (f.) See **code de la nationalité**

navette (f.) A commute; hence, *un(e) navetteur(euse),* a commuter. The word is not really in common use, however; it seems to be more of a journalistic coinage. A commuter is more likely to call him- or herself *un(e) banlieusard(e).*

navette (f.) **spatiale** Space shuttle.

néfaste food (m.) A term applied, in semiplayful protest, to the onslaught of *fast food* (m.) in France; *néfaste,* of course, means "harmful." See **Burger King; McDonald's; restauration rapide**

neige (f.) **artificielle** Or *neige de culture,* artificial snow. *Quand il n'y a pas assez de neige, les stations de ski ont recours à de la neige artificielle;* "When there is not enough snow, ski resorts resort to artificial snow." *Elles utilisent un canon à neige;* "They use a snow gun."

ne se prononcent pas (m./f. pl.) A collective noun: the "don't knows" or "no opinions" among the individuals questioned by a poll. *Par exemple, Pour: 43%; contre: 27%; ne se pro- noncent pas: 30%.*

network (m.) *Faire du network,* to network, engage in networking.

nettoyage (m.) **ethnique** Term used first by Valéry Giscard d'Estaing, the former president, in 1992 to refer to ethnic cleansing in Bosnia. Also called **purification** (f.) **ethnique.**

ni-ni (m.) *Le ni-ni du Parti socialiste: ni nationalisation ni privatisa- tion,* position taken by the Socialist Party in 1990: no further nationalization but no further privatization, either, of banks, enterprises, and so on. *Ni-ni* has given rise to similar phrases in other fields. *Le ni-ni bancaire: ni rémunération ni tarifica-*

tion; "Banks' policy is to not pay interest but on the other hand not to charge for certain services."

nippon(ne) Adjective often used by the media instead of *japonais(e)*. The country itself is either *le Japon* or (unofficially) *le pays du soleil levant,* "the land of the rising sun."

nivellement (m.) **par le bas** What modern education is frequently accused of causing or fostering: a general leveling down. *Certains spécialistes cependant rétorquent qu'en fait il y a un nivellement par le haut, puisque tant d'élèves vont jusqu'au Baccalauréat et, parmi eux, un pourcentage très élevé continue dans le supérieur;* "But some specialists retort that in fact there is a leveling up, since so many pupils go as far as the *baccalauréat,* and then a very high percentage of them go on into some form of higher education."

Noah, Yannick Half-French, half-Cameroonian tennis player who won the French Open in Paris in 1983 and instantly became a hero. Captain of the French team that won *la coupe Davis* in 1991 in Lyons. He coached the 1996 French team to another Davis Cup victory, in Malmö, Sweden, and the 1997 French women's team to victory in the Fed Cup. See **Coupe Davis; Roland Garros; saladier d'argent**

noctambus (m.) A word coined to designate night-time bus service in Paris; based on *noctambule* (m. or f.), "night owl," "reveler."

nocturne (m. or f.) A night or evening opening. *L'exposition Manet est ouverte en nocturne tous les mercredis. Pour relancer la consommation, de plus en plus de magasins prévoient maintenant une ou deux nocturnes par semaine;* "To encourage people to buy, more and more stores are scheduling late night opening hours once or twice a week."

noir (m.) Informal, illegal, undeclared. *Le travail au noir,* work paid for under the table. *Le travail au noir constitue une part beaucoup trop importante de l'économie française,* say the economists, "Illegal employment accounts for far too large a share of the French economy." *On blanchira l'argent au noir;* "Illegal funds will be laundered illegally," punned *Rien à cirer,* a satirical radio program, in 1993. (Its name comes from the very colloquial phrase *j'en ai rien à cirer,* "I don't give a hoot.") *Pendant la guerre, le marché noir était florissant;* "During the war years, the black market flourished."

nomade (m. or f.) Gypsy, vagrant, homeless person. *"Stationnement interdit aux nomades,"* say signs warning these people not to park their *caravanes.* A building that is occupied by squatters is said to be *nomadisé. Cet immeuble de bureaux, qui est vide depuis deux ans, vient d'être nomadisé.*

nono From mid-1940 to November 1942 the northern half of France and the Atlantic coast constituted *la zone occupée par les troupes allemandes.* The rest was *la **zone libre*** or *la zone* *non-occupée,* and *zone non-occupée* was shortened (in spoken French) to *zone nono.* The term is still heard in countless talk shows and films.

nos chères têtes (f. pl.) **blondes** Our darlings, our children; a cliché that was often used to designate the younger generation and therefore France's future. *Il faut toujours agir dans l'intérêt de nos chères têtes blondes;* "We must always bear in mind the interests of France's youth." It reflected the demographic fact that a large portion of the French population traditionally derived from northern European, as opposed to southern or Latin, sources. Today, it is used only with irony because it obviously does not include the children of immigrants from the Maghreb and other former French colonial regions in Africa.

notaire (m.) One of the most powerful professions in France. You cannot purchase a house, apartment, land, and so on, without paying *des frais de notaire,* "fees," which until recently were as high as 11 percent of the selling price. (The fees on newly built real estate are lower.) The *notaire*'s function in such a transaction is to look into title and have the transaction registered with the central, nationwide *registre de l'immobilier.* See **immobilier**

nourrice (f.) *Trouver une nourrice (ou une place à la crèche) est la préoccupation numéro un de la plupart des jeunes mamans qui travaillent;* "The number one concern for most young working mothers is to find a woman to look after their infants (or find room in a day care center)." See **AGED**

Nous sommes tous des juifs allemands "We are all German Jews." One of the many slogans spawned, and chanted, during the **événements de mai 68.** It expressed support for **Daniel Cohn-Bendit,** one of the most vocal student leaders during that period; he is of German-Jewish origin.

nouveaux pauvres (m. pl.) A term coined in the early 1980s to designate *d'anciens cadres* (m. pl.), "former executives," and other individuals who had sunk below the poverty line, chiefly as a result of unemployment. *Dans cette catégorie entrent des personnes ayant fait des études supérieures et ayant accumulé les diplômes, qui autrefois n'avaient jamais à craindre le chômage et la pauvreté;* "This category includes individuals who have gone to college and gotten degrees and who never used to have to be afraid that they would become unemployed and poor."

nouvelle vague (f.) A nostalgic term today, referring to a period of moviemaking in the late 1950s and early 1960s exemplified by François Truffaut (*Les 400 coups, Baisers volés*), Claude Chabrol (*Les cousins, Le beau Serge*), and others.

noyau (m.) **dur** Literally, the hard nucleus; the hard core. *Lors de la privatisation d'une banque ou d'une société, le noyau dur* *ce sont les investisseurs institutionnels qui s'engagent à ne pas vendre leurs actions avant la fin d'une certaine période;* "When the government privatizes a bank or company, the hard core consists of the institutional investors who pledge not to sell their shares before a given period has elapsed."

NTM The name of a rap group. *NTM* stands for *Nique ta mère,* "Fuck your mother." In July 1996 NTM gave a concert in Toulon, in southern France, one of the three cities at that time (along with Orange and Marignane) to have a *Front national* mayor since the *FN* had won the local elections earlier in the year. *Au cours du concert, en présence de policiers qui étaient là pour empêcher des débordements, des paroles soudainement ajoutées disaient, Nique ton policier;* "During this concert, while policemen were on hand to keep order, lyrics were suddenly added to one song, saying, 'Fuck your policeman.'"

The group's leaders were arrested, tried, sentenced to a six-month prison term (mostly suspended) and forbidden to perform for six months. The judge was accused of being an *FN* sympathizer. Howls of protest against the verdict, in the name of free speech, came from civil rights groups around the country; the **Garde des Sceaux** (part of the then *RPR* government) came out with a statement objecting to the verdict. Some commentators alleged that there was *une hystérisation de la situation* and objected to *l'interdiction de chanter imposée à un groupe de rap à cause de propos hors texte,* objected that a rap group should not be forbidden to sing because of words that were not part of the lyrics. *NTM* became famous overnight.

On appeal, in 1997, *NTM* was given a two-month suspended sentence and fined 25,000F (approximately $4,000).

nuancer To qualify a statement (one's own or someone else's); to clarify, make distinctions, or water down, as in a talk show debate when a speaker says, *"Je voudrais nuancer un peu ce que Monsieur X vient de dire."*

nucléaire (m.) Nuclear energy; *l'énergie* (f.) *nucléaire. Une grosse partie de l'électricité produite en France provient du nucléaire;* "Much of the electricity produced in France comes from nuclear energy." *Mais les médias demandent souvent, "Faut-il avoir peur du nucléaire?"* "But the media often ask, 'Should we be afraid of nuclear power?'"

*Le nucléaire est de plus en plus contesté depuis que les résultats d'une étude scientifique ont été révélés au début de 1997: chez les habitants de **La Hague** (près de Cherbourg), où se trouve une usine de traitement des déchets nucléaires, le taux de leucémie parmi les enfants serait trois fois plus élevé que la norme;* "Nuclear energy has become more and more debatable since the results of a scientific study concerning the inhabitants of La Hague (near Cherbourg), where there is a nu-

clear waste treatment plant, were revealed early in 1997: it would seem that the leukemia rate among the local children was three times higher than the normal rate."
See **plateau d'Albion; Superphénix**

nuisance (f.) Not just a nuisance (i.e., a source of irritation) but something harmful, *quelque chose qui nuit. La nuisance sonore,* noise pollution. *Les émissions de gaz toxiques constituent une nuisance grave;* "Toxic gas emissions are a serious source of pollution."

numérique Digital. *Enregistrement* (m.) *numérique,* digital recording. *Numérisation* (f.), digit(al)ization. *France Télécom vise une numérisation plus élevée de son réseau;* "France Télécom aims to put a larger portion of its network on a digital basis."

numéro (m.) **de code secret** The PIN number you need to use your **carte de crédit.** *Il vous le faut non seulement pour retirer de l'argent mais aussi pour payer un achat ou une addition au restaurant; par contre il vous dispense de signer.* "You need it not only to withdraw money but also to pay for any purchase or pay a restaurant bill; on the other hand, your signature is no longer necessary."

numéro un (m.) Informal term for leader. *La visite de Yasser Arafat, le numéro un de l'OLP, est attendue aujourd'hui;* "A visit by Yasser Arafat, the PLO leader, is expected today."

numéro (m.) **vert** A free telephone number, the equivalent of an 800 number in the United States; and, indeed, since late 1996, when all of France converted to ten-digit telephone numbers, *un numéro vert* begins with 0800 followed by six digits.

O

OAS (f.) The *Organisation de l'Armée secrète,* created in 1961 and active in the early 1960s; its policy was to oppose Algerian independence by all possible means, including terrorism, and keep Algeria French. It was outlawed by President de Gaulle's government and its leaders were tried; three of them were executed. See **Petit Clamart**

obédience (f.) This is not the word for obedience in the usual sense, which is *l'obéissance. Une obédience* is "an allegiance, an affiliation to some religious, political, or spiritual organisation," as in *Les pays d'obédience communiste se comptent aujourd'hui sur les doigts d'une main.* Often used in speaking of *la franc-maçonnerie,* which is considered as a more underground movement and viewed with more suspicion than are the

Freemasons in the United States. *La franc-maçonnerie est une obédience à caractère secret.* See **franc-maçon; Grand Orient**

objecteur (m.) **de conscience** Conscientious objector (CO). *Un objecteur de conscience a toujours l'option de remplacer le service militaire obligatoire par une période de service communautaire;* "A CO can always do a period of community service instead of complying with the draft."

obligation (f.) **alimentaire** Requirement to provide support for one's spouse or ex-spouse, children, parents, or other relatives. *A présent que la famille éclatée ou monoparentale devient la norme, l'obligation alimentaire ne va plus de soi; elle est souvent contestée ou rejetée.* "With split or single-parent families becoming the norm today, the maintenance obligation no longer goes without saying; it is often challenged or ignored." *Pension* (f.) *alimentaire,* alimony or child support. See also **soutien**

obligation (f.) **pourrie** Junk bond.

obole (f.) A very small contribution, usually financial but also, by extension, contribution of opinion. *Apporter son obole,* to chip in, put in your two cents' worth.

obtention (f.) **de papiers** The fact of obtaining (official residence) papers. *L'obtention de papiers par des immigrés en situation irrégulière n'est pas considérée par les mouvements de droite comme une chose souhaitable;* "The rightist political movements do not believe that illegal immigrants should be able to obtain official residence papers." See **régulariser sa situation; sans-papiers**

occase (f.) Colloquial for occasion (f.), opportunity: *C'est une bonne occase.* Also, colloquial for second-hand, that is, *d'occasion,* as in *une voiture d'occase.*

Occident A far right movement in the 1960s, before the emergence of the *Front national.* It was dissolved in 1968, then replaced by *Oeuvre française,* whose leader was Pierre Sidos and whose emblem, painted on walls, was a cross inscribed in a circle.

occidental(e) West or Western, as in *la Virginie occidentale,* West Virginia. *Le monde occidental,* the Western world. *Les pays occidentaux ou les pays de l'ouest. Oriental(e),* East or Eastern. See **Allemagne occidentale; Allemagne orientale**

occulté(e) Overshadowed, eclipsed. *Vers la fin de 1990 la proposition de réforme de l'orthographe, qui pourtant avait soulevé beaucoup de discussion, a été totalement occultée par la guerre du Golfe;* "Although the proposed spelling reform had given rise to heated discussion, it was completely overshadowed at the end of 1990 by the Gulf War."

oeuvrer pour la paix To work toward peace, make efforts to achieve peace. *Les pays européens devraient faire davantage afin d'oeuvrer pour la paix au Moyen Orient,* say some commentators; "The European countries should do more to promote peace in the Middle East."

oléagineux (m. pl.) The oil-seed plants or crops, notably *le tournesol*, sunflowers. They were at the heart of the last GATT negotiations, ending in 1993, and of much bitterness in rural France. Having been urged ten or twenty years earlier to plant more and more acreage to sunflowers, they were now told to stop planting them and to let their fields lie fallow. *Les cultivateurs français avaient l'impression que les technocrates à Bruxelles et le gouvernement américain étaient en train de leur donner des ordres—et de quel droit?* "French farmers felt that the technocrats running the European Community in Brussels, plus the American government, were giving them orders, and what right did they have to do that?" See **friche**

OLP (f.) *Organisation de libération de la Palestine;* the PLO.

Olympia Major concert hall in Paris (and one of the oldest), along with *le Bataclan, Bercy, Bobino, le Palais des Congrès,* and *le Zénith. C'est ici que se produisent les plus grandes vedettes de la chanson;* "This is where the really big-name singers appear."

OM (f.) *L'Olympique de Marseille,* one of the best-known and most ardently supported soccer teams, *équipes de football,* in France. Owned in the early 1990s by Bernard Tapie, a self-made man and flamboyant businessman turned politician. *Lui et son équipe étaient au coeur d'un scandale en 1993, l'affaire OM-Valenciennes, où l'on accusait l'OM d'avoir offert de fortes sommes d'argent aux joueurs de Valenciennes pour laisser gagner l'OM;* "He and the team were the crux of a scandal in 1993 in which the *OM* was accused of having offered heavy bribes to *Valenciennes* players to throw the game in favor of the *OM.*"

Oncle (m.) **Picsou** Any tight-fisted individual; specifically, Uncle Scrooge in Donald Duck cartoons.

ONG (f.) *Organisation non gouvernementale,* nongovernmental organization (NGO). *La Croix rouge et le **Croissant rouge,** par exemple, sont des ONG;* "For instance, the Red Cross and the Red Crescent are NGOs."

ONU (f.) *Organisation des Nations unies,* the United Nations (UN). *Onusien(ne),* having to do with the UN. *Les forces onusiennes de maintien de l'ordre seraient entrées dans la capitale;* "It appears that the UN peacekeeping force has entered the capital."

onze (m.) **tricolore** *L'équipe qui joue officiellement pour la France lors de toute rencontre internationale, comme par exemple la Coupe du monde;* "The official French soccer team in the World Cup and all other international encounters." See **bleus; Coupe du monde; pluriel(le)**

OPA (f.) *Offre publique d'achat,* a takeover bid. *Contre OPA,* counter-takeover bid. *OPA hostile,* hostile takeover bid. The word *opéable* was coined to designate *la cible probable d'une OPA,* "the likely target of a takeover bid," as in *Cette chaine de supermarchés est éminemment opéable.*

OPCVM (m.) *Organisme de placements collectifs en valeurs mobilières*—a type of investment fund.

Opération (f.) **Mains propres** Anticorruption ("clean hands") campaign in Italy in the mid-1990s; it received considerable attention in France.

Opération (f.) **Vacances propres** A campaign led by national or local government to combat litter on streets, beaches, mountain paths, and so on, in popular resort areas. *Dans le cadre de cette opération les autorités ont installé davantage de corbeilles* (f. pl.) *à papiers et distribué gratuitement des sacs* (m. pl.) *poubelle;* "As part of this effort the government installed more litter bins and distributed free garbage bags."

opposition (f.) Crucial notion in French politics. *Etre dans l'opposition,* to be in the party or parties that is/are not in power. Always to be viewed in relation to *la majorité,* who are in power. *Dans un interview à la radio réalisé vers le début de 1997, à une époque de gouvernement RPR, c'est-à-dire de droite-centre droite, Bruno Mégret, le numéro deux du Front national, a affirmé que la gauche (essentiellement le Parti socialiste et le Parti communiste) étaient dans une opposition déclinante, alors que le Front national était dans une opposition montante;* "In a radio interview early in 1997, at the time of an *RPR* (right–center right) government, Bruno Mégret, second in command of the *Front national,* claimed that the Left (chiefly the Socialist and Communist Parties) constituted a declining opposition force while the *Front national* constituted a rising opposition force."

Ordre (m.) **du Temple solaire** *Une secte qui a des ramifications internationales, puisqu'en 1994 des membres de la secte se sont donné la mort ensemble en Suisse romande, en 1995 seize personnes sont mortes dans un suicide collectif parmi ses adeptes dans le Vercors, et en 1997 cinq autres morts dont plusieurs d'origine française ont été trouvés au Québec;* "A sect with international ramifications, as shown by the fact that in 1994 several of its members in French-speaking Switzerland died together, in 1995 sixteen of the faithful died in a mass suicide in the *Vercors* in eastern France, and in 1997 five other sect members, including several of French origin, were found dead in Quebec."

Les médias ont posé beaucoup de questions concernant le financement des sectes en général, les pouvoirs de leurs gourous et la psychologie de leurs adeptes, les abus sexuels qui auraient été commis sur des enfants, ce que pouvaient faire les familles des membres d'une secte, et ainsi de suite; "The media were filled with questions about how sects in general are financed, their leaders' influence and their followers' psychology, whether children had been sexually abused, what the families of sect members could do, and so on."

ordures (f. pl.) *Le ramassage (ou la collecte) des ordures est devenu(e) une des tâches les plus pressantes des autorités municipales;* "Garbage collection has become one of the most urgent tasks facing municipal authorities." *Le tri des ordures par catégorie de déchets (verre, papier, etc.), sans être toujours obligatoire, est fortement encouragé;* "Sorting waste into categories (glass, paper, etc.) is not always compulsory but is strongly encouraged."

Conséquence de la forte consommation de repas à emporter ou livrés à domicile et des surgelés, des pizzas et autres produits pré-emballés, le volume des ordures a augmenté dans les mêmes proportions; "Because people are consuming so many take-out or delivered meals and frozen foods, pizzas, and other prepackaged products, the sheer volume of waste has swelled in the same proportions."

Orsec *Le Plan Orsec (Plan pour l'organisation des secours) est déclenché chaque fois qu'une catastrophe naturelle se produit— par exemple, incendie de forêt dans le Massif des Maures dans l'arrière-pays de la Côte d'Azur;* "The relief organization system goes into effect whenever some natural disaster occurs, such as forest fires in the mountains of Provence, just above the Riviera." See **Plan Orsec**

orthographe (f.) At irregular intervals, it is announced that French spelling needs to be reformed, and each planned *réforme* (f.) *de l'orthographe* arouses controversy. It involves ministerial approval and publication in *le Journal officiel.* The latest reform was mooted about in 1990 and would have involved *la suppression de l'accent circonflexe,* "doing away with the circumflex accent." There was strong reaction to that suggestion. But see **occulté(e)**

OS (m.) *Ouvrier spécialisé,* unskilled or semiskilled worker. *Ouvrier qualifié,* skilled worker. *Le salaire d'un OS est nettement moins élevé que celui d'un ouvrier qualifié;* "An unskilled worker gets paid much less than a skilled worker." *A noter: ouvrier qualifié* is never abbreviated as *OQ.*

Oslo *Les accords d'Oslo* refers to the agreements reached in Oslo in 1993 and 1995 with the aim of furthering peace in the Middle East. *Le processus d'Oslo,* the peacemaking process outlined in those agreements. *Suite aux accords d'Oslo, Hébron a été rendu aux Palestiniens en janvier 1997;* "In accordance with the Oslo agreements, Hebron was given back to the Palestinians in January 1997." Sometimes the word Oslo

is used by itself, just as **Maastricht** can be used to mean the
Traité de Maastricht.

OTAN (f.) *L'Organisation du Traité de l'Atlantique Nord,* the
North Atlantic Treaty Organization (NATO). *En 1996–97 la
tension était très forte entre Washington et Paris parce que les
Français voulaient obtenir le commandement du secteur sud de
la défense européenne, y compris la 6e flotte américaine, alors
que les Américains s'y refusaient absolument;* "In 1996–97
feeling ran high between Washington and Paris because
France wanted to be given control of the southern European
defense sector of NATO, including the U.S. Sixth Fleet, while
the United States was adamant in its refusal."

*L'Europe pourrait partager plus la prise de décision dans le
sud de l'Europe; il faudrait que les Etats-Unis acceptent,* said
one analyst on a radio talk show; "Europe could play a bigger
role in the decision-making process in southern Europe; the
United States ought to agree to that."

outre- Adverb generally used in combination with *mer* (f.) or with
names of other major bodies of water. *Outremer,* overseas, as
in **DOM-TOM.** *Outre-Atlantique,* (in) Canada, the United
States, and/or Latin America. *Outre-Manche,* across the
English Channel, (in) England and/or (in) the United Kingdom as a whole. *Outre-Méditerranée,* (in) North Africa. *Quelle
est aujourd'hui la véritable influence de la France outre-
Méditerranée?* "How much and what kind of influence does
France actually have today in North Africa?" *Outre-Rhin,* (in)
Germany. *Nos homologues outre-Rhin,* our opposite numbers
in Germany. *Nos amis d'outre Quiévrain,* the Belgians (Quié-
vrain is a small town in Belgium on the French border).

Passer outre is "to disregard advice," as in *La candidate a
passé outre aux avertissements de son état-major politique;*
"The candidate disregarded her staff's warnings."

ouverture (f.) **à la concurrence** Said of a sector or activity that has
hitherto been regulated or enjoyed a monopoly but is no
longer so protected. *Avec la déréglementation du ciel européen
en 1997, c'est l'ouverture à la concurrence des compagnies
aériennes;* "Airlines operating in Europe have been exposed
to competition since 1997, when air transport in Europe was
deregulated."

ouverture (f.) **dominicale** Sunday opening hours for stores. A hot
issue, as Sunday opening had always been forbidden (except
for shops and stores selling food) to respect the traditional
principle of a weekly day of rest. The prohibition was successfully challenged by *le **Virgin Mégastore*** on the *Champs-
Elysées,* which has been open on Sundays since 1993.

overdose (f.) Overdose, of course, in a drugs context; and *dans le
langage familier,* an excess of something in other contexts.

OVNI (m.) *Objet volant non identifié,* an unidentified flying object (UFO). *Bien qu'il y ait peut-être moins d'intérêt en France pour les OVNI qu'aux Etats-Unis, la célèbre série télévisée américaine* Au-delà des frontières du réel (Les X-Files) *a fait un tabac en France, au point d'être un phénomène de société;* "Although the French may take less interest in UFOs than the Americans do, the famous American TV series *The X-Files* was a smash hit in France and even indicative of a social trend."

P

PAC (f.) *Politique agricole commune,* the common agricultural policy (CAP) decided in 1992 by what was then *la Communauté européenne* before it became *l'Union européenne. Elle obligeait entre autres de laisser une partie des terres en friche pour éviter une surproduction;* "It required among other things letting a certain amount of land lie fallow to avoid overproduction." *Les cultivateurs français étaient farouchement opposés à cette politique décidée par Bruxelles; à la campagne on voyait un peu partout des pancartes avec une tête de mort et le sigle* PAC. "French farmers were fiercely opposed to this policy laid down by Brussels; in the countryside it was common to see signs showing a skull (death's head) and the initials *PAC.*" See **friche; paysan**

Paca *Paca* is short for *Provence–Alpes–Côte d'Azur,* considered as a region for political and administrative purposes. There are nearly two dozen other *régions* in France and the **DOM-TOM:** *Aquitaine, Champagne-Ardennes, Midi-Pyrénées, Nord-Pas de Calais, Poitou-Charentes, Rhône-Alpes,* and so on. The regions in France are vying with those in other European countries to obtain subsidies from Brussels and have also acquired new political significance within France itself (see **région**). Some *régions* are claiming affinities with and/or creating economic links with regions elsewhere in Europe.

Pacs *Pacte civil de solidarité.* See **CUCS**

pacte (m.) **de stabilité** This stability pact was agreed on by the member countries of the European Union at a Dublin meeting in December 1996; its purpose was to keep the financial and fiscal situation in each of them under close supervision in the final two years leading up to adoption of the **euro,** the **monnaie unique,** at the beginning of 1999. At the Amsterdam summit six months later, however, France's newly elected Socialist government *a voulu y ajouter un chapitre social,* "sought to have the pact rewritten so as to place more emphasis on job creation and growth." See **pensée unique**

pacte (m.) **républicain** A sort of covenant or pact between the Republic and all of its inhabitants. As *Le Monde* noted on July 31, 1997, about the new Socialist government's wish to come to grips with the status of immigrants, *"Jospin fait de l'intégration des immigrés un des principaux enjeux du pacte républicain qu'il proposait aux Français";* " 'For the prime minister, the integration of immigrants is one of the main pillars of the covenant he proposes between this country's government and its inhabitants.' "

PAF (f.) *Police de l'air et des frontières,* French border police.

PAF (m.) *Paysage audiovisuel français,* the French radio and television broadcasting situation. *Au cours de la présidence de François Mitterrand, le nombre de radios locales privées a grandement augmenté;* "During François Mitterrand's years as president, the number of private local radio stations greatly increased."

page (f.) **de publicité** On the radio, this is a break for a commercial. *Avant de vous apporter la suite de ces informations nous allons marquer une pause pour une page de publicité;* "We will continue with the news after this word from our sponsor." A neat case of one medium using a metaphor based on others (newspapers and magazines).

Palais (m.) **Bourbon** Home of the *Assemblée nationale.*

Palais (m.) **Brogniart** Home of *la Bourse,* the Paris stock exchange.

Palais (m.) **du Luxembourg** Home of the *Sénat.*

Palais (m.) **Garnier** *L'Opéra,* the old opera house in Paris, built in 1875, where both ballet and opera were performed. In 1989 *l'Opéra Bastille* was built, and the intention was that all opera in Paris would henceforth be performed there while the *Palais Garnier* would be reserved for ballet despite a number of *places sans visibilité,* "seats from which you cannot see." But after four or five years it was decided to move some opera performances back to the *Palais Garnier.*

palmarès (m.) Hit parade or record of achievements. *Cet avironneur a trois médailles d'argent et deux de bronze à son palmarès;* "As a rower he has three silver medals and two bronze to his credit." *Le palmarès de la chanson européenne donne toujours Johnny Hallyday en tête dans la catégorie tous publics;* "The hit parade of European singers shows that Johnny Halliday is still number one in the family entertainment category."

pantalonnade (f.) Colorful expression—like *bouffonnerie* (f.)— for farce, unsubtle comedy. Used scornfully, for instance by a *Front national* spokesman in October 1996 on the radio program called *Le rendez-vous politique,* to criticize *l'expulsion des sans-papiers de l'**Eglise Saint-Bernard** en août 96* and *l'interdiction de syndicats émanant du FN,* "the prohibition of labor unions founded or led under *FN* influence."

pantoufler To leave a government post and enter the private sector. *Le pantouflage,* the fact of doing so. In this context, *une pantoufle* is not "a slipper" but "a penalty." *Pour être précis, c'est le dédit que vous devez payer si, une fois que vous avez été formé(e) aux frais du gouvernement, dans une des grandes écoles, pour une carrière de haut fonctionnaire, vous décidez que vous voulez quitter le service public pour le secteur privé où vous gagnerez davantage;* "Specifically, this is the fine or refund you must pay if you have been trained at government expense, in one of the *grandes écoles,* for a high-level career in government service, and then decide you want to leave for the private sector, where you will earn more." Once you have made this decision, and if you are among the top-ranking graduates, other alumni of *l'Ecole nationale d'administration* and other *grandes écoles* who have *pantouflé* like you will tend to hire you in the private sector and, if necessary, bail you out of one executive job and find you another. *Un pantouflard,* however, is "an unambitious stay-at-home."

National *pantoufle* factory. "If they privatize it, that's going to throw more people out of work!"

by EsCaro in *Le Canard enchaîné,* February 2, 1997

PAO (f.) *Publication assistée par ordinateur,* desktop publishing. See **CAO; TAO**

PAP (m.) (1) *Prêt d'accession à la propriété,* special low-interest loan intended to facilitate and encourage home ownership. (2) *Le **prêt-à-porter,*** the ready-to-wear industry.

Papon, Maurice *Secrétaire-général de la préfecture* in Bordeaux under the Vichy government, in close contact with the German authorities. However, toward the very end of the war, he successfully claimed that he had played a role in the Resistance. After the war, he served under de Gaulle as *Préfet de police de Paris* (see below), as well as in the Barre and Pompidou governments.

　　Not until 1997 was it announced that he would be tried for his activities during the war years including, allegedly, having been responsible for the deportation of approximately 1,600 people, including many Jewish children. Immediately, in pretrial interviews, he denied all wrongdoing and maintained that he had had no choice but to carry out orders from higher up. By 1997 he was the last prominent Vichy figure still alive. See **Bousquet, René; Touvier, Paul.** Papon's trial for *crimes contre l'humanité,* which began in October 1997, triggered soul-searching at all levels of French society; massive media attention and countless books and interviews attempted to grapple with the Vichy period, what it stemmed from, the degree of responsibility of French *fonctionnaires,* the silence of the French Church at the time, and other issues. In April 1998 the jury found Papon *coupable de complicité d'arrestation et de complicité de séquestration* but cleared him of charges of *complicité d'assassinat.* He was sentenced (at the age of eighty-seven) to *dix ans de réclusion criminelle* but not to *la réclusion perpétuelle,* "a life sentence." The verdict was felt in some quarters to be too harsh, in others too lenient. See **Pétain, Philippe; repentance; Vél d'hiv**

In 1997, just as Papon's trial concerning World War II was beginning, the government decided to open official archives on the events of October 17, 1961, which until then had virtually never been publicly mentioned. In 1961 the Algerian war was still in progress. On that October date the **FLN** had called a peaceful proindependence demonstration in Paris and the Algerians who turned out for it were unarmed. They were nonetheless charged and pursued by the Paris police, which was under Papon's authority. The next day, some sources have said, the bodies of some two hundred Algerians were found floating in the Seine.

parabole (f.) Satellite dish. *Grâce à la parabole, les Algériens—qui chez eux ne sont pas bien informés par leurs autorités sur les activités des terroristes islamiques intégristes—peuvent capter des émissions européennes et ainsi recevoir des informations sur ce qui se passe dans leur propre pays;* "Thanks to satellite dishes, the Algerians in Algeria—who are not well informed by their government about the activities of the fundamentalist Islamic terrorists—can receive European programs and get some information that way about what is going on in their own country."

parachutage (m.) This occurs when a political party decides to slot one of its candidates into *une **circonscription,*** "an electoral district," any district, where he or she has a good chance of beating the other party(ies), regardless of whether the candidate comes from that district or has any connection with it. *Se faire parachuter; être parachuté(e).*

paramètre (m.) Parameter—that is, factor or characteristic. A fashionable word to use, along with or instead of *élément* (m.), *aspect* (m.), or *caractéristique* (f.). *Il faut connaître tous les paramètres de la situation avant de pouvoir en parler utilement;* "You have to be familiar with every aspect of the situation before you can talk about it to any purpose."

parc (m.) **automobile** This does not mean a parking lot! (That is *un parking.*) It is a collective noun, meaning the total number of cars in France. *Le parc social,* stock of low-rent housing. *Le parc nucléaire,* all of France's nuclear equipment: *centrales* (f. pl.) *nucléaires, usines* (f. pl.) *de retraitement des déchets, sites* (m. pl.) *de stockage de déchets nucléaires . . . ,* nuclear power stations, waste treatment plants, and nuclear waste storage sites. *Le parc d'autobus,* bus fleet. *La gestion de votre parc informatique,* managing your "fleet" of computers/computerized equipment.

Parc (m.) **des Princes** Soccer stadium on the western edge of Paris.

parcours (m.) Itinerary in both the physical and the figurative sense. *En septembre 94, à la suite de certaines révélations, Mitterrand a été contraint de justifier son parcours (concernant Vichy en général et René Bousquet en particulier) à la télévision;* "In September 1994, when certain revelations had been made concerning Mitterrand's role in the days of the Vichy government in general and René Bousquet in particular, Mitterrand was obliged to go on television to explain his earlier attitude and activities." See **Bousquet, René; Ile d'Yeu**

Accomplir son parcours du combattant, to get through an obstacle course (figurative).

parfum (m.) **du jour** Flavor of the day; in other words, something (or someone) that is suddenly in fashion.

Paris-Dakar (m.) *Le Paris-Dakar est un raid où participent voitures, camions et motos et qui a lieu tous les ans,* a yearly motor vehicle race that goes south through the African desert and ends in Senegal. It is hotly criticized by human rights advocates, who claim it disturbs and distorts the lives *des populations locales,* and by environmentalists, who claim it disturbs local ecosystems.

parité (f.) A term used during the presidential election campaign of 1995 and still more so in 1997 during the legislative election campaign and then by the newly elected Socialist government. It expresses the goal of having more women candidates and more women occupying government posts than had been the case—indeed, ultimately, of having equal numbers of female and male candidates and officials. The question arose, or arises, *Est-il réaliste d'inscrire cette parité hommes-femmes dans la Constitution?* "Is it realistic to write the principle of such male-female parity into the Constitution?"

parler d'une seule voix A phrase introduced by President Chirac (*RPR*) in June 1997, when the Socialists won the legislative elections and he was therefore obliged to appoint a Socialist prime minister, thus beginning a period of what is informally called *la cohabitation* due to last until the next presidential elections, in 2002. He said that *"la France parlerait d'une seule voix,"* "'France would speak with a single voice,'" in European and other matters, meaning that the internal political cleavage or split personality would be overcome and harmony achieved.

parler vrai (m.) *Le parler vrai,* straight talk, the truth; telling it like it really is; *le parler faux* is doublespeak, similar to *la **langue de bois**. Le parler vrai est une chose que l'on rencontre rarement dans la classe politique;* "You rarely hear straight talk from politicians."

parquet (m.) The office of *le procureur général,* "the prosecutor," and the activity of the various levels of judges; in other words, the actual activity of the judicial system, as distinct from *la chancellerie* (another name for *le Ministère de la justice*), which is the government or administrative view of the judicial system. *Le parquet s'est rendu sur les lieux du crime pour une reconstitution des circonstances exactes du meurtre;* "The judge went to the scene of the crime, where the exact circumstances in which the murder took place were to be reconstituted."

parrain (m.) Godfather—in both the mafia and nonmafia senses —and also sponsor. *Le parrainage,* sponsorship; also called *le sponsoring.* The verb is *parrainer. Marraine* (f.), "godmother," is not used in the sense of corporate sponsor. There is no verb *"marrainer."*

partage (m.) **du travail** Job sharing. Often proposed as a way of reducing unemployment, since, *en principe,* it would take a greater number of workers, each with reduced hours, to complete a task. See **réduction du temps de travail; temps choisi**

partenaire (m.) **outre-Rhin** Germany. See **couple franco-allemand; outre-**

partenaires (m. pl.) **sociaux** Workers, employers, and unions. *Un accord entre les partenaires sociaux, afin de mettre fin au conflit, est attendu cette nuit;* "It is expected that labor and management will reach an agreement tonight to settle the dispute." *Un groupe de travail mixte entre partenaires sociaux et pouvoirs publics vient d'être mis en place avec pour mission de réfléchir aux conséquences qu'aurait la retraite à 55 ans;* "A joint working party has just been set up among representatives of labor, management and unions, and the government to examine what the implications of retirement at fifty-five would be."

partenariat (m.) Partnership in the figurative sense; the fact of working in unison toward a common goal. *Le partenariat franco-allemand,* cooperation between Bonn and Paris. *Il faut* *renforcer le partenariat entre l'université et les partenaires sociaux;* "Higher education must work hand in hand with labor and management." See **-ariat**

partie (f.) **civile** A legal term: *se constituer (se porter) partie civile,* to associate in a court action with the public prosecutor; to take part in a class action suit; to be civil plaintiff(s).

partisan (m.) An advocate of something. *Les partisans du oui,* those in favor; *les partisans du non,* those against. During World War II *un partisan* was a member of *la Résistance;* their song was *Le chant des partisans.*

Pasqua, Charles *Ministre de l'Intérieur* in the Balladur government (1993–1995). *Les lois Pasqua, datant de 1993, ont imposé des conditions plus strictes concernant l'entrée, l'accueil et le séjour des étrangers en France;* "The so-called Pasqua laws, passed in 1993, laid down more stringent conditions concerning the way foreigners could enter and reside in France." See **code de la nationalité; vrai faux passeport**

passage (m.) **à la monnaie unique** The fact or the prospect of adopting a single currency, the **euro,** of seeing it come into effect throughout the European Union and thus seeing the French franc become a thing of the past. *Le passage à la monnaie unique est-il une bonne chose? ou signifie-t-il la fin de l'identité française?* See **report**

passer aux actes To take action. *Assez parlé! Il est temps de passer aux actes/temps pour le gouvernement de passer aux actes;* "Enough palaver! Now it's time (for the government) to take action/do something about it."

passerelle (f.) Footbridge or gangway; so, by extension, a link of any kind. *Trop souvent à l'université en France on constate qu'il n'y a pas de passerelle entre les diplômes ou les cursus,* say critics; "In the French university you find out all too often that there is no way to connect one degree or program with another." *Il faudrait créer des passerelles entre le monde des études et le monde du travail;* "Links should be created between the world of higher education and the labor market."

pastille (f.) **verte** A green windshield sticker, intended as an anti-pollution measure. Early in 1998, Dominique Voynet, *la Ministre de l'Environnement,* announced that all owners of electric cars or of cars either (1) equipped to use *le gaz pétrole liquéfié (GPL)* instead of *l'essence,* "gasoline," or (2) equipped with three-way catalytic converters for gas or diesel fuel, would be entitled to place this sticker on their windshield and thus would be allowed to drive *même les jours de pic* (m.) *de pollution,* "even on days of peak pollution." See **pot catalytique.**

On those days the principle of *la circulation alternée* would continue to apply to older vehicles, which are not so equipped.

Seuls ceux dont la plaque se termine par un chiffre pair auraient le droit de circuler les jours pairs, alors que ceux dont la plaque se termine par un chiffre impair n'auraient le droit de circuler que les jours impairs; "Only those whose license plates end with an even figure could be driven on even days while those whose license plates end with an odd figure could only be driven on odd days." However, in an attempt to encourage **le covoiturage,** "car pooling," older cars carrying at least three or four people might be allowed to circulate, regardless of their license plate number.

patrimoine (m.) For an investment banker, this is your personal wealth or your investment portfolio; *gestion* (f.) *de patrimoine,* personal portfolio management.

In a broader sense, this is the French heritage—cultural, architectural, and so on. *Tous les ans, au cours de la journée du patrimoine, le public peut visiter gratuitement toutes sortes de monuments nationaux (musées, palais de l'Elysée . . .),* "Every year, on national heritage day, the public can visit museums, the *palais de l'Elysée,* and other national monuments free of charge."

patronat (m.) Refers to all employers (*les patrons*) collectively. *Le président du Conseil national du patronat français* (**CNPF**) is often referred to (unofficially) as *le patron des patrons,* "the bosses' boss." *L'Etat pousse le patronat à s'engager à embaucher davantage de jeunes;* "The government is urging management to commit itself to hiring more young people."

pavé(s) (m. sing. or pl.) Dice-shaped paving stones. During *les événements de mai 68,* particularly in the Latin Quarter, rioters ripped up *pavés* to hurl them at the police. One of the most durable slogans from that period was *"Sous les pavés la plage,"* a poetic vision whereby if only artificial constraints imposed by society could be abolished, life would be lovely. Nearly thirty years later, in the summer of 1997, a cheese manufacturer photographed a plate of salad and feta cheese, with a child's beach shovel and rake on either side, by way of knife and fork, and captioned it *"Sous le feta la plage."*

Etre sur le pavé, to be down and out, living in the street.

pavé (m.) **dans la mare** *Lancer/Jeter un pavé dans la mare* is a set phrase: "to let all hell break loose," "to make a big splash," since *un pavé* is "a paving stone" and *une mare* is "a pond or puddle." *En faisant grève à l'échelle nationale les chauffeurs de poids lourds ont lancé un pavé dans la mare du gouvernement;* "The teamsters' nationwide strike has been a bombshell for the government."

pavés (m. pl.) **du nord** A notorious spine-jolting stretch of road between *Tourcoing* and *Roubaix,* in northern France. Cyclists who must endure it during a race know it as *l'enfer du nord.*

As part of the taste for *commémorations de toutes sortes* that has gripped France in the past decade, the *pavés du nord* were officially designated *un **lieu de mémoire.***

pays (m.) **de droit** A law-abiding country, a country that recognizes the rule of law. During *l'affaire OM-Valenciennes,* a corruption scandal involving two soccer teams, *l'Olympique de Marseille* and *Valenciennes,* one commentator noted, *"Il faut que la justice fasse son travail, nous sommes dans un pays de droit."* See **OM**

pays (m. sing. or pl.) **de l'est** East European country/countries. *Les pays de l'est sont ceux qui étaient autrefois derrière le rideau de fer,* "those that used to be behind the Iron Curtain."

pays (m. sing. or pl.) **en (voie de) développement** *(PVD),* developing country/countries.

pays (m.) **émergeant** Newly developed country.

paysage (m.) **politique** The political scene or landscape. *Mme Dominique Voynet, à la tête des Verts, est relativement une nouvelle venue dans le paysage politique français;* "Ms. Dominique Voynet, at the head of an environmentalist party, is a relative newcomer on the French political scene."

paysan(ne) Although the word *peasant* sounds antiquated in English, French farmers often talk about themselves as *paysans.* *"Paysans en colère!" dit une pancarte contestant une politique décrétée par Bruxelles;* "'French farmers up in arms!' a sign may read, protesting against a policy laid down by the European authorities in Brussels." Commenting on the official view that farmers should farm less and provide more accommodations for tourists instead, one *cultivateur* said, in a radio interview, *"Trop de touristes en milieu agricole, ça tue le paysan;"* "'Encouraging tourists to overrun the countryside is death to farming.'" See **PAC; technocrate**

PC (m.) or **PCF** *Parti communiste (français),* French Communist Party. Very powerful after World War II because *bon nombre de résistants étaient au PC,* "many French resistants were Communists." *Aujourd'hui cependant le PC est en perte de vitesse, au profit de l'extrême droite, semble-t-il;* "But today the French Communist Party has lost a lot of ground, to the benefit of the far right, apparently.

La PC in Paris means *la petite ceinture,* "a bus," that goes all around *le boulevard périphérique,* "the ring road around the city."

PDG (m. or f.) *Président(e)-directeur(trice)-général(e),* the CEO of a conglomerate or any firm. Sometimes, in the satirical mode, it is written the way it is pronounced, *pédégé.* In his play called *Le boulanger, la boulangère et le petit mitron,* Jean Anouilh gave one of his characters the facetious title of *Président-Directeur-Général-Evêque,* President-Chief-Executive-Bishop.

pédophilie (f.) *La France a été très sensibilisée à l'existence de réseaux pédophiles suite à l'affaire Dutroux en Belgique en 1996;* "The French became keenly alert to the existence of pedophilia networks after the Dutroux case broke out in Belgium in 1996."

Au moins cinq des personnes accusées d'avoir chez elle des cassettes vidéo montrant des abus sexuels pratiqués sur des enfants se sont suicidées; "At least five of the individuals accused of having at home videotapes showing sexual abuse of children committed suicide." See **Ados 71**

peine (f.) **capitale** Capital punishment; abolished in France in 1981. Also called *la peine de mort.*

Une peine de prison, prison sentence. *Une peine incompressible de trente ans est maintenant requise contre toute personne reconnue coupable de viol d'enfant;* "A thirty-year prison sentence whose duration cannot be reduced for good conduct or any other reason is now sought against any person found guilty of raping a child." *Une peine avec sursis,* a suspended sentence. *Une remise de peine,* a reduction of sentence. See **perpétuité réelle**

pensée (f.) **unique** The doctrine whereby the only criterion that counts in shaping employment policy or any other policy is one that furthers the interests of world capital as expressed on the world's financial markets; workers' interests are ignored, or secondary to those of shareholders. The monthly *Monde diplomatique* first applied this term toward the end of 1994 to the "neoliberal ideology" recommended by international economic organizations and think tanks and redefined it in mid-1997; by then it had become one of the major buzzwords on the political scene, even though people who use it—and also those who decry it—are sometimes vague as to what it means.

percepteur(trice) (m. or f.) Tax collector. *Les percepteurs savent à l'occasion se montrer compréhensifs quand un contribuable vient leur demander un délai;* "Sometimes tax collectors take an understanding attitude when a taxpayer asks them to extend the payment deadline."

pérenne (adj.) Lasting, durable; the noun is *pérennité* (f.). *Chercher une solution pérenne, posséder une qualité pérenne. La laïcité fait partie des valeurs pérennes de la nation;* "Secularism is one of this country's lasting values." *Les gens n'ont plus confiance en la pérennité de leur emploi;* "People no longer believe that their jobs are going to last for a long time."

perfide Albion See **Albion**

périmé(e) Expired. *Apportez vos médicaments périmés à la pharmacie pour les faire détruire;* "Bring your outdated medicines to the local drug store so that they can be destroyed." *Date de péremption,* expiration date. (Good until . . . , use by . . .).

période (f.) **rouge/bleue/blanche** *La SNCF et France Télécom uti-lisent ces termes pour distinguer les tranches horaires où vous payez plein tarif et celles où vous payer tarif réduit;* "Both the **SNCF** and **France Télécom** use these terms to designate times of the day or days of the week when you pay the full fare or rate and those when you can pay a reduced fare or rate."

permis (m.) **à points** *Le permis de conduire, nouvelle manière:* since 1992 a driver's license has comprised twelve penalty points; for each offense, a varying number of points is de-ducted. *La conduite en état d'alcoolémie coûte six points. Un excès (un dépassement) de vitesse de plus de 40 km/heure coûte quatre points; un refus (non-respect) de priorité en coûte quatre également, et ainsi de suite.* "Drunken driving costs six points. If you're caught for exceeding the speed limit by more than 25 mph, you lose four points; refusing to yield to another driver who has the right of way, according to *le Code de la route,* also makes you lose four points; and so on. *Si un(e) conducteur(trice) perd tous ses points, il ou elle doit attendre six mois avant de repasser son permis de conduire;* "When a driver has lost all of his or her points, he or she must wait six months before taking his or her driver's license all over again from scratch."

perpétuité (f.) **réelle** A genuine, unreducible sentence of life im-prisonment. This is what was recommended in some quarters in the early 1990s as punishment *pour les assassins et violeurs d'enfant, puisque la peine capitale a été supprimée,* "for anyone who killed or raped a child, since capital punishment no longer exists." See **peine capitale**

perquisitionner To carry out a search in a person's home or busi-ness premises. *Avant de faire une perquisition, il faut un man-dat;* "A search warrant is required before a search can be car-ried out."

personnel (m.) **volant** Flight crews (also called *personnel navi-gant*), as distinct from *le personnel au sol* or *personnel ram-pant,* ground crews. *Le personnel volant d'Air France à déposé un préavis de grève de quarante-huit heures;* "The Air France flight crews have given forty-eight hours' notice of a strike."

perspective (f.) Outlook. *Perspective à terme,* final or long-term outlook. *Dans la perspective d'une perte de popularité pour son parti, le RPR, bien avant la date normalement prévue en 1998 pour les élections législatives, le Président Chirac a décidé de dissoudre le parlement en avril 1997 pour provoquer des élec-tions anticipées, à une date qu'il croyait plus favorable pour son parti;* "Since a decline in his party's popularity was foreseeable before the scheduled date in 1998 for legislative elections, President Chirac decided to dissolve the legislature in April 1997, thus necessitating earlier elections, at a date that he believed would be more advantageous to the *RPR.*" See **dissolution.**

La perspective de l'élargissement de l'Europe, the prospect of including more member countries in the European Union.

La perspective monumentale is a specialty of French city planning: it entails the deliberate creation of awe-inspiring vistas by the positioning of avenues, esplanades, and buildings so as to lead the eye along to a culminating point, as, for instance, from the *Arc du Carrousel* in the *Louvre* gardens, through the *Tuileries,* across the *Place de la Concorde,* and up the *Champs-Elysées* to the *Arc de Triomphe.*

perturbations (f. pl.) Disturbances or dysfunctioning; a word often used in talking about the effects of a strike. *Des perturbations sont attendues dans le Métro et les autobus parisiens au cours de la grève prévue pour jeudi;* "Metro and bus service is expected to be reduced/disturbed by next Thursday's strike."

peste (f.) **brune** Literally, the brown plague; a phrase still sometimes used to designate Hitler's brown-shirted troops, as in a January 1997 radio interview with Philippe de Villiers, a right-of-center politician, who referred to *"la collaboration avec la peste brune"* in connection with the recent announcement that **Maurice Papon** would soon be brought to trial.

Pétain, Philippe Leader of the Vichy government. *En juin 1940, à l'armistice mettant fin officiellement à la débâcle, le Maréchal Pétain s'adressa aux Français à la radio dans un discours célèbre: "Je fais don de ma personne à la France";* "In June 1940, when the armistice was signed with Germany, officially concluding France's military defeat, Marshall Pétain spoke to the nation over the radio; the most famous sentence was 'I sacrifice myself entirely to France.'" Pétain was eighty-four years old in 1940 but still carried great prestige—especially among *les anciens combattants,* "veterans"—as the hero of World War I, *le vainqueur de Verdun* (1916), the victor in the battle of Verdun against the German army. Charles de Gaulle in 1940 was a fifty-year-old colonel and unknown to the public; he had been a soldier in World War I, and at one time his commanding officer had been Pétain.

One famous apology for the Vichy government is summed up in the phrase *le bouclier et le glaive,* "the shield and the sword"; in this claim, the shield was Pétain, who remained in France and collaborated with the occupying forces so as to lessen the impact of war on the French population, while the sword was de Gaulle, who preferred to leave France and lead French resistance efforts from London. See **Appel du 18 juin; Bousquet, René; Ile d'Yeu; Papon, Maurice; repentance; Touvier, Paul**

petit boulot (m.) Odd job, or any type of illegal employment, *où* *on est payé sous la table,* "where there is no payslip"; you are paid in cash. Normalement *un petit boulot ne suffit pas pour vivre; il faut en avoir plusieurs.* "Usually this kind of job is not enough to live on; you need several of them." *Un petit boulot permet tout au plus de vivoter;* "At most a job like this lets you scrape by, just barely."

The recent term, *emploi* (m.) *de proximité,* is an official one, and is sometimes a euphemism for *petit boulot,* but with a payslip.

Petit Clamart Suburb just south of Paris; in 1962 it was the scene of the most famous failed attempt (instigated by the **OAS**) to assassinate President de Gaulle. Still spoken of with a certain amount of awe, as proof of de Gaulle's invulnerability.

petit écran (m.) Television, as distinct from *le grand écran,* "movies, the movie industry."

petit peu A verbal crutch, a sort of modest qualifier, very commonly used by speakers in all contexts ranging from sports to strikes. Sometimes it may really mean "a little bit"; sometimes it is more like "like" in English. *Regardons un petit peu les retombées de cette victoire* (the French Davis Cup victory in 1996); "Let's, like, look at what the fall-out of this victory will be." *On va regarder un petit peu les résultats du sondage;* "We'll just, like, take a little look at the results of that poll." *Je veux un petit peu compléter ce que X a dit;* "I'd like to, like, add to what X has just said." *Il faut remettre un petit peu les choses dans leur contexte;* "Things have to be, like, considered in their context." See also **quelque part**

petit porteur (m.) Literally, small bearer; hence, small (i.e., individual) shareholder. See **actionnaire; privatisation.** But see also **gros porteur**!

pétrole (m.) Oil. Since France has virtually no domestic oil reserves, a still-famous slogan appeared in the mid-1970s, *à l'époque de la première crise pétrolière,* "at the time of the first oil crisis": *"En France on n'a pas de pétrole mais on a des idées";* "'France may be poor in oil but it's rich in ideas.'"

peuple (m.) **de gauche** One of the **politologues'** favorite phrases; it designates France as an essentially left-leaning country, a country whose heart is on the left of the political spectrum.

phénomène (m.) **de société** A major social issue or trend. *La façon dont les Français ont adopté le fast food est un phénomène de société.*

phocéenne (adj.) *La cité phocéenne* means Marseilles because its precursor, Massilia, was founded in the seventh century B.C.E. by traders from Phocaea (*Phocée* in French) in Asia Minor.

Piat, Yann *Une députée UDF (après avoir été au Front national), assassinée sur la Côte d'Azur en 1994;* "a *UDF* (and former

Front national) member of parliament, assassinated on the Riviera in 1994." In 1997 a book by two journalists alleged that two *UDF* ex-*ministres* (unnamed but lavishly described and very thinly disguised) had ordered the killing, perhaps to prevent the revelation of what the *Nouvel Observateur* (October 9–15, 1997) suggested may have been *une gigantesque ma-gouille politico-mafieuse pour réaliser de juteux projets im-mobiliers,* "a huge scheme by politicians hand in hand with the Mafia to make juicy real estate profits." One of the two ex-*ministres* demanded that the incriminating passages be deleted from the book.

pied-noir (m.) A French settler in North Africa (Morocco, Tunisia and chiefly Algeria) and especially a French settler who came back to France. *En 1962, l'année de l'indépendance algérienne, ou peu après, la France a vu une arrivée massive de pieds-noirs;* "In or soon after 1962, when Algeria became independent, there was a massive influx of *pieds-noirs* in France." *Ils se sont installés surtout dans le sud de la France et en Corse et n'ont pas toujours été bien accueillis;* "They settled mostly in southern France and in Corsica and were not always warmly received." *Certains Français de la métropole avaient le sentiment que les pieds-noirs faisaient main basse sur les meilleures terres agricoles;* "Some people in France felt that the *pieds-noirs* were gobbling up the best farming land." *Parmi les pieds-noirs eux-mêmes certains avaient prévu les événements et pris la précaution d'ouvrir un compte ou d'acheter du bien en France; d'autres au contraire sont arrivés les mains vides;* "Some of the *pieds-noirs* had seen how the wind was going to turn and had taken the precaution of opening bank accounts or buying property in France, but others arrived empty-handed."
La phrase viendrait du fait que les colons européens en Al-gérie portaient des chaussures alors que les populations autoch-tones portaient des sandales ou allaient pieds nus; "The term is said to derive from the fact that European settlers in Algeria wore shoes, whereas the native population wore sandals or went barefoot." See **Algérie**

pierre (f.) Stone, of course; and, by extension, buildings, real estate. *Investir dans la pierre,* to invest in real estate. *La pierre a toujours été considérée un placement de père de famille;* "Real estate has always been considered a safe investment." *Cepen-dant, depuis que les prix de l'immobilier ont chuté à Paris, au milieu des années 90, la pierre est moins cotée;* "Nonetheless, since the mid-1990s, when real estate prices in Paris dropped sharply, real estate has been less sought after."
Pierre de taille, hewn stone; *les promoteurs vous disent fièrement que la façade du nouvel immeuble qu'ils vont livrer*

à la fin de l'année est en pierre de taille, developers tell you proudly that the new building they will complete by the end of the year is faced with hewn stone.

pifomètre (m.) *Le pif* is slang for *le nez,* so *juger quelque chose au pifomètre* is "to follow your nose, evaluate something on the basis of a hunch." *Au pifomètre, je dirais que la gauche va perdre les prochaines présidentielles;* "On a hunch I'd say the parties on the Left are going to lose the next presidential elections."

pilule (f.) *La pilule anticonceptionnelle est disponible en France, sur ordonnance, depuis 1966;* "The birth control pill has been available in France, by prescription, since 1966." *Le coût de la pilule est remboursé en grande partie par la Sécu;* "The price of the pill is refunded, to a large extent, by the *Sécurité sociale.*" See **avortement; contraception; IVG**

piraterie (f.) **aérienne** The hijacking of an airplane, *par un(e) ou plusieurs pirates de l'aire,* by one or more hijackers.

Piratage de logiciel (m.)/*de l'informatique* (f.), software/computer hacking. *Pirate* (m. or f.) *informatique,* computer hacker.

piste (f.) Theory, explanation. *En juillet 96 quand un avion de la TWA qui devait relier New-York à Paris explosa peu après le décollage, les commentateurs notaient, "La piste du terrorisme reste au conditionnel";* "In July 1996, when a plane blew up soon after take-off on TWA flight 800 from New York to Paris, commentators noted, 'The assumption that the explosion was caused by a terrorist act is still only a theory.'"

PJ (f.) *La police judiciaire,* criminal investigation bureau, crime squad.

place (f.) Similar to **rôle à jouer,** as in *Il faut assurer la place de la France en Europe et dans le monde.*

placard (m.) **doré** *Se faire mettre dans un placard doré,* to lose your job at one level and be given a title at a higher level; to be kicked upstairs.

Place du Colonel Fabien Where the **PCF** has its headquarters, in the tenth *arrondissement* of Paris.

plafonnement (m.) **des dépenses** Putting a ceiling on expenditures, especially in the context of *la Sécurité sociale.*

plage (f.) Not only the beach but also a range or spectrum. *"Il y a toute une plage de salaires possibles,"* said union leader Marc Blondel on the radio on October 1994; "'There's a whole range of salary possibilities.'" See also **pavé(s)**

planche (f.) **à voile** Windsurfing board. *Véliplanchiste* (m. or f.), windsurfer. *Tous les ans au début de l'été les services de sauvetage en mer mettent en garde les véliplanchistes contre les dangers de s'éloigner trop de la côte;* "Every year at the beginning of summer French lifeguards and sea rescue crews warn windsurfers about the dangers of venturing out too far from the coast."

planche (f.) **de surf sur neige** Snowboard.

Plan d'épargne logement (PEL) (m.) *Pour faciliter l'accession à la propriété, le gouvernment a lancé ces plans vers la fin des années 70;* "To make it easier for people to buy their own homes, the government launched this special savings scheme in the late 1970s." *L'épargnant doit verser de l'argent sur son PEL à intervalles réguliers et ne peut récupérer son argent avant quatre ans; en échange, il touche des intérêts non imposables plus une prime d'Etat et au moment d'effectuer son achat il a droit à un prêt à taux avantageux.* "The individual must pay money into his or her *PEL* at regular intervals and cannot touch the money for four years; in exchange he or she receives tax-free interest plus a government premium and, when the time comes to purchase a house or apartment, can borrow money at a relatively low rate."

plan (m.) **de sauvetage (redressement) du Crédit Lyonnais** Government plan to reduce the enormous debts incurred by this bank after a period of unsuccessful investments (including a scheme intended to give it control of a Hollywood studio) and debatable loans. *Le gouvernement a assuré les contribuables qu'ils n'auraient pas à payer des impôts supplémentaires pour éponger cette dette puisqu'elle serait couverte par les recettes provenant des privatisations;* "The government assured taxpayers that they would not have to pay higher taxes to absorb this debt since it would be covered by income from the privatization of nationalized firms."

planète (f.) **rouge** The planet Mars. *La sonde américaine Pathfinder a atteint la planète rouge en 1997;* "Pathfinder, the American space probe, reached Mars in 1997." *Est-ce que la météorite trouvée récemment sur notre planète est réellement venue de la planète rouge?* "Did the meteorite that was recently found on Earth really come from Mars?" *Y a-t-il des indices de vie microbienne?* "Are there indications of microbial forms of life?"

planification (f.) **familiale** Family planning. See **avortement; contraception; IVG; pilule; PMI**

Plan (m.) **Orsec** *Plan officiel pour l'organisation des secours lors des catastrophes naturelles et urgences collectives,* official plan to deal with emergencies of all kinds—*incendies* (m.) *de forêt, attentats terroristes, congères* (f. pl.) *sur l'autoroute . . . ,* "forest fires, terrorist attacks, and snowdrifts on the thruway and so forth." *Déclencher le Plan Orsec,* to apply the emergency measures provided under the plan. See **Orsec.** *Orsec-Tox, organisation des secours en cas de pollution toxique. Orsec-Rad, contre irradiation et contamination radioactives accidentelles.*

**ROCKY LE ROBOT N'A PAS ENCORE RÉPONDU
À TOUTES LES QUESTIONS**

There are some questions the robot hasn't been able to answer yet.

Jospin wonders, "Are there jobs on Mars?"

by Lefred-Thouron in *Le Canard enchaîné*, July 9, 1997

plan (m.) **quinquennal** Any five-year plan, such as *le Plan quinquennal pour l'emploi* launched in September 1993 to foster employment.

plan (m.) **social** Not at all friendly or sociable, this is the plan drawn up by an employer for the dismissal (firing) of part of the employees. *Un plan social prévoit parfois, mais pas toujours, des mesures d'accompagnement;* "Sometimes but not always, such a plan makes provision for some compensation or benefits for the people being dismissed."

(se) planter Colloquial way of saying, to misjudge a situation. Talking about **Daewoo**'s offer to buy **Thomson** in 1996, one commentator noted, *"Il y a de grandes entreprises coréennes qui se sont plantées";* "'Some of the big Korean firms have been known to misjudge the market.'"

plastique (m.) The explosive used in certain types of bomb; hence, *un plastiquage,* explosion using plastic bombs, carried out by *des plastiqueurs. Plastiquer veut dire, déposer une charge de plastique,* to set a plastic explosives charge.

Also, plastic money, **cartes de crédit.**

plateau (m.) Stage or set. *Parmi nos invités sur le plateau ce soir* *nous avons trois prix littéraires;* "Among our guests on this program tonight we have the winners of three literary prizes."

plateau (m.) **d'Albion** A site in *Haute Provence*, near Apt and the Lubéron, where ground-ground ballistic nuclear missiles were stored from 1971 to September 1996.

plomb (m.) Lead, contained in *l'essence* (f.) *ordinaire*, regular gasoline. *Essence sans plomb*, unleaded gasoline. By now all *postes d'essence*, "gas stations," except a few in small, remote towns have *le super sans plomb 95 et 98*, "95 and 98 octane unleaded gasoline."

Le saturnisme is an illness affecting children brought up in housing painted with lead-based paint.

plongée (f.) **sous-marine** Deep-sea (scuba) diving, one of the most popular leisure activities. *Le masque, le tube, les palmes* (flippers), *la bonbonne* (tank of compressed air). *On n'a pas besoin d'aller au bord de la mer pour apprendre; on peut s'entrainer et obtenir son brevet dans un bassin spécial.* "You don't have to go to the seashore to learn; you can practice and get your certification in a special, very deep pool."

pluie (f.) **acide** Acid rain. *On parle moins aujourd'hui de pluie acide en Europe qu'il y a dix ans parce que dans l'intervalle l'industrie a fait des efforts pour réduire ses émissions toxiques;* "There is less talk of acid rain in Europe today than there was ten years ago because meanwhile industry has made efforts to clean up its emissions."

pluriel(le) (adj.) This term has come into wide use since the mid-1990s. On the political scene it is applied to the Left, *la gauche plurielle, composée de différentes sensibilités* (*Communistes, Socialistes, Verts, Radicaux . . .*). *Courants* (m. pl.) and *tendances* (f. pl.) are used interchangeably with *sensibilités*.

La France plurielle sums up the country's demographic situation today, very far from the one of two generations ago that used to be described in **nos chères têtes blondes;** school children throughout France and its colonial empire used to repeat together in history class, *"Nos ancêtres les Gaulois."* Immigration from former colonies and other parts of the world has now created a multi-hued France, described as **black blanc beur.**

When *l'équipe de France,* also called *le onze tricolore* or *les bleus,* won *la Coupe du monde* (also called *le Mondial*) in July 1998 by defeating Brazil 3–0, the French public was jubilant over the upset victory and the press exulted. *"C'est une France résolument plurielle fêtant sa victoire aux rythmes conjugués de la trompette et du tam-tam,"* noted *Le Monde* on July 14. The team's twenty-two players, all French citizens, could trace their ancestry back to Algeria, Armenia, the Basque country, Brittany and other parts of mainland France, Guadeloupe, Pacific islands, Portugal, sub-Saharan Africa, and the West Indies. Zinedine Zidane (nicknamed Zizou), Lilian Thuram, Thierry Henry, Marcel Desailly, Fabien Barthez, Laurent Blanc, and the others all became French heroes, and some in particular role models for children in the **banlieues.**

PMA (m. pl.) *Les pays les moins avancés,* the least developed countries. See **pays émergeants; PVD**

PME (f. pl.) *Les petites et moyennes entreprises,* small and medium-sized firms; similarly, *PMI* (f. pl.), *les petites et moyennes industries. Les PME sont une locomotive de notre économie; elles permettent la création d'emplois et des avancées sociales.* "Small and medium-sized firms are the driving force of our economy; they are a source of new jobs and allow labor to improve its situation/status by acquiring more perks/ benefits."

PMI (f.) *La protection maternelle et infantile,* a government health care policy for mothers and young children. *Il y a des consultations gratuites dans les centres de PMI;* "Free visits to the doctor are available in PMI centers."

PMU (m.) *Pari mutuel urbain.* Common form of betting on horseraces.

poche (m.) Paperback (i.e., pocket) edition of a book. *Ce titre est maintenant disponible en poche;* "This book is now available in paperback."

pognon (m.) Slang for "money." Used derogatorily by those who are against the capitalist system, as in *Le pognon c'est le synonyme de tout ce qui ne va pas dans la société capitaliste; tout ce qui compte c'est le pognon, et la dimension humaine n'existe plus.* "Money is a synonym for everything that is wrong with capitalism; the only thing that counts is money and there's no human dimension any more." See **AMI; pensée unique**

poils (m. pl.) *Nos amis à poils et à plumes,* our furred and feathered friends, a phrase often heard *lors de l'ouverture de la chasse,* when the hunting season opens.

point (m.) A percentage point, as in *La popularité du Premier ministre a reculé de onze points;* "The prime minister's popularity has slipped eleven points."

pointe (f.) Cutting edge, as in *industrie de pointe, technologie de pointe.*

pointu(e) Subtle or penetrating, as said of a question, for instance. *Les questions posées par cette journaliste sont toujours pointues; il est difficile d'y répondre au pied levé.* "That journalist always asks very sharp questions; it's hard to answer them if you're not prepared."

policier (m.) *Un (roman) policier* is "a detective novel"; the most famous collection is still perhaps *la Série noire* (published by Gallimard), which includes many novels translated from English and other languages. *Un film policier* is a detective film. An amazing number of more or less old American films have been sold relatively cheaply to French television channels, *qui les passent à 20h45, l'heure de grande écoute,* which show them at 8:45 P.M., prime time. *Par exemple,* Hawaii Five-O *est devenu* Hawaï police d'état.

politique (m.) A politician; the word is often used in the plural, to designate male, or male plus female, politicians. It is not used in the feminine singular or plural.

politiquement correct(e) Adjective or noun based directly on the American term *politically correct. Le souci du politiquement correct est très en retrait en France par rapport aux Etats-Unis;* "There is nothing like the concern with political correctness in France that there is in the United States."

politologue (m. or f.) Political analyst or pundit.

pompidolien(ne) Adjective coined from the name of Georges Pompidou, *Président de la République* from 1969 to 1974.

pontage (m.) Coronary bypass operation. *Il a subi un triple pontage;* "He underwent a triple bypass."

portable (m.) Portable telephone *Téléphone* (m.) *cellulaire,* cell phone.

port (m.) **d'armes** The fact of carrying weapons. *Avoir un permis de port d'armes,* to have a gun permit. *"L'arme est un faux problème; le garde-chasse, le garde-pêche, le douanier sont tous armés. Nous ne sommes pas ici au Texas!"* noted one commentator on a radio talk show, *Le téléphone sonne.* "'Guns themselves are not the issue; game wardens, fishing wardens, and customs officers all carry guns. France is not the Wild West!'" See also **armes.**

    "Le port d'armes est proscrit dans les lieux publics, les transports publics et les établissements scolaires," noted *Le Monde* in April 1996; "'It is forbidden to carry weapons in public places, public means of transportation, and schools.'"

port (m.) **du voile** The fact of wearing the Muslim head scarf in school, banned as *un signe ostentatoire d'appartenance religieuse,* "a visible sign of religious affiliation." See **chador; foulard; laïcité; signes ostentatoires; tchador; voile à l'école**

porteurs (m. pl.) **de valises** Sympathizers in France who, during the late 1950s and early 1960s, helped to collect and carry funds to support the independence movement in Algeria. Literally, suitcase carriers.

Port Royal A station on the *Réseau* (m.) *Express Régional* (*RER*) the regional commuter train system in and around Paris, where an explosion took place during the evening rush hour in December 1996 *au moment où la rame entrait en gare,* "just as the train was pulling into the station." *Aussitôt à la radio, en même temps qu'ils ont décrit les dégâts (vitres soufflées, etc.),* *indiqué le nombre de morts et de blessés graves, et evoqué l'éva-cuation en cours des passagers et des personnes se trouvant dans la station, ils ont dit qu'il s'agissait probablement d'un attentat d'origine islamique;* "On the radio, at the same time as they described the damage (windows shattered, etc.), stated the number of persons killed and seriously injured, and reported that passengers and people in the station were being evacuated, they immediately declared that the explosion was probably due to an Islamist terrorist action."

Généralement, quand il y a un attentat, une cellule de crise est mise en place et l'on évoque la prise en charge psychologique des survivants; "Usually, when a terrorist incident takes place, a crisis unit is set up and the media note that psychologists have been appointed to deal with the survivors." *Après Port Royal on a beaucoup parlé de réactiver le plan Vigipirate,* after the Port Royal incident, there was much talk of reactivating an antiterrorist plan involving, among other things, *des escadrons de la gendarmerie mobile et la récolte des informations dans le but de débusquer les éventuels terroristes,* "the use of squads of special gendarmes and intelligence operations to flush out possible terrorists."

POS (m.) *Le Plan d'occupation des sols,* zoning (land use) regulations. *Les promoteurs, dans leur rage de bétonner toute la Côte d'Azur, ont plus d'une fois piétiné le POS;* "In their haste to put up (concrete) hotels and apartment buildings all along the Riviera, developers have frequently trampled on the zoning regulations."

post-soixante-huitard(e) A person who took part in *les événements de mai 68.* Also said of an opinion influenced by first-hand experience of that period.

pot (m.) **catalytique** Three-way catalytic converter (exhaust pipe). It has been mandatory in France since January 1993 for new gas engine cars and since 1996 for new diesel engine cars. See **pastille verte**

pote (m.) Pal or buddy. *"Touche pas à mon pote"* ("He's my buddy—lay off him") became famous as the slogan used by **SOS Racisme** in an antiracism campaign; it was symbolized by adhesive "handprints" that came in all colors of the rainbow and that participants wore conspicuously on their clothing.

poudreuse (f.) The kind of light, fluffy snow that all skiers hope for *quand ils partent aux sports d'hiver;* see **remonte-pente.**

poussée (f.) Upsurge or thrust forward; gain in numbers or support. Chiefly heard in *la poussée du Front national. Maîtriser la poussée de l'inflation,* bring the inflationary tendency under control.

pouvoir (m.) **d'achat** Purchasing power. *Economistes et hommes* *politiques sont d'accord pour augmenter le pouvoir d'achat des consommateurs afin de favoriser la relance mais—par quel moyen? En augmentant le SMIC? En baissant la TVA?* "Economists and politicians agree that to boost economic recovery, people's purchasing power must be increased—but how? By increasing the minimum wage? Lowering the value-added tax?"

pouvoirs (m. pl.) **publics** The authorities; in other words, the government. *Les pouvoirs publics prêchent la maîtrise des dépenses mais c'est à eux de montrer le chemin,* note critics; "The government calls on everyone to cut down on expenditures, but it's up to the government to lead the way."

préavis (m.) **de grève** Notice of intention to strike. *Les principaux syndicats de fonctionnaires ont déposé un préavis de grève pour le jeudi 30;* "The major unions of government workers have given notice that they intend to strike on Thursday, the 30th." *Le préavis de grève déposé pour demain a été levé;* "The strike notice given for tomorrow has been canceled."

précaire Precarious—that is, offering no guarantees as to future employment or benefits. *Le contrat à durée déterminée (**CDD**) est le type même de l'emploi précaire;* "A short-term contract that can very well not be renewed is the perfect example of a job that may have no future." *Etre précarisé(e),* to be hired on such a basis or retrograded to it; *la précarisation. La précarité est le maître mot aujourd'hui dans le domaine de l'emploi;* "Nonrenewable jobs are the key notion in the employment situation today."

See **flexibilité; jetable**

pré (m.) **carré** Someone's special preserve or special field of action. *Chacun défend son pré carré;* "Everyone's defending their own personal territory."

précathodique Applies to the period before television, before the cathode-ray tube. *Ah, les heureux parents de l'époque précathodique! Ils n'avaient pas besoin de surveiller à chaque instant leurs chers bambins installés devant le petit écran.* "How lucky parents were in the days before TV! They didn't have to keep an eye on their little darlings every minute as they watched the box."

préférence (f.) **nationale** *Donner la préférence nationale* is one of the planks in the *Front national* platform: giving systematic preference to *les Français de souche,* "native-born French-(wo)men," rather than to immigrants, *à tous les niveaux, que ce soit l'emploi, la santé, les allocations . . . ,* "in every respect, be it employment, health care, government allowances, and so on."

prélèvements (m. pl.) Deductions from pay, *prélevés à la source,* "withheld at source." *Depuis les dernières années du gouverne-*

ment socialiste ils comprennent la **CSG,** *contribution sociale généralisée, et depuis le début du gouvernement RPR-UDF, ils comprennent également la CRDS, contribution au remboursement de la dette sociale, tous deux destinés à combler le trou de la Sécu,* both intended to catch up on the Social Security deficit. *Les prélèvements obligatoires sont une forme d'impôt direct;* "Deductions are a form of direct taxation." (*La CRDS* is also called *le* **RDS:** *le remboursement de la dette sociale.*)

premier(ière) Can be misleading because it does not always mean first in chronological order; instead, it can mean "leading," "number one." *Bull* (pronounced like *bulle* (f.), bubble) *est le premier constructeur informatique français;* "Bull is number one among French computer manufacturers."

prendre un arrêté To issue a decree. *L'arrêté a été pris hier, comme prévu;* "The decree was issued yesterday, as expected."

préréglé(e) Preset, as, for instance, a radio set to a certain station or a thermostat at a certain temperature.

préretraite (f.) *Partir en préretraite,* to take early retirement. *Les employeurs espèrent réduire leur personnel sans licenciement sec, par le jeu des préretraites;* "Employers hope to cut back their staff without actually firing anyone, by offering early retirement." See **embaucher**

"If you only buy one car, I get fired."

"Really? What if I buy two?"

"They give me early retirement."

by Lefred-Thouron in *Le Canard enchaîné,* July 9, 1997

présentateur(-trice) TV anchorman (woman). *Certains sont devenus des vedettes à part entière;* "Some of them have become stars in their own right." *Certains ont été accusés d'avoir accepté des avantages en nature (voyages, séjours, rembourse-*

*ment de frais fictifs ou gonflés . . .) de la part d'hommes poli-
tiques ou d'hommes d'affaires;* "Some have been accused of
accepting favors (trips, vacations, reimbursement of fictitious
or exaggerated expenses, etc.) from politicians or businesspeople."

préservatif (m.) A condom. (See **Condom.**) Hence, preservatives
in food products are definitely not *préservatifs;* they are *agents*
(m. pl.) *conservateurs* or *agents de conservation.*

   *Les préservatifs sont au coeur même de la campagne d'in-
formation et de protection contre le Sida;* "Condoms are the
crux of campaigns to inform the public about AIDS and protect the public against it." *En 1995, un certain nombre d'ecclé-
siastiques français ont déclaré leur soutien à l'utilisation des
préservatifs comme mesure de prévention contre le Sida malgré
leur opposition aux préservatifs en tant que contraceptifs;* "A
group of French ecclesiastics came out in support of the use of
condoms as protection against AIDS even though they were
opposed to the use of condoms as a means of contraception."
See **Sida**

Président (m.) **du Conseil** An old term for *Premier ministre* that
has not been in official use since *la Quatrième République*
(1946–1958) but is still heard in a historical context or in talking about other countries, particularly Italy.

présidentiable (m. or f.) Likely or plausible presidential candidate.

présidentielles (f. pl.) Presidential elections.

présomption (f.) **d'innocence** The principle whereby a person is
assumed to be innocent until legally proven guilty. *Mais étant
donné la récente vague de **mises en examen** de personnalités
politiques et de PDGs, la détention provisoire de certaines personnes et la médiatisation de ces pratiques judiciaires, il est difficile de préserver la présomption d'innocence dans l'esprit du
public;* "But because a considerable number of politicians and
top executives have recently been placed under investigation
and a number of these people have been taken into custody,
and because the media have given ample attention to these
measures taken by the judicial system, it is difficult to keep
the public from assuming that people who make the headlines
for such reasons are guilty."

presse (f.) **écrite et presse parlée** A useful distinction that is still
used, although less often than before, between newspapers
and magazines, on the one hand, and the radio, on the other.
Now the umbrella word *les médias* is used to cover them all,
plus television.

prestation (f.) A very versatile word; the general idea is performance or a service that is provided. *La prestation télévisée du
candidat fut sévèrement critiquée;* "The candidate's performance on TV came in for heavy criticism." *Est-il possible de*

maintenir les prestations de santé sans en augmenter les coûts?
"Is it possible to maintain health care services without increasing their cost?"

prêt-à-porter (m.) Ready-to-wear clothing; sometimes shortened (by the younger generation) to *prêtap.* A sarcastic spin-off from this word is *le prêt-à-penser,* "ready-made ideas." See **PAP**

prévisionniste (m. or f.) Economic forecaster.

prise (f.) **de bénéfices** Profit-taking.

prise (f.) **de participations croisées** A share swap; cross shareholding.

privatisation (f.) In the years immediately after World War II, many French industries were nationalized. Then came a reversal of government policy. *Les privatisations se sont succédé au cours de la première moitié des années 90. Chaque fois qu'une banque ou une société a été privatisée, les Français ont été fortement encouragés à acheter des actions mais le nombre d'actions que pouvait acquérir chaque particulier était fortement limité, laissant ainsi de gros blocs d'actions pour les investisseurs institutionnels.* "A series of privatizations were carried out in the first half of the 1990s. Each time a bank or company was being privatized, the French were strongly encouraged to buy shares but the number that each individual could acquire was sharply limited, leaving large blocks of shares available for institutional investors." See also **actionnaire.**

La SNCF, Air France-Air Inter, l'EDF-GDF, et la Poste ne sont toujours pas dénationalisés; quant à France Télécom, 25% de son capital a été privatisé en 1997.

privilégier To give preference to (something). *Pour vaincre la pollution en ville il faudrait privilégier les transports en commun, aux dépens de la voiture de tourisme;* "To overcome urban pollution, public transport should be given preferential treatment over individual motorists and their cars." *Les vacanciers semblent privilégier de plus en plus la route;* "When people go away on vacation, they seem more and more inclined to drive instead of taking the train or the plane." *L'incinérateur est aujourd'hui privilégié pour se débarrasser des déchets;* "Today incinerators are the preferred means of getting rid of trash."

Les privilégiés generally means *"les riches."*

prix (m. pl.) **littéraires** The most important ones—*le Goncourt, le Renaudot, le Médicis, le Fémina,* and *l'Interallié,* among others—are awarded in November according to an immutable ritual. The Goncourt jury makes its first selection early in September, then narrows it down from week to week; on the fatal day it always has lunch at the same Paris restaurant, *chez Drouant,* where the winner's name is then announced. The whole process and the winners get great play in the media. See **Galligrasseuil**

Parmi d'autres prix littéraires il y a le Prix Inter, le prix des lectrices de Elle, *le Prix Goncourt des lycéens, le Grand prix de l'Académie française, et le Prix de Maisons de la Presse . . . ;* "Other literary prizes include the *Prix Inter;* the prize awarded by the readers of *Elle* magazine; the Goncourt awarded by a jury of high school students; the Grand Prize of the French Academy; the Booksellers' Prize, and so on."

problème (m.) **de société** A major social issue or trend, one so important that to a certain extent it defines or influences the type of society. *La justice/La façon dont le capitalisme fonctionne actuellement/La **mondialisation** peut être considérée aujourd'hui comme un problème de société.* "The legal system/ The way capitalism functions today/Globalization can be considered a major social issue."

processus (m.) **de paix** The process leading to or maintaining peace. *Peut-on encore sauver le processus de paix au Moyen Orient?* "Is there still hope for peace in the Middle East?" *La France souhaite que tout soit mis en oeuvre pour faire avancer le processus de paix;* "France urges that every possible step be taken to achieve peace."

procréation (f.) **médicalement assistée** Medical techniques devised and used to assist human fertility and childbirth; they are regulated by *la loi de 1993.*

produits (m. pl.) **blancs** Household appliances, also called *l'électroménager,* including *la cuisinière, le réfrigérateur-congélateur, le lave linge, le lave vaisselle, et le (four à) micro-ondes,* "stove, refrigerator plus freezer, washing machine, dishwasher, and microwave oven." *Les produits bruns* include *le téléviseur, le magnétoscope, l'ensemble* (m.) *stéréo,* "TV set, VCR, and stereo system."

profanation (f.) Desecration of a religious edifice or site. *Le cimetière juif à **Carpentras** a été profané en 1990; des crânes-rasés ont avoué en 1996 et leur procès a eu lieu en 1997.* "The Jewish cemetery in Carpentras was desecrated in 1990; in 1996 some skinheads confessed, and their trial took place in 1997."

programme (m.) **spatial** In 1965, the first rocket that was neither American nor Soviet was launched; it launched the first French satellite, *Astérix,* from Hammaguir, in the Sahara desert. In 1979 *Ariane,* the first European rocket, was launched for the first time. In 1982 Jean-Loup Chrétien became the first French astronaut to take part in a space flight. In 1993, Claudie André Deshaye became *la première Française cosmonaute,* "the first French woman astronaut." The word *spationaute* (m. or f.) is also used.

In 1980 *Arianespace,* a private company, was set up, to produce, launch and commercialize *Ariane,* the satellite-launching rocket. It has carried out over 180 contracts. See **Kourou**

progresser A term that is often misleading to English-speaking people since it does not carry the idea of progress (*amélioration*) but only the idea of increase (*croissance, augmentation*). *Le nombre de vols à main armée a progressé de 3% depuis l'année dernière;* "The number of armed robberies has increased 3 percent since last year." *La progression du nombre de demandeurs d'emploi est moins prononcée dans certaines régions que dans d'autres;* "The increase in the number of jobseekers is less marked in some regions than in others."

proportionnelle (f.) Proportional representation as a way of acknowledging election scores, instead of awarding seats only to the party winning a majority of votes. *On dit souvent que c'est grâce au PS que le FN a pu avancer, puisque le PS a choisi la proportionnelle aux élections de 86 et le FN a pu en profiter;* "It is often said that the Socialist Party is responsible for the *Front national*'s breakthrough because for the 1986 elections the *PS* chose proportional representation, which proved beneficial to the FN." *La classe politique s'interroge beaucoup: faudrait-il introduire une dose de proportionnelle? Elle serait plus juste envers les écologistes, entre autres.* "Politicians are in a quandary: should a certain amount of proportional representation be introduced? It would be fairer to the environmentalist parties, among others."

propos (m.) Words; what someone says whether in a public or a private capacity. *Ce ne sont que des propos en l'air* is a common phrase expressing distrust or scepticism: "That's just a bunch of words, not to be taken seriously."

Prost, Alain Very popular French racing car driver in the early and mid-1990s. *Maintenant il dirige sa propre écurie;* "Now he runs his own racing car stables."

protection (f.) **rapprochée** Bodyguards. *Assurer la protection rapprochée d'une personnalité politique,* to provide bodyguards for/to act as bodyguard of a prominent political figure. A bodyguard is *un(e) garde du corps.*

protection (f.) **sociale** The nationwide system of benefits—*congés payés, allocations familiales, congé maternité prénatal et postnatal, allocations chômage, versement de retraites par l'Etat, et ainsi de suite*—paid for by *les **prélèvements** sur les salaires, les **cotisations** des travailleurs indépendants, et les **charges salariales** payées par les employeurs.*

protestant(e) *Les protestants sont une très petite minorité en France, a peine un million sur presque soixante millions;* Protestants are a very small minority in France, barely one million out of a population of nearly sixty million. *Néanmoins, le protestantisme est la troisième religion en France, après le catholicisme et l'islam;* "Nonetheless, Protestantism is the third largest religion in France, after Catholicism and Islam/the Muslim religion." See **Edit de Nantes.**

A Protestant church (the building) is *"un temple";* the Protestant church (the institution) is *"l'Eglise protestante."*

province (f.) A word still used with scorn by some Parisians to mean everything in France that is not Paris and the Paris region. It used to be assumed that *l'ambition de tout(e) provincial(e) était de monter à Paris,* "the ambition of any person living *en province* was to get away and go to Paris." *Mais aujourd'hui beaucoup de personnes estiment que la province est non seulement moins chère que la capitale mais plus saine, plus propre, plus proche de la nature;* "Today however many people believe that not only is the cost of living outside the Paris area lower but also that you can live a healthier, cleaner life outside Paris, closer to nature."

proximité (f.) Neighborhood, as in small neighborhood stores, *les magasins/commerçants de proximité. On essaie actuellement de revaloriser les commerces de proximité par opposition à la prolifération des grandes surfaces, qui sont la mort des petits commerçants et de toute vie de quartier;* "People today are being urged to patronize small local stores because there is a danger that supermarkets will drive them out of business and put an end to neighborliness." *On parle même de la petite délinquence de proximité et de la police de proximité.*

Pour recréer une vie de quartier et combattre le chômage, on essaie de promouvoir les emplois de proximité; "In an attempt to bring city neighborhoods back to life and combat unemployment, the value of local jobs (home helps, etc.)— but *en tant qu'emplois déclarés,* as 'jobs on a legal basis'—is being touted." See **petit boulot**

prud'hommes (m.) Dispute-settlement tribunal in the field of labor relations. Elections to the *conseils de prud'hommes* are held every few years and any person who is legally employed, including immigrants, is entitled to vote. *Si vous estimez que vous êtes victime de licenciement abusif, vous pouvez traîner votre ancien employeur devant les prud'hommes;* "If you believe that you have been wrongfully dismissed, you can drag your former employer before the *prud'hommes.*" The procedure is free of charge.

PSA The Peugeot company, also called Peugeot Sochaux because of the factories located in **Sochaux.**

PSG (m.) *Le Paris-Saint-Germain,* one of the best known *équipes de football,* "soccer teams." Saint-Germain refers to Saint-Germain-en-Laye, just outside Paris. *Les supporters du PSG seront présents en masse;* "There will be a huge turnout of *PSG* fans."

psy (m. or f.) A shrink; short for *psychanalyste* (m. or f.). The *p* before the *s* is pronounced.

publireportage (m.) An advertising feature in the form of an article.

puce (f.) Silicon chip. *Carte* (f.) *à puce,* microchip card.

Pucelle (f.) *Jeanne d'Arc, la Pucelle d'Orléans,* "Joan of Arc, the Maid of Orleans," a symbol of French national identity and purity and of resistance to foreign (i.e., English) perfidy ever since the end of *la Guerre de Cent ans,* "the Hundred Years' War," in the fifteenth century. (See **Albion.**) *Mais depuis la fin des années 80 le Front national a largement récupéré la Pucelle;* "Since the end of the 1980s, however, the *Front national* has succeeded to a large extent in appropriating Joan of Arc as its own symbol," thereby effectively establishing itself in many voters' minds as the embodiment of the combat to safeguard French national identity and resist a new foreign "perfidy," this time that of immigrants from Africa and North Africa.

purification (f.) **ethnique** Ethnic cleansing. *Le terme est apparu au cours de la guerre en ex-Yougoslavie;* "The term came into use during the war in the former Yugoslavia."

puritain(e) What all Americans are reputed to be—that is, prudish.

PVD (m. sing. or pl.) *Pays en voie de développement.*

quadra (m. or f.) Short for *quadragénaire* (m. or f.), a forty-year-old, someone fortyish.

quai (m.) **de Javel** Synonymous even today with Citroën cars because the factories used to be located on the *quai de Javel* in Paris. See **Boulogne-Billancourt; Sochaux**

quarante-cinq tours (m.) Almost extinct, this is the old 45-rpm record on which so many jazz hits and popular songs were available. They are now found only on compact disc (CD) and **K7.**

quantité (f.) **négligeable** On *Le téléphone sonne,* a phone-in radio talk show, one listener claimed bitterly, *"En Allemagne, la France est tenue pour une quantité négligeable; le partenaire, c'est Washington";* "In Germany, France is considered insignificant; the country that counts is the United States.'"

quarté (m.) Term for betting on four horses in a race; *le quarté plus, le quinté* (five horses), and *le quinté plus* are variations on the same theme. See **tiercé**

quartiers (m. pl.) **en difficulté** A euphemism to designate urban districts or suburbs with a high rate of *chômage, criminalité, délinquence parmi les jeunes,* and so on. Also called *quartiers difficiles* or *défavorisés. Dans ces quartiers les commerçants menacent de mettre la clé sous la porte car ils en ont assez de* *devoir baisser leur rideau de fer;* "In these neighborhoods storekeepers threaten to close their shops for good because they're tired of having to roll down their metal shutters."

Quart monde (m.) Whereas *le Tiers monde* includes all underdeveloped countries outside of Europe, *le Quart monde* refers to the most poverty-stricken of them. By extension it has recently come to be used to designate *ceux qui en France vivent au-dessous du seuil de la pauvreté, les sans abri, les exclus, les marginalisés,* "people in France itself who live below the poverty line, the homeless, and the social outcasts." *La quart-mondisation.* See **exclusion; SDF**

quatre-quatre (4 × 4) (f. or m.) Pronounced *"quatre-quatre."* A four-wheel drive car.

quatre-vingt-dix (90) Maximum speed (ninety kilometers/hour) at which new drivers are allowed to drive for the first year after they obtain their *permis de conduire.*

In Belgium and French-speaking Switzerland, ninety is called *nonante,* the logical culmination of the series *quarante, cinquante, soixante, septante, octante, nonante.* In France, the series goes *quarante, cinquante, soixante,* but then *soixante-dix, quatre-vingts, quatre-vingt-dix.*

quatrième âge (m.) Also called *le très grand âge,* referring to very elderly people, usually those over eighty. See **troisième âge**

Québec (m.) The French obviously have a special place in their hearts for *les québécois,* who are living proof that *la francophonie existe vraiment.* On October 31, 1995, when French television was presenting the previous day's referendum in Canada, in which Quebec independence was turned down by a margin of only about fifty-thousand votes, one commentator said accusingly, *"Les Etats-Unis, géant voisin avec une population d'un quart de milliard, restent indifférents au sort des cinq ou six millions de francophones au Québec;"* "'The United States, the gigantic neighbor with a population of one quarter billion, is indifferent to the fate of the five or six million French-speaking people of Quebec.'"

quelque part A phrase that can become a verbal tick, like "like" or "somehow." *C'est un cinéma quelque part qui essaie de cerner le phénomène guerre;* "Somehow it's the type of film that tries to come to grips with what war is." See also *un petit peu*

querelle (f.) **scolaire** The ever-present tension between *l'école publique et l'école privée, l'école laïque et l'école religieuse.* See **Clovis; laïcité; loi Falloux**

quinquennal, -ale Five-year, as in *la loi quinquennale pour l'emploi.*

quinquennat (m.) A five-year term of office. It has often been suggested, with regard to the *Président de la République,* that the septennat stipulated in the Constitution be replaced by *un quinquennat.* Because it could coincide with the five-year term of office of *les Députés,* it could put an end to *la* **cohabitation.** Under the current Constitutional provision, a president elected to a seven-year term, *un septennat,* can run for and be elected to another *septennat,* thus remaining in office for fourteen years as the result of only two elections.

quinze (m.) **de France** French rugby team (*l'équipe de rugby à quinze*).

R

rabibocher Colloquial. To reconcile people after a quarrel. The reflexive form has a similar meaning. *Est-ce que les tendances divergentes dans le camp écologiste vont pouvoir se rabibocher à temps pour faire front commun lors des élections?* "Will the different factions among the environmentalists be able to patch things up in time to put up a united front during the elections?"

racisme (m.) Racism; racialism; race discrimination. *Peut-on légiférer contre le racisme?* "Is it possible to take action against race discrimination by passing laws?" *Est-ce que les Français sont plus racistes ou moins racistes que les autres peuples?*

rafle (f.) Police raid or round-up. The most famous one in France, even today, occurred on July 16, 1942; see **Vél d'hiv.** See also **repentance**

RAID (m.) *Recherche, assistance, intervention et dissuasion,* a specialized antiterrorist police unit.

Rainbow Warrior (m.) The Greenpeace vessel that French government agents sank in the harbor at Auckland, New Zealand, in 1985. Greenpeace had been opposed to French nuclear weapons testing in the Pacific—and still was in 1995; see **Mururoa.**

ranger au magasin des accessoires To stop using a given tactic. *Il faudrait que les politiques rangent (or remisent) au magasin des accessoires la langue de bois;* "Politicians must give up using double-talk."

rappeler à l'ordre To reprimand. *Le Ministre a été rappelé à l'ordre* is more official and veiled than, for instance, *Le Ministre s'est fait taper sur les doigts.*

rapport (m.) **de forces** Power struggle or balance of power. Not at all the same as *une épreuve de force,* "a showdown." *Aujourd'hui, où il faut à tout prix relancer l'économie, il y a un nouveau* *rapport de forces entre consommateur, vendeur et fabricant; le pouvoir est du côté du consommateur;* "Today, with the top priority being economic recovery, the power center/struggle among consumer, seller, and manufacturer has shifted; the ball is in the consumer's court."

rapport (m.) **coût-efficacité** Cost-effectiveness.

rapport (m.) **qualité-prix** Value for money. *Ce restaurant offre un excellent rapport qualité-prix;* "This restaurant gives you top value for your money." *Est-ce que le contribuable n'est pas en droit de demander si son gouvernement offre un bon rapport qualité-prix?* "Aren't taxpayers entitled to ask whether their government is giving them decent value for their money?"

Ras l' Front The name of a movement whose position, as stated on posters that appeared early in 1998, was *"Contre le fascisme."* The posters' two-line message read, *"Si tu ne t'occupes pas du FN, Le FN s'occupera de toi."* "'If you don't do something about the *Front national,* the *FN* will do something about you.'" The latter line was printed against a background showing barbed wire. *Ras l' Front* is a variation on a very commonly used phrase of colloquial French, *ras le bol,* meaning "fed up," as in *Ah, j'en ai ras le bol de. . . .* " See **Front national**

ratonnade (f.) A very pejorative word, one that it is never wise to use. During the Algerian war, *une ratonnade* was "a punitive raid against Arabs"—"Arab bashing," so to speak—since, in spoken French, *raton* (m.) was a pejorative word for "Arab." Today, by extension, the fact of beating up or attacking (Arab) immigrants. See **bougnoule**

RATP (f.) *Régie autonome des transports parisiens,* the heavily subsidized agency that runs the Paris Metro and bus system.

Ravel *Recensement automatisé des voeux des élèves,* automatic census of pupils' wishes. *Ravel* is the computerized system whereby *les élèves de terminale font leur demande d'entrée à l'université,* "high school seniors apply to college"; they express their wishes as to *l'établissement et la filière,* "the university or institute and the field of study." All high school seniors are required to use this system by certain specified dates in the spring; they then take their *Bac* in June and July and, if they pass it, can enter *l'enseignement supérieur,* "higher education," in September–October. Ravel makes it compulsory to use the **Minitel;** no handwritten or other types of application are accepted.

raz (m.) **de marée** Tidal wave or (figuratively) landslide. *Le résultat des élections n'a pas été le raz de marée escompté par la droite;* "The elections did not give the Right the overwhelming victory it had been counting on."

RDA (f.) *République démocratique allemande,* official name of former East Germany. Still talked about today, as in *Dans l'ex-RDA les gens étaient habitués à avoir un emploi à vie;* "The people of East Germany were accustomed to having a job for life." See **RFA**

RDS (m.) *Remboursement de la dette sociale,* a payroll tax introduced in 1996 for purposes of paying off the *deficit of la Sécurité sociale.* Also called *Contribution au remboursement de la dette sociale (CRDS). Le RDS et la CSG sont prélevés du salaire brut à un taux d'ensemble de 2,9% de 95% du brut;* "It is deducted from gross salary together with the **CSG** at a combined rate of 2.9 percent of 95 percent of the gross."

réactualiser To update.

rebelote (f.) Always heard together with **belote.**

rebondissement (m.) New development or twist. *Le procès dans l'affaire OM, maintenant dans sa troisième journée, a connu un nouveau rebondissement;* "The **OM** case, whose trial is now in its third day, has taken a new turn."

recadrer To realign a policy (*la politique sur l'immigration, la politique du franc fort,* etc.).

recentrage (m.) Attempt to achieve new or sharper focus. *Grâce à sa récente prestation à 7 sur 7, le Premier ministre espère réussir un recentrage de son image;* "With his recent appearance on *7 sur 7,* the prime minister hopes to bring his public image into new focus." (*7 sur 7* was a 7 P.M. Sunday TV classic on which Anne Sinclair interviewed political figures, who also commented on the events of the previous week.)

réchauffement (m.) **de la planète** Global warming. *Les scientifiques ont l'air de dire maintenant que le degré de réchauffement de la planète sera moindre qu'on ne l'avait craint il y a quelques années et que par conséquent le niveau de la mer augmentera moins;* "Scientists now seem to believe that global warming will not be as extreme as was feared a few years ago and that as a result the sea level will not rise as much." See also **effet de serre**

recherche (f.) **dans l'intérêt des familles** Police search for a missing person.

récidiver To repeat an offense. *A peine les cambrioleurs ont-ils été relaxés qu'ils ont récidivé;* "Hardly had the burglars been released when they committed another burglary." *Un(e) récidiviste,* repeat offender. *La récidive,* the fact of repeating an offense.

reclasser *Le reclassement d'un travailleur,* finding work for an employee (or ex-employee) in another sector.

réclusion (f.) **criminelle** Prison sentence handed out to a criminal. *La réclusion criminelle à perpétuité,* Life sentence. *La réclusion criminelle assortie d'une peine de sûreté de trente ans;* "Prison sentence for a minimum duration of thirty years."

reconduire To renew or extend the duration of something. *L'ac-*

cord a été reconduit pour une nouvelle période de trois ans. Reconductible, renewable. *Un **CDD** n'est pas reconductible;* "A short-term employment contract cannot be extended."

reconduire à la frontière Official euphemism for *expulser du territoire,* since it means "to accompany an undocumented immigrant," *un(e) immigré(e) en situation irrégulière,* back to the border (i.e., put him or her on a flight back to his or her country of origin). See **charter; Eglise Saint-Bernard; régulariser sa situation; sans-papiers**

recordman (m.) Record holder in any field of sports. *Recordwoman* (f.).

Rectorat (m.) School board that can make some decisions at the local (district) level but is appointed by the *Ministère de l'Education nationale* and answers to it, applying ministerial decrees and so forth.

reculer To back up; also, to decrease. *Malgré toutes les déclarations mirobolantes des candidats de tous bords, le chômage n'a pas plus reculé sous un gouvernement de droite que sous un gouvernement de gauche;* "Notwithstanding the great claims made by candidates of all stripes, unemployment has not decreased under a government by the Right any more than it did under a government by the Left."

Les ventes d'automobiles neuves ont reculé de 18% par rapport au mois dernier; "New car sales are down by 18 percent over last month."

récupérer To take over, appropriate, or coopt a movement, an event, or a person. During a student demonstration, one student explained, *"On a préféré faire ça en indépendant; si on avait fait appel aux syndicats on se serait fait récupérer";* "'We preferred to organize our own demo; if we'd relied on the unions, they would have taken everything out of our hands and taken over.'" See **Pucelle.**

Faire de la récup(ération), to salvage discarded objects or materials so as to either sell them or turn them into something else.

redressement (m.) The fact of straightening something out, bringing it back to normal. *Il y a une telle crise de confiance chez les électeurs à l'égard de la classe politique que le redressement de la situation ne sera pas facile à obtenir;* "Voters are so mistrustful of politicians that it will be no easy task to overcome their skepticism." *Le redressement des pays d'Europe après la deuxième guerre mondiale était loin d'être acquis jusqu'en 1947, quand le Plan Marshall a été introduit;* "The countries of Europe were nowhere near being back on an even keel after World War II, until the Marshall Plan was brought into effect in 1947." See **plan de sauvetage (redressement) du Crédit Lyonnais.**

Un redressement fiscal, the requirement to pay back taxes.

réduction (f.) **du temps de travail** Time-sharing measure put forward as a means to combat unemployment. *En réduisant le temps de travail de 40 à 35 ou même à 32 heures par semaine, on créera plus d'emplois, disent certains;* "Some people claim that reducing the work week from forty to thirty-five or even thirty-two hours will create more jobs." By 1997 the rallying cry had become *35 heures payées 39,* a thirty-five-hour week for thirty-nine-hour pay." This measure was officially adopted at the *Conférence de Matignon sur l'emploi, les salaires et le temps de travail,* whereupon the president of the **CNPF** resigned in protest, saying that he had been *berné,* "fooled." See **tueur**

rééquilibrage (m.) Effort to achieve a new balance. *S'agissant de l'implantation des grandes écoles, l'idéal serait d'arriver à un rééquilibrage Paris-province;* "Ideally, the **grandes écoles** should be more evenly distributed between Paris and the rest of the country."

refuge Adjective meaning "safe," in stock market terms. *Les valeurs refuge,* blue chip shares, safe investments.

régalien,(ne) Sovereign, related to the governement's inherent functions. *"La justice, la police, la défense, la fiscalité, l'éducation sont les attributs régaliens de l'Etat"* (*Le Point,* 1992); "'It is incumbent on the State to provide and administer justice, the police, defense, taxation, and education.'"

régime (m.) **de retraite** Retirement system or plan. See **fonds de pension; retraite par capitalisation; retraite par répartition**

régime (m.) **social** Overall system governing health benefits, retirement, and allowances of various kinds. *Le déficit de notre régime social constitue notre plus grand problème budgétaire.*

région (f.) As a general rule, regional elections, held by direct universal suffrage every six years, arouse little interest. (See **Paca.**) The March 1998 elections put the parties of the Left in the lead in most of the regions, although often without an absolute majority. During the week that followed, however, a complete reversal occurred as winning candidates maneuvered among themselves to choose the president of each *conseil* (m.) *régional.* Some *RPR* and chiefly *UDF* winners negotiated with or were approached by the *FN;* as a result, several regions suddenly had a president from the Right but placed in office thanks to support from the far Right. *Donc, ont dit certains commentateurs, le suffrage direct a été bafoué par ces alliances avec le Front national;* "Therefore, said some political analysts, the voters' wishes as expressed through universal suffrage were overridden by these deals with the *FN.*" Media and politicians alike used terms such as *"convulsion," "implosion," "crise politique la plus importante depuis le début de la Cinquième République,"* and *"cassure du tabou contre des alliances avec le Front national";* Jacques Chirac, *Président de la*

République, felt compelled to address the nation twice to warn against the gravity of the situation and specifically designated the *Front national* as *raciste* and *xénophobe;* see **xénophobie.**

regroupement (m.) **familial** A key phrase in the debate over immigration, and specifically over the question as to whether and to what extent immigration should be limited. *Faut-il favoriser le regroupement familial?* "Should measures be encouraged that would make it easier for families to be reunited?"

régulariser sa situation To officialize one's residence status by acquiring the required papers. *Faut-il régulariser la situation des enfants d'immigrés si les enfants sont en France depuis plus de dix ans?* "When immigrants' children have been living in France for over ten years, should they be given official residence status?" In October 1997 *Le Monde* reported that *"les régularisations dans les préfectures n'avançaient pas aussi vite que prévu, que certaines préfectures exigeaient encore des bulletins de salaire alors que d'autres ne les exigeaient pas, et ainsi de suite,"* " 'the clarification-of-status process was not proceeding as fast as had been expected, that some police headquarters were still requiring applicants to present payslips while others did not require them, and so on.' "

    Also, to get married to the person one has been living with.

(se) réinsérer To become part of (society, the labor market, etc.) again. *Se réinsérer dans la vie active,* to find a new job after having been *au chômage* or having voluntarily stopped working (e.g., to raise a child). *Il faut travailler à la réinsertion des exclus;* "Efforts are needed to help those who are marginalized to reenter mainstream society." See **exclusion; insertion**

réinventer To think along completely new lines. *"Pour combattre l'exclusion il faudra réinventer le travail ou le concept de travail"* (*Le téléphone sonne,* September 1994); " 'If we don't want to lock people out of society/the mainstream, we must come up with a brand new definition of work or of the concept of work.' "

relance (f.) What politicians and businesspeople desperately want: the revival of economic activity. *Afin d'activer la relance, il faut diminuer l'impôt sur le revenu et la **TVA** afin d'augmenter le pouvoir d'achat des consommateurs, préconisent certains économistes;* "To get the economy moving again, income taxes and the VAT must be lowered so as to increase consumers' purchasing power, some economists urge." *Relancer la croissance/la consommation.* See also **reprise**

relever le défi To meet the challenge. *Relever le défi de la mondialisation est la tâche la plus urgente pour les pays de l'Europe aujourd'hui;* "The most urgent task facing the European countries today is to meet the challenge of globalization."

remise (f.) **de peine légale** Reduction of prison sentence—*par ex-*

emple, trois mois pour un an de peine, "three months off for each year to be served."

remiser See **ranger au magasin des accessoires**

remonte-pente (m.) Ski lift; much in the news every winter. *L'académie de Paris est en vacances cette semaine, les remonte-pentes seront pris d'assaut;* "With schools in the Paris district on vacation this week, the ski lifts are going to work overtime."

Renault French car manufacturer that made headlines late in 1996 by announcing abruptly that it was going to close its plant in **Vilvoorde** (or Vilvorde) in Belgium. See **camouflet; eurogrève**

rendez-vous, être au To exist, to be on hand or available. *La transparence n'est pas toujours au rendez-vous—comme par exemple ici en Europe après Tchernobyl;* "Full and honest information is not always available—here in Europe, for instance, after the accident at Chernobyl."

rendez-vous (m.) **citoyen** Concept launched in 1996, when it was announced that the draft would be done away with; see **armée de métier.** The *rendez-vous citoyen* was to enter into effect in 1999 for men born after January 1, 1979, and in 2003 for women. *Si on avait entre 18 et 30 ans on pouvait aussi faire 24 mois de volontariat;* "Anyone between eighteen and thirty could also do twenty-four months of volunteer service."

rendez-vous (m.) **social** Meeting among government officials, employers, and unions to discuss salary levels, age of retirement, job creation measures, and other labor relations issues. *"Pourquoi proposer le Smic jeunes à trois jours seulement d'un grand rendez-vous social?"* asked one commentator; "'What's the point of suggesting a special minimum wage for young people just three days before a major meeting on labor issues?'" The *Conférence nationale sur l'emploi, les salaires et le **temps de travail,*** in 1997, was an important *rendez-vous social.*

rentrée (f.) **sociale** The resumption of labor unions' demands, strikes, demonstrations, negotiations, and so on, in September–October, after the summer hiatus. *La rentrée sociale promet d'être chaude;* "There's going to be a lot of labor unrest in the fall."

renvoyer l'ascenseur (m.) To return a favor. *Autrefois le maire a aidé le Sénateur à se lancer dans la carrière politique; aujourd'hui il attend un renvoi de l'ascenseur.* "Some time back the mayor helped launch the senator's career; now he's waiting for the senator to do him a favor in return."

repentance (f.) At the end of September 1997, *l'Eglise de France,* "the French Catholic Church," issued a formal *déclaration de repentance* for the fact that during the first half, especially, of World War II, it did not speak out against the anti-Jewish measures taken by the Vichy government. *"Aujourd'hui nous confessons que ce silence fut une faute,"* said the bishops of the Paris region in this statement. It was read aloud by the bishop of the diocese of Saint-Denis, north of Paris, where Drancy is located. From the *camp d'internement* at Drancy some seventy-six thousand Jews were deported to concentration camps; approximately two thousand survived. Similar *camps d'internement* in France included Beaune la Rolande, **Gurs,** and Pithiviers, among others. See also **rafle; Vél d'hiv**

repère (m.) Landmark or any reliable form of guidance. *Aujourd'hui, dans un contexte de Sida, de chômage et de famille éclatée, où voulez-vous que les jeunes cherchent leurs repères?* "Today's young people are surrounded by AIDS, unemployment, and broken families; where on earth can they look for guidance?" *Dans un monde de changement hyper-rapide, que ce soit technologique, démographique, linguistique ou économique, beaucoup de Français cherchent des repères forts;* "In a world of ultrarapid change, be it in terms of technology, population patterns, language, or economics, many French people are looking for something strong to identify with."

report (m.) Postponement. *Jacques Santer,* president of the European Commission, stated in an early 1997 radio interview, *"Tout report (de l'introduction de la **monnaie unique,** prévue par le **Traité de Maastricht** pour le 1er janvier 1999) serait la mort de l'Union monétaire pour au moins une génération";* "'If the introduction of the single currency, scheduled for January 1, 1999, under the Maastricht Treaty, were to be postponed to any extent, that would spell the death of the European monetary union for at least a generation to come.'"

Another, strictly electoral meaning stems from *le système français à deux tours,* "the two-round system of elections in France." *Ce qui est en jeu au deuxième tour c'est le report d'une partie des voix du premier tour;* "What is at stake in the second round is the way some of the votes cast in the first round are going to swing." For instance, *Les voix des divers droite vont se reporter sur le RPR-UDF;* "Votes that went to the various fringe parties on the Right are now going to be cast for the *RPR* and the *UDF.*" *D'après certains **politologues,** la gauche devrait sa victoire lors des législatives de 97 au report des voix de l'extrême droite;* "According to some pundits, the Left won the 1997 legislative elections because the far Right instructed its voters not to give their votes to the *RPR.*"

reprise (f.) Economic recovery.

République (f.) See **Cinquième République**

rescapé(e) (m. or f.) Someone who has survived or has been rescued from a dire situation. *Les rescapés de l'Eglise Saint-Bernard,* a phrase coined by people sympathetic to the illegal immigrants who occupied a church in Paris to protest their uncertain status and who were not expelled from France after that episode. See **Eglise Saint-Bernard**

réseau (m.) Network, as in *Comment démanteler les réseaux natio-nalistes en Corse?* "How can the nationalist networks in Corsica be dismantled?" See **Corse**

résistant(e) (m. or f.) **de la onzième heure** Any person who claimed, at the very end of World War II, when collaborating with the enemy was no longer a healthy thing to do, that he or she had been in the resistance movement all along.

respectueux(euse) de l'environnement Environment-friendly or -sensitive.

responsabiliser To make or let someone take responsibility for his or her actions. *Si les gens ne font que recevoir des allocations mais n'ont jamais l'occasion de prendre leur destin en main, on ne pourra jamais les responsabiliser;* "If people just receive government allowances but never have a chance to take control of their own lives, it will never be possible to give them a sense of responsibility." See **assisté(e)**

responsable mais non coupable Georges Habache was the leader of a Palestinian liberation organization who was based in North Africa and was not officially welcome in France. Early in 1992, however, because he was ill, *la Croix rouge,* "the International Red Cross," flew him to France for treatment in a Paris hospital. The episode instantly became *l'affaire Habache;* its political fallout was considerable. President Mitterrand was abroad at the time and was not informed; it was immediately asked why he was not informed and who had authorized Habache's entry into France. An official at the *Ministère de la santé* declared that she was *"responsable mais non coupable,"* "'responsible but not guilty,'" a phrase which has since been abundantly parodied. She resigned.

ressourcer, se Reflexive verb meaning "to find new inspiration, new strength." *Chaque fois qu'un membre haut placé du gouvernement se sent à court d'inspiration il fait une tournée en province pour se ressourcer;* "Every time a high government official feels that he or she's going stale, he or she goes on an official visit somewhere outside Paris to recharge his or her batteries."

restauration (f.) **rapide** An attempt to replace the all-pervading phrase *le fast food* by a French term. See **Burger King; fast food; McDonald's; néfaste food**

Restos (m. pl.) **du coeur** An organization founded in 1985 by a comedian known as *Coluche;* it operates soup kitchens for homeless and other needy people. (*Resto* is a truncated word for *restaurant.*) An offshoot in Paris is *la Péniche du coeur,* "a boat moored on the Seine which can sleep a number of homeless people."

restructuration (f.) Restructuring (i.e., downsizing) of a firm. *Dès qu'un employeur envisage de restructurer son entreprise les salariés craignent pour leur emploi et souvent ils font grève pour protester d'avance;* "As soon as an employer begins to consider downsizing his or her firm, the employees fear for their jobs and often go on strike to protest in advance."

rétention (f.) Detention, as of individuals who attempt to enter the country without papers. *La rétention d'immigrés en situation irrégulière est limitée à un certain nombre de jours; ils sont maintenus dans des zones de transit.* "Undocumented immigrants are held in transit zones; they cannot be kept there for more than a specified number of days." *Les retenus* (m. pl.), the individuals so held.

retenues (f. pl.) The various amounts withheld from a paycheck; also called *prélèvements* or *cotisations obligatoires.*

retour (m.) **de bâton** A strong reaction to something disappointing or unpopular. *Si les mesures que doit prendre le gouvernement concernant les augmentations de salaires se révèlent décevantes, il faudra s'attendre à un retour de bâton;* "The government will be making decisions on the question of salary increases; if they turn out to be disappointing, a backlash can be expected."

retours (m.) **de vacances** Days on which traffic is heavy and airports and railway stations are crowded because people are coming home from *un pont, ou les vacances scolaires, ou leurs congés annuels,* "a long weekend, or school vacation, or their annual vacation." *Les départs en vacances et les retours de vacances les plus chargés se situent au début et à la fin août;* "The days when the greatest numbers of people are traveling occur at the beginning and end of August." See **bison futé**

retraite (f.) **anticipée** Early retirement. *Encourager ses employé(e)s à prendre une retraite anticipée est une façon d'éviter des licenciements secs quand on veut réduire ses effectifs;* "An employer who wants to make cutbacks but prefers to avoid firing employees will offer them incentives to take early retirement." *La direction compte sur une centaine de départs à la retraite volontaires;* "Management is counting on the idea that about a hundred employees will voluntarily opt for retirement." See **embaucher; préretraite**

retraite (f.) **par capitalisation** Prefunded retirement system. *Chacun épargne individuellement et pour lui seul;* "The payments made by each individual are used to fund only his or her future retirement." See **retraite par répartition**

retraite (f.) **par répartition** Pay-as-you-go system, such as *la Sé-*

curité sociale and *les retraites complémentaires. Les cotisations versées par les adhérents aujourd'hui paient les retraites actuelles;* "The amounts currently being paid into it by all of the people included in the system fund the retirement benefits of those who used to pay into it." See **retraite par capitalisation**

rétrograder To bring or put down into a lower category. *L'enjeu de ce match est énorme puisque l'équipe sera rétrogradée ou non selon le score final;* "The team has a lot riding on this game because if it loses it drops down into second division."

revaloriser To upgrade or raise the status of. *Il faut revaloriser le travail manuel;* "Manual labor must be allowed to regain a certain amount of prestige."

revendications (f. pl.) **sociales des chômeurs** Starting in December 1997, groups of jobless people organized sit-ins at des *antennes de l'Assedic,* "Assedic offices," in various cities, engaged students at two elite institutions in Paris—the *Fondation nationale des sciences politiques ("Sciences Po")* and the *Ecole normale supérieure ("Normale Sup,"* in the *rue d'Ulm)*—in discussion, etc. The jobless demanded *une prime de fin d'année* from the government—analogous to *la prime de Noël,* "Christmas bonus," or **treizième mois** paid by a number of employers to the people on their payrolls—and higher unemployment allowances. *Les chômeurs ont demandé entre autres que le gouvernement fasse des dépenses actives pour favoriser l'emploi et combattre la paupérisation de la population française, au lieu de verser en permanence des allocations chômage (dépenses passives);* "The jobless urged among other things, that the government engage in active expenditure to foster employment and combat pauperization instead of continuing endlessly to pay unemployment allowances (passive expenditure)."

Together, the aims of these and other demands, *"revendications,"* were called *le relèvement des minima sociaux,* "increased minimum income levels." These *journées* (f. pl.) *d'action* and these *revendications* suddenly took on a nationwide character and were publicly supported by at least one government minister, speaking on television.

revendiquer To claim credit for. *Aucun mouvement n'a encore revendiqué l'attentat d'hier soir qui a fait au moins une dizaine de morts dans le centre d'Alger;* "No movement has yet claimed credit for the terrorist incident that killed at least ten people in downtown Algiers yesterday evening."

Also, to demand, to proclaim one's right to something. *Revendiquer le droit à une cinquième semaine de vacances/à ouvrir le dimanche,* to demand a fifth week of paid vacation/the right to stay open on Sundays. *Les ouvrières dans cette usine n'ont pas encore réussi à faire entendre leurs revendications par la direction;* "The women who work in that factory have not yet been able to get management to listen to their demands."

revirement (m.) A reversal of opinion or situation. *Un homme politique, accusé de revirement et comparé à une girouette, déclara que ce n'est pas la girouette qui change mais le vent;* "One politician who was accused of changing his mind (frequently or radically) and was compared to a weather vane, retorted that it was not the weathervane that turned—it was the wind."

révisionniste (m. or f.) Person who challenges or denies the authenticity of events during World War II, *notamment l'existence des camps de concentration, des chambres à gaz, et des fours crématoires,* "particularly the existence of the concentration camps, gas chambers, and crematory ovens."

revoir sa copie An image borrowed from the schoolroom and very commonly used to mean "to revise or even overhaul one's policy or approach." *Vu l'ampleur du vote de protestation enregistré au premier tour des élections, la majorité actuelle devra revoir d'urgence sa copie;* "There were so many protest votes during the first round of ballotting that the current (governing) majority must revise its policies immediately."

révolution (f.) **verte** The fact of making the land yield more. *"La révolution verte s'est produite en Asie—pourquoi pas en Afrique?"* asked one listener on a radio talk show; "'Agricultural output has been increased in Asia—why hasn't it happened/why shouldn't it happen in Africa?'"

RFA (f.) *République fédérale d'Allemagne,* official name of reunified Germany, including the former *République fédérale allemande (**RFA**),* (West Germany) and the former *République démocratique allemande (**RDA**)* (East Germany).

RG (m. pl.) Or *DCRG, Direction centrale des renseignements généraux,* security branch of the police, with functions somewhat similar to those of the FBI in the United States.

Rhin-Rhône *Le canal Rhin-Rhône, qui devait relier les deux fleuves (à travers la Saône) entre Dole et Mulhouse, a suscité une forte opposition de la part des écologistes;* "The canal that was to link the Rhine River with the Rhône (via the Saône) between Dole and Mulhouse was fiercely opposed by environmentalists." In June 1997 the project was put on hold by the new Socialist government.

RIB (m.) *Relevé d'identité bancaire,* a sort of official checkbook stub showing your bank's name, address, and ID number and your name and account number; you show it to your employer or to any agency, association, and the like, that is supposed to transfer money directly into your account rather than sending you a check; also to a utilities company or any other party whom you authorize to deduct money from your account. A *relevé d'identité postal* (*RIP*) serves the same purpose with regard to your postal checking account.

riche (adj.) *Une semaine riche en rebondissements/événements,* a week in which a great many new developments have occurred.

ripoux (m. pl.) **Verlan** for *pourris* (i.e., corrupt police officers who take protection money, etc.). *Les ripoux* was a successful screen comedy on the subject; it spawned an even more cynical sequel, *Ripoux contre ripoux.*

riverain (m.) Person living alongside or in the immediate vicinity not only of a river or stream but of whatever installation or building project is being discussed. *Les riverains du nouvel héliport se plaignent du bruit en invoquant le Plan d'exposition aux bruits récemment adopté;* "People living near the new helicopter airport complain about the noise and justify their complaints on the basis of the recently adopted regulation on exposure to noise."

RMI (m.) *Le revenu minimum d'insertion,* government allowance intended to provide a statutory minimum income to *les plus démuni(e)s, surtout ceux ou celles qui ont épuisé leurs droits aux allocations de chômage et n'ont strictement aucune source de revenu,* "the poorest individuals, especially those whose unemployment benefits have run out and who have no source of income whatsoever." Introduced by the socialist government in 1988, it now stands at approximately 2,300 francs (between $400 and $450) per month. *Un(e) RMIste,* person receiving *le RMI.* The weekly *Marianne* commented (August 17, 1997) on *"un chef d'entreprise gagnant 15,000,000F par an (soit 578 RMI chaque mois),"* "'a business executive paid 15,000,000F a year who was in effect getting 578 times the statutory minimum income allowance each month.'"

Rocher, le Unofficial name for Monaco.

Roland Garros Tennis stadium in the *Bois de Boulogne,* on the western edge of Paris. Scene of the French Open tournament, *les internationaux de Roland Garros,* every year in May–June. *Roland Garros est à la terre battue ce que Wimbledon est à l'herbe;* "Roland Garros is to clay courts what Wimbledon is to lawn tennis." See **Noah, Yannick**

rôle (m.) **à jouer** A part to play. *Il est impératif que l'Europe et particulièrement la France aient un rôle plus important à jouer dans la définition de la politique de défense de l'OTAN;* "Europe in general and France in particular must be able to play a larger part in defining NATO's defense policy." See **tenir son rang**

roman (f.) **de gare** A potboiler, the type of romantic novel you can pick up at a train station (or airport or supermarket), read on your trip, and then leave behind. *Après une longue carrière* *d'auteur de romans de gare, voici que Mme X a produit un volume d'un mérite littéraire certain;* "Until now Ms. X had written a long string of potboilers; now she has come out with a book that has definite literary merit."

rond point (m.) Rotary junction or traffic circle. A great many of them were built on country roads in the 1990s to replace four-way intersections without traffic lights. See **giratoire, sens**

rose (f.) **au poing** A red rose clutched in a fist, emblem of the *Parti socialiste* since 1981, when François Mitterrand was elected president.

routier (m.) Truck driver; teamster. See **transports routiers**

RPR (m.) *Rassemblement pour la République,* a Right–center Right political party founded in 1976 by Jacques Chirac. One of the three largest parties in France today, along with *le Parti socialiste (PS)* and *l'UDF.*

rue (f.) **de Grenelle** The Paris street where the *Ministère de l'Education nationale* has its offices.

rue (f.) **de Rivoli** This used to be synonymous with *the Ministère des Finances,* until its offices were moved from the wing of the *Louvre* that fronts the *rue de Rivoli* to **Bercy,** in eastern Paris.

rue (f.) **de Solferino** Headquarters of the *Parti socialiste (et républicain).*

rue (f.) **de Valois** The *Ministère de la Culture et de la Communication,* whose offices are on this street, next to the *jardin du Palais-Royal.* It was de Gaulle who in 1958 created the first *Ministère de la Culture* and appointed André Malraux to fill the post.

rustine (f.) A patch used to repair a flat tire; hence, a hasty, short-term measure. *Ceux qui sont censés nous gouverner persistent à mettre des rustines au lieu de trouver une vraie volonté politique;* "The people who are supposed to be running the country keep on adding patches here and there instead of demonstrating real political determination." A variation heard in connection with the immigration question was *"Nous mettons sans arrêt des Tricostérils® sur des plaies béantes";* "'We keep putting Band-Aids® on gaping wounds.'"

S

sabrer To make vicious or drastic cuts in expenditure.

Saint Père (m.) The pope. See **Saint Siège; Sa Sainteté; souverain pontife**

Saint Siège (m.) The Holy See. See **Saint Père; Sa Sainteté; souverain pontife**

saladier (m.) **d'argent** The silver salad bowl—in other words, an informal name for the Davis Cup trophy, won by the French team in 1991 (for the first time since 1932) and again in 1996. See **Coupe Davis; Noah, Yannick**

salle (f.) **obscure** Movie theater. Almost always used in the plural: *Le nombre d'entrées dans les salles obscures aurait augmenté de 3% le mois dernier;* "The number of moviegoers is said to have increased by 3 percent last month."

Samu (m.) *Service d'assistance médicale d'urgence. En moins de deux minutes le SAMU était sur les lieux de l'incendie;* "In less than two minutes there were ambulances at the scene of the fire." Concerning the disillusionment of French voters with their political leaders, *L'Express* noted in July 1996, *"Les Français ne croient plus au Samu politique";* " 'The French have lost faith that any dramatic rescue will occur on the political front.' " *"Le Samu social, c'est trop peu et trop tard,"* commented *Marianne,* a weekly, in August 1997; " 'Stop-gap welfare measures are too little and they come too late.' "

sang (m.) **contaminé** Blood contaminated by the AIDS virus and used in blood transfusions in France in the 1980s without having been heated, even after it was scientifically established that heating beyond a certain temperature would destroy the virus. This was the subject of a major and long-lasting scandal: *Le directeur du Centre national de la transfusion sanguine, les responsables de la santé publique et le Premier ministre à l'époque où l'utilisation du sang contaminé a été autorisée, en 1984–85, savaient-ils à l'époque qu'il était contaminé?* "Did the director of the National Blood Transfusion Center, the public health officials and the prime minister who were in office in 1984–85, when the blood was authorized for use, know then that it was contaminated?" The trial in 1992, and subsequent appeals, drew nationwide attention.

sans *Sans* can introduce a term denoting an individual or a category of individuals (e.g., the *sans-culottes* during the French Revolution). Un/Les *sans-abri* or *sans-logis* or *sans-domicile,* a homeless person/the homeless. See **sans-papiers; SDF**

sans-papiers (m. pl.) Unofficial term for undocumented immigrants; see **Eglise Saint-Bernard**

sans plomb (m.) Lead-free gasoline. It began to be available in France in about 1985, and, to encourage people to use it, its price was made lower than that of the leaded gasoline that had prevailed until then. By 1995 about half of all gasoline sold in France was lead-free.

Sa Sainteté (f.) His Holiness, the pope. See **Clovis; Saint Siège; souverain pontife**

saucissonner The traditional French way of picnicking: *du saucis-*

LA POLICE AUX PETITS SOINS POUR LES SANS-PAPIERS
GRÉVISTES DE LA FAIM

UNE CUILLÈRE POUR LA
LIBERTÉ, UNE CUILLÈRE
POUR L'ÉGALITÉ, UNE,

The police look after the hunger-striking illegal immigrants with TLC. "One spoonful for
freedom, one for equality, one [for brotherhood]."

The traditional way of urging an infant to eat is to say, *"Une cuillerée pour Maman, une
cuillerée pour Papa . . ."*

by Wojniak in *Le Canard enchaîné,* August 14, 1996

son, du camembert, et du vin rouge. Said condescendingly by
people who have more sophisticated tastes; *les saucissonneurs,*
the lower class.

    Saucissonner also means to slice up or break into sections
as, for instance, a budget. *Le saucissonnage, le fait de découper
une émission de radio ou de télévision en tranches pour la publicité,* slicing up a radio or TV program into segments so as
to fit in the commercials.

saut (m.) **à l'élastique** Bungee jumping.

sauvage Often synonymous with *féroce,* as in *une concurrence sauvage.* But also synonymous with *spontané, non officiel,* as in
une crèche sauvage, "an unofficial day care center for infants,"
of the kind that sprang up among students during the **événements de mai 68.** *Faire du camping sauvage,* to camp away
from authorized sites.

Schengen The name Schengen (a place in Luxembourg) designates *la convention de Schengen,* the Schengen convention
signed in 1990 by member countries of the then European
Community to complete the 1985 *accords de Schengen. Ces
accords prévoient la libre circulation des biens et des personnes
et suppriment les contrôles aux frontières communes des pays
signataires;* "Under these agreements any individual or any
goods from any member country can cross any border into

any other member country, throughout the European Community." The agreements have been criticized as making it too easy for terrorists, drug dealers, illegal immigrants, and false political refugees to escape detection. The agreements' entry into force was postponed several times between 1993 and 1995. See **Europe passoire**

Scientologie (f.) Controversial movement created by L. Ron Hubbard. *Les partisans de la Scientologie prétendent que c'est une église en bonne et due forme, alors que ses opposants clament qu'il s'agit plutôt d'une secte et même d'une arnaque;* "Supporters of Scientology say that it is a church in the fullest sense of the word, whereas its adversaries say it is really a sect and even a swindle." *Un procès à Lyon en septembre 1996 a condamné certains responsables du mouvement à des peines de prison avec sursis, d'autres à des amendes;* "In September 1996 a trial in Lyons gave some of the movement's leaders suspended prison terms and fined others." In 1997 the case came up on appeal, *un procès en appel; le mouvement de Scientologie était accusé d'escroquerie et d'homicide involontaire. Le tribunal à Lyon décida que la Scientologie était une église; le Ministre de l'intérieur rétorqua que le tribunal n'était pas compétent pour décider du caractère cultuel ou non d'un mouvement.* "The movement was accused of fraud and manslaughter. The court in Lyons ruled that Scientology was a church; the minister of the interior retorted that the court did not have jurisdiction to decide whether a movement was a religion." See **culte; secte**

scolariser To enroll in school; to provide an education to. *Être scolarisé(e),* to be enrolled in school; to be receiving an education. *Un des buts principaux de l'aide étrangère accordée à ce pays d'Afrique occidentale est d'assurer la scolarisation de tous les enfants d'âge scolarisable;* "One of the chief aims of the foreign aid which goes to that West African country is to ensure that all school-age children actually go to school."

SDF (m. or f. sing. or pl.) *Sans domicile fixe,*—that is, homeless. *Les SDF sont devenus une catégorie de la population à part entière;* "Homeless people are now a population category in their own right." *Pour qu'un SDF puisse voter lors d'élections présidentielles ou législatives, il a été proposé qu'il puisse donner comme adresse celle du centre administratif ou d'hébergement qui s'occupe de lui;* "Homeless people cannot vote in presidential or other elections because they do not have an address; to remedy this it has been suggested that they could use the address of the welfare center or shelter they go to." *L'hiver, pour empêcher des SDF de mourir de froid, certaines stations de Métro parisien leur sont ouvertes la nuit, et un véhicule de la Ville de Paris circule pour repérer des SDF qui dor-*

ment dehors et les amener, de force parfois, dans un abri; "In wintertime, to prevent homeless people from dying of cold, some Metro stations are open for them at night, and a special municipal vehicle drives around to spot homeless people sleeping outdoors and bring them—by force, if necessary—to a shelter."

Il existe plusieurs journaux de SDF, généralement des hebdomadaires (Macadam, le Lampadaire, l'Itinérant . . .). *Ils constituent à présent un nouveau média, et les vendeurs, qui sont des SDF, peuvent garder 60% du prix de chaque exemplaire vendu.* "There are several homeless newspapers, usually weeklies. They have become a new part of the media, and the homeless people who sell them are entitled to keep 60 percent of the price of every copy they sell."

See **galère**

Sécam The process used chiefly in France and certain other European countries to record videocassettes. It is not compatible with the PAL system, used in most European countries and elsewhere, or with NTSC, used in North America, Mexico, and elsewhere. Therefore, a standard French **magnétoscope** (m.) cannot show American videotapes, and a standard American VCR cannot show French videotapes.

sécheresse (f.) Drought. *La sécheresse très prolongée du printemps 1997, venant à la suite d'autres sécheresses de ces dernières années, faisait sérieusement craindre pour les nappes phréatiques;* "The very prolonged drought of spring 1997, coming on the heels of other droughts in recent years, appeared to pose a real threat to groundwater levels." *On commençait à craindre qu'il faudrait payer en fin d'année un impôt sécheresse, comme en 1976;* "People began to fear that at the end of the year they would have to pay a drought tax, as they had in 1976."

second couteau (m.) Team member whose job is to put the team leader in the most favorable position possible. *Au Tour de France, les seconds couteaux sont les **coureurs** qui sont au service du chef de l'équipe.*

secret (m.) **de l'instruction** The right of *un juge d'instruction* not to reveal the information that his or her investigation has produced. This right is challenged by journalists. *Les média ont-ils le droit de révéler des éléments de l'instruction? Le public a le droit de savoir.* See **juge d'instruction; secret de Polichinelle**

secret (m.) **de Polichinelle** An open secret. *"Le **secret de l'instruction** est devenu un secret de Polichinelle,"* complained one judge during a radio discussion about the media and the judicial system; "'The findings that a judge has the right to keep secret have become an open secret.'"

secte (f.) Religious sect. See **Ordre du Temple solaire**

In August 1997, after the decision about *la **Scientologie,*** a radio debate called *"Religion ou secte?"* on *Le téléphone sonne* discussed the following criteria for distinguishing between the two: *Comment le mouvement recrute-il ses membres? Sont-ils libres d'aller et venir? Est-ce que le mouvement respecte l'ordre public? Y a-t-il un maître ou un gourou? une structure hiérarchisée? Comment l'argent du mouvement est-il acquis? Une secte se livre a des pratiques objectivement illégales ou frauduleuses. Les groupes cultuels jouissent d'avantages fiscaux; les dons sont déductibles des impôts.* "How does the movement recruit its members? Can they come and go as they please? Does the movement respect public order? Is there a master or a guru? A hierarchy? How does the movement acquire its money? A sect indulges/engages in practices that are objectively illegal or fraudulent. Religious institutions have a special tax status; gifts are tax deductible." See **culte**

secteur (m.) **public** Public sector—that is, in terms of employment, the civil service, *"les fonctionnaires."* A sector that carries enormous weight in France. Often said to be jealous of *le secteur privé—et inversement,* and vice versa. *Les fonctionnaires affirment que les employés du secteur privé ont de plus gros salaires, alors que les employés du secteur privé envient la sécurité d'emploi des fonctionnaires. Le secteur public serait un secteur protégé, alors que le secteur privé serait un secteur exposé.* "Civil servants claim that private sector employees have higher salaries, but private sector employees envy civil servants their job security. The public sector is said to be protected and the private sector to be exposed."

Said one commentator on a radio talk show in late November 1996, *"Lors de la récente grève des **routiers**, l'état a réglé un conflit dans un secteur exposé. Pour éviter le grand incendie social, il a même écorné sa politique sociale en accordant un départ à la retraite à 55 ans.* [See **social**.] *Existe-il un privilège pareil dans le secteur public? Est-ce que le fossé n'est pas en train maintenant de se creuser entre le secteur public et le secteur privé?"* "'Concerning the recent teamsters' strike, the government has settled a dispute in an exposed sector. To prevent a huge social explosion, it even betrayed some of its own social policy by allowing truck drivers to retire at fifty-five. Does the public sector enjoy any such privilege? Isn't the gap now widening between the public sector and the private sector?'"

sécurité (f.) Public safety, particularly with regard to a perceived threat of terrorist activity. *L'insécurité* (f.), (fear of) inadequate public safety. *Quand un grand magasin place à toutes les portes d'entrée une personne qui fait ouvrir son sac à chaque client qui entre, cela ne sert peut-être pas à grand'chose dans la réalité mais pour le public c'est sécurisant;* "When a department store posts someone at every entrance to open and look into the bag of every customer who comes in, it may not do much good in practical terms but it makes the public feel safer."

(se) sédentariser To abandon a nomadic way of life, or to cause (or compel) someone else to do so. *A cause de la sécheresse grandissante dans le Sahel ces dernières années, des populations nomades sont amenées à se sédentariser;* "Because of the increasing drought in the Sahel, in Africa, in recent years, nomadic peoples are having to live a more settled life."

SEITA (f.) The *Société nationale d'exploitation industrielle des tabacs et allumettes,* former government monopoly on the sale of tobacco and matches. *La SEITA a été privatisée en 1995.* The same year the *SEITA* was also sued, for the first time, by the widow of a man who had been a heavy smoker and had died of lung problems. See **tabac**

séjour (m.) **linguistique** *Il est courant pour les élèves des collèges et des lycées en France d'effectuer au cours de leurs études un ou plusieurs séjours, allant de huit jours à un mois, dans le pays dont ils étudient la langue.* "Junior and senior high school pupils in France often go to the country whose language they are studying. They may go several times during their school years and usually spend between a week and a month there each time." *La destination la plus courante est la Grande Bretagne;* "Great Britain is their most common choice." *Souvent ils sont reçus dans une famille et font un échange, recevant l'année suivante chez eux le fils ou la fille de la famille en question;* "Often they go to host families on an exchange basis, whereby the son or daughter of that family comes to stay with them the following year."

sélection (f.) French education authorities proudly state that *l'université est complètement démocratique puisqu'elle est ouverte à tous. Il n'y a pas de sélection; tout élève ayant obtenu son Bac est admis en fac s'il en fait la demande.* "College is completely democratic since it is open to anyone who has completed high school and got their *Bac;* they can apply to college and are accepted without going through any selective admissions process." Many people feel that the word *sélection* has become a synonym for *antidémocratique* and are prepared to **descendre dans la rue** to defend the absence of selective admissions criteria.

Mais les possibilités d'accueil des facultés sont souvent insuffisantes pour le nombre d'étudiants: pas assez de places assises dans les amphi(théâtre)s ou en bibliothèque, pas assez de conseillers. Par conséquent, au cours de la première année de fac un pourcentage élevé d'étudiants et d'étudiantes abandonne les études, et la sélection se fait donc par le décourage-

ment. D'autres sont parfois obligés de redoubler la première année. "But university facilities are often inadequate to handle the number of students: not enough seats available in lecture halls or libraries, not enough advisers. As a result, the dropout rate among first-year college students is high, and so the system is selective anyhow, through discouragement. Other students may be obliged to repeat the first year."

Les grandes écoles, les instituts d'études politiques, les instituts de gestion et autres ont au contraire des critères très sélectifs; l'entrée se fait sur concours et seul un petit nombre de candidats est admis. "On the other hand, the *grandes écoles* (*Polytechnique, ENA, les Mines, Ponts et chaussées, Hautes études commerciales,* etc.), *Sciences Po,* and other political science institutes, business schools, and so on, have very stiff entrance criteria, applied through competitive exams; only a few applicants are admitted." Most have spent a year or two in a *prépa* (*école préparatoire*), after the *Bac,* to prepare for the **concours.**

sellette (f.) *Etre sur la sellette,* to be in an acutely uncomfortable situation; to be held responsible, called upon to explain. *Mettre quelqu'un sur la sellette,* to put someone else in such a position. From the name of the small wooden seat on which a defendant had to sit while appearing in court.

semaine (f.) **de 35 heures** A proposal put forward as a time-sharing and therefore job-creating measure by various unions as well as the *Parti socialiste* and the *Parti communiste: la semaine de 35 heures payée 39 heures,* "a thirty-five-hour work week but with a thirty-nine-hour wage." *Le* **patronat** *ne s'est pas montré enthousiaste.* A variation on the theme is *la semaine de 32 heures.* See **Conférence nationale sur l'emploi, les salaires, et le temps de travail**

semeuse (f.) The symbolic figure of a woman draped in an ankle-length dress and striding along, rhythmically sowing seeds; long depicted on French postage stamps and still found on several coins: five francs, two francs, one franc, fifty centimes.

sensibiliser To raise awareness. *Le public n'a pas été suffisamment sensibilisé sur cette question;* "The public has not been made sufficiently aware of // sensitive to this issue." *La sensibilisation des consommateurs sur cette question de fraîcheur est primordiale;* "Getting consumers to care about freshness is vital." (*Sensibiliser à* is considered better usage.)

Sept (f.) *La Sept* was TV channel 7, a cultural channel created in 1986. In 1992 it was succeeded by **Arte.**

septennat (m.) Seven-year term of office, specifically the one to which *le Président de la République* is elected. In 1997, when President Chirac, who was elected in 1995, decided to dissolve the parliament and hold legislative elections a year early, one commentator sardonically said, *"Le but est d'assurer le septennat d'Alain Juppé à Matignon";* "'The purpose is to make sure that Juppé will serve a seven-year term as prime minister'" (by making it more likely that his and Jacques Chirac's party, the *RPR,* will win the elections and thus remain in office for the next five years). *Il n'y a évidemment rien dans la constitution qui prévoit un tel mandat puisque le Premier ministre n'est pas élu; il est nommé par le Président, qui peut ensuite, en principe, lui demander sa démission.* "Of course there is no provision in the Constitution for any such term, since the prime minister is not elected; he is appointed by the president who, theoretically, can ask him or her later to resign." See **cohabitation; quinquennat**

série (f.) **noire** Not only the famous mystery novel series published by Gallimard but also any unremitting series of problems. *A propos de la station Mir, en août 1997, on a parlé de série noire parce que les problèmes techniques en tout genre se succédaient;* "In August 1997, with regard to the Mir space station, the media talked about a run of bad luck because technical problems kept occurring one after another."

seringue (f.) Syringe. *Se shooter,* to shoot up. *Mourir d'une overdose,* to die of an overdose.

séronégatif(ive) HIV negative. *La séronégativité,* the fact of being HIV-negative.

séropositif(ive) HIV positive. *La séropositivité,* the fact of being HIV-positive. See **Sida**

serveur (m.) Computer server.

service (m.) **militaire** Compulsory military service; the draft. In 1996 President Chirac announced that it would be brought to an end in France before the year 2000. *Effectuer/Faire son service militaire,* to do your stint in the army. *Etre libre des obligations militaires,* to have done your stint. See **armée de métier; rendez-vous citoyen**

shakehand (m.) A time-honored franglais term meaning "handshake." In May 1995, right after the presidential election campaign, *le 13–14,* a France Inter radio program from 1 P.M. to 2 P.M. (*de 13 heures à 14 heures*), compared the relatively reserved Edouard Balladur with the extroverted Jacques Chirac, commenting, *"Jacques Chirac a le shakehand facile";* "'Chirac loves to work a crowd.'"

shooté(e) On drugs. *"Aux J.O., six athlètes sur dix sont shootés";* "'Six out of every ten athletes at the Olympics are on drugs,'" claimed one journalist in 1996.

SICAV (f.) *Société d'investissement à capital variable,* mutual fund, a prominent form of investment in the 1980s and 1990s.

Sida (m.) AIDS. A person with AIDS is *"un(e) sidéen(ne)"* or *"une personne atteinte du Sida ou malade du Sida"* or, more rarely, *"un(e) sidatique." La peur du Sida est une des raisons principales pour lesquelles les jeunes ont tendance à former des couples beaucoup plus stables qu'il y a quelques années;* "Fear of AIDS is one of the main reasons why the younger generation tends to form more long-lasting couples than they did a few years ago." *Le fait de porter un ruban rouge est devenu un signe reconnu internationalement qui indique que l'on participe à la lutte contre le Sida;* "Wearing a red ribbon has become an internationally recognized sign that you're doing something to fight AIDS." See **séropositif**

Une campagne publicitaire pour encourager l'utilisation du préservatif avait comme slogan, "On peut aussi lutter contre le Sida en portant autre chose qu'une blouse blanche"; "The slogan of one advertising campaign urging couples to use condoms was, 'You can combat AIDS by wearing something else besides a doctor's white coat.'"

Sidaction (f.) Annual fund-raising **téléthon** for AIDS, launched in 1995; during the evening devoted to it, *toutes les chaines de télévision ont un programme unique,* "all TV channels carry the same program."

Sidi Brahim A chain of small grocery stores in France generally run by Tunisians or Moroccans and which in the 1980s and 1990s replaced earlier long-established chains with such French names as *Goulet Turpin* and *Félix Potin. Sidi Brahim* and similar local stores have created a niche for themselves by staying open until 10 or 11 P.M. and all day Sunday, whereas *les supermarchés en ville* generally close by 7:30 P.M. and on Sunday afternoons. The nonimmigrant population generally calls such stores *le petit Arabe,* as in *J'ai oublié les pommes de terre; va voir si le petit Arabe est encore ouvert.* See **Arabe**

signalétique (f.) System of signals or symbols. *En 1996 on a introduit une nouvelle signalétique à la télévision contre la violence, et* le Parisien, *un quotidien, a expliqué: un rond vert au début de l'émission signifie que l'accord parental est souhaitable, un triangle orange signifie que l'accord des parents est indispensable, et un carré rouge signifie que l'émission est réservée à un public adulte.* "In 1996, in an attempt to curb TV violence, a new system of symbols began to be used on each program, and *Le Parisien,* a daily paper, explained them as follows: a green circle appearing on screen at the beginning of the program means it is advisable for children to watch the program only if the parents consent; an orange triangle means the parents' consent is indispensable, and a red square means that the program is for adult viewers only."

signes (m. pl.) **ostentatoires** Controversy arose when some Muslim girls in France came to school wearing the **chador.** Since state schools in France are officially nondenominational, thus reflecting *les vertus républicaines, c'est-à-dire laïques,* the *Ministre de l'Education nationale* responded with a decree forbidding anyone to wear *des signes ostentatoires d'appartenance religieuse,* "visible signs of religious affiliation," to school. See also **Clovis; foulard; laïcité; loi Falloux; tchador; vertus républicaines; voile à l'école**

sinistrose (f.) The ailment from which the French themselves say they have been suffering in the 1990s: pessimism; a tendency to view the present and the future in a sinister or catastrophic light. *Est-ce le résultat de la crise ou une (des) cause(s) de la crise?* "Is it the result of the current economic crisis or one cause of the crisis?"

Un sinistre is "an accident" (*explosion, incendie,* etc.); *un(e) sinistré(e)* is "a person who has suffered property or other damage in such an accident." The suffix *-ose* often denotes ailment, as in *mycose, narcose, psychose,* and *tuberculose.*

See also **morosité**

SMIC (m.) *Salaire minimum de croissance,* the minimum gross hourly wage for any employee aged eighteen or over. It amounts to approximately 6,600 francs ($1,100) a month. *Un(e) smicard(e),* person who is paid the minimum wage. The *SMIC* was created in 1970 to replace the *SMIG* (*salaire minimum national interprofessionnel garanti*) in an attempt to avoid distortion between the minimum wage and the general salary trend. *Les employeurs prétendent que le SMIC est trop élevé et les empêche donc d'embaucher; les syndicats au contraire considèrent qu'il est trop faible. Certains économistes demandent s'il faudrait augmenter le SMIC afin d'augmenter la consommation et ainsi relancer l'économie.*

SNCF (f.) *Société nationale des chemins de fer,* the French railway system. Nationalized after World War II, it is still nationalized, and heavily subsidized, today. See **cheminot; Socrate**

Sochaux Site of Peugeot car factories, in the *département* of *le Doubs* in eastern France, bordering on Switzerland. Also a famous soccer team. See **Boulogne-Billancourt**

social (m. and adj.) *L'immense domaine des relations entre employeur et employé(e) plus les prestations sociales en général et la protection sociale,* the vast field of labor relations, social services, and protection measures. *Le climat social est tendu;* "Things are tense on the labor relations front." See **partenaires sociaux; plan social.** *Si le chômage ne diminue pas, y aura-t-il une explosion sociale?* "If the unemployment situation doesn't get better, will all hell break loose?" *Après le 2e tour des élections, y aura-t-il un 3e tour social?* "After the second round of voting, will there be a third round in the form of strikes?" See **mouvement de grève**

société (f.) One of the keywords in all political discourse. *Quelle* *société pour demain?* "What kind of society will we have/do we want tomorrow?" *Il faut oeuvrer pour une société apaisée et décrispée;* "We must make every effort to soothe social tensions." *Dans la société actuelle les liens se distendent; il faut recréer la solidarité.* "In our modern society the links between people are getting very faint; we must revive the idea of solidarity."

société (f.) **à deux vitesses** See **deux vitesses**

Socrate A computerized reservation system that the **SNCF** introduced in 1993 but which soon came in for heavy criticism: *trop compliqué, pas fiable, logiciel (acheté à American Airlines) non adapté aux besoins . . . ,* "too complicated, unreliable, software (purchased from American Airlines) that was not suited to the purpose, and so forth."

soixante-huit Not just any 68 but May 1968, the period of student riots and sit-ins that transformed French society. *Un(e) soixante-huitard(e),* a person who took part in or witnessed those events. See **événements de mai 68**

soldats (m. pl.) **du feu** When a forest fire broke out between Marseilles and Aubagne in the summer of 1997, the media constantly referred to *les pompiers* as *"les soldats du feu."*

soleil (m.) **levant** *Le pays du soleil levant* is Japan, "the land of the rising sun." See **nippon**

solidarité (f.) *La solidarité* is often referred to as a goal, as is *la cohésion sociale.* The idea is to combat *la **fracture sociale*** and *la **pensée unique;*** to help people in distress and work for a more egalitarian society. *Il faut que nous soyons tous solidaires.*

solide (m.) *C'est du solide;* "It's reliable; you can count on it." *Quand le candidat X promet quelque chose, ce ne sont pas des paroles en l'air—c'est du solide.*

solitaire, en This does not mean "to be in solitary confinement," which is *être au secret. Solitaire* means "solo," as in *gagner la course à la voile en solitaire. Gérard d'Aboville est un Breton qui est devenu célèbre d'abord en 1980 quand il a traversé l'Atlantique à la rame, depuis Cape Cod jusqu'à Brest, en solitaire, et encore en 1991, quand il a fait la traversée du Pacifique à la rame, toujours en solitaire, d'ouest en est;* "Gérard d'Aboville, from Brittany, became famous in 1980, when he rowed single-handedly across the Atlantic from Cape Cod to Brest, and again in 1991, when he rowed single-handedly across the Pacific."

Solutré A place name made famous during Mitterrand's two terms as president, since *grimper à la roche de Solutré*—"doing a mild hike to the top of the rock at *Solutré,*" in Burgundy—was a ritual with him and his *entourage* every year.

sommet (m.) Summit, as in summit conference. *Le sommet du G7,* summit meeting of G7 countries' leaders. *Le sommet de la FAO à Rome en 1996 devait examiner le problème de la faim dans le monde; est-ce qu'il est question que ce sommet se prononce contre l'embargo contre l'Irak?* "The FAO summit meeting in Rome in 1996 was expected to discuss the problem of hunger throughout the world; would it come out with a statement condemning the embargo against Iraq?"

Somport Site of a highway tunnel built through a valley in the Pyrenees; it was completed in 1997 despite opposition by *des écologistes*. See **Rhin-Rhône; tunnel de Somport**

Sonacotra *Société anonyme de construction pour les travailleurs*, the agency in charge of supplying housing to immigrant workers of all ages. *Foyer* (m.) *Sonacotra*, hostel or residence for immigrant workers (generally without their families).

sondage (m.) Opinion poll or survey. *Les sondeurs*, poll takers, polling institutes. *Les sondé(e)s*, people who are polled. *Un sondage effectué hier auprès de 2.738 personnes montre la popularité du Président en hausse de 6% par rapport au mois dernier;* In a survey taken yesterday, with 2,738 people polled, it appears that the president's popularity has gained 6 percent since last month. *Est-ce que les sondages suivent seulement l'opinion ou est-ce qu'ils la façonnent?* "Do opinion polls merely reflect public opinion, or do they shape it?" *Sondage intentions-de-vote*, preelection poll. *Sondage sortie-des-urnes*, exit poll.

97% of French people have never been questioned by an opinion poll. "How am I supposed to know what I think?"

(Note the *charentaises* this man is wearing on his feet, designating him as the perfect *beauf*.)

by Nicoulaud in *Marianne*, May 19–25, 1997

sonde (f.) Space probe. *Pathfinder, la sonde américaine, est arrivée sur Mars en juillet 1997.* See **planète rouge**

sonner l'hallali In hunting, to blow the horn to signal that the animal is at bay or has been killed. Hence, *Le Monde* spoke, in October 1993, of *"sonner l'hallali et faire ainsi la chasse à tous les présidents (de sociétés nationalisées),"* "'hunting down the heads of all nationalized firms and bringing them to the kill.'"

sono (f.) *La sonorisation,* sound system, as at a club, rally, or party.

Sophia-Antipolis Industrial and science park in southeastern France, just inland from *la Côte d'Azur,* "the Riviera"; specialized in computer science and electronics. See **technopôle**

sortant(e) Incumbent or outgoing. *Le maire sortant, qui devait gagner ces élections haut la main, n'a récolté que 39,6% des voix au premier tour;* "On the first round, the outgoing mayor, who was expected to win the election hands-down, got only 39.6 percent of the votes."

SOS Racisme Organization founded in 1984 to combat intolerance. See also **droits de l'homme; Désir, Harlem; Licra; MRAP; pote**

souche (f.) A stump with roots; a vinestock; in other words, the living basis for something. *Les Français de souche* is the term used by the *Front national* to designate native-born French-(wo)men, as distinct from naturalized French people and other immigrants.

souris (f.) Not the mouse that roared but the infinitely more powerful computer mouse. *Cliquer avec la souris.*

sous-informer To underinform. *A l'époque de Tchernobyl en avril 1986 les populations européennes se sont plaintes qu'elles avaient été sous-informées par leurs gouvernements s'agissant des conséquences possibles, de ce que le vent apportait en Europe, et ainsi de suite;* "When the accident occurred at Chernobyl in April 1986, the people of Europe complained that they were underinformed by their governments about what the consequences might be, what the wind was blowing toward Europe, and so on." *Des traces de radioactivité auraient été trouvées trois mois plus tard dans du thym qui poussait en Haute-Provence;* "Traces of radioactivity were reported to have been found three months later in some thyme growing in Haute Provence." *La sous-information.* See also **surinformer**

sous-médicalisé (m.) Adjective used to describe a country with inadequate health care and inadequate means by which to detect and prevent health problems. *Un pays sous-médicalisé est un pays où les soins médicaux et les moyens de dépistage et de prévention sont insuffisants.*

soutien (m.) Support, as in *le devoir de soutien alimentaire,* the duty to provide, or share in providing, basic support to one's offspring and parents. *Par exemple, participer aux frais d'hé-*

bergement des enfants ou des parents. Autrefois il était courant pour les parents d'être pris en charge par leurs enfants adultes, mais à présent que les familles sont éclatées et que la notion d'entr'aide est très affaiblie, les autorités soulignent le devoir de soutien alimentaire; "It used to be fairly common for parents to be looked after by their grown children, but today families are split up and the idea of family members helping one another no longer goes without saying, so officials are emphasizing the family's obligation to provide basic support."

souveraineté (f.) A source of much concern. *Est-ce qu'avec l'Europe la France perdra sa souveraineté nationale?* "When Europe comes into existence, will France lose its national sovereignty?" *Les Allemands seraient hostiles à l'euro parce qu'ils ne veulent pas que le deutschemark perde sa souveraineté;* "The Germans are said to be opposed to the **euro** because their own national currency will no longer be supreme in Europe."

Souverain Pontife (m.) The pope; the Supreme Pontiff. See **Clovis**

spationaute (m. or f.) Astronaut. Also *astronaute* (m. or f.) or *cosmonaute* (m. or f.).

speaker(erine) TV anchorman or -woman. Also *présentateur-(trice)*.

spécificité (f.) *La spécificité de la France,* the attributes that make France unique. Also, *la spécificité de la culture française.* Like *l'exception culturelle et l'identité culturelle,* the phrase is often invoked to explain/justify/urge French resistance to *l'hégémonie américaine,* the overwhelming influence of all things American, from motion picture distribution, to international diplomacy, to fast food.

speedé,(e) High-powered, fast-track. *Un jeune cadre speedé,* high-powered young executive.

sponsoriser To sponsor something or someone. *Sponsoriser un match de football, un récital . . . ,* to sponsor a soccer game, a recital, etc. *Un sponsor. Le sponsoring* or *la sponsorisation.*

squatter *Occuper un logement ou autre surface sans y avoir de titre légal,* to occupy housing or some other structure or space without having legal title to it. *Un squat,* the premises that are occupied. *Squatter(teuse).*

Stade (m.) **de France** Purpose-built soccer stadium erected in the Seine-Saint-Denis, just outside Paris, in time for the **Coupe du monde.** Its seating capacity is 80,000.

station (f.) **de travail** Workstation. *Une station de travail intelligente est connectée à des ordinateurs centraux.*

station (f.) **terrienne** Ground station for satellite communications.

stérilet (m.) Intrauterine device (IUD). See **contraception; planification familial**

St Nicolas du Chardonnet See **intégrisme; Monseigneur Lefebvre**

Strasbourg Seat of the European Parliament.

stressé(e) *Etre stressé(e),* to be under pressure.

structures (f. pl.) This does not always mean "buildings or other tangible structures"; it can mean "arrangements, measures, or provisions," as in *des structures d'accueil* or *des structures d'accompagnement pour les* **SDF.**

stups (m. pl.) Short for *stupéfiants,* narcotics. *La brigade des stups a fait une descente dans un labo de fortune;* "The narcotics squad raided a makeshift drugs lab."

subsaharien(ne) Sub-Saharan. *Suite aux événements au Rwanda et au Zaïre, la politique du gouvernement français vis-à-vis de l'Afrique subsaharienne est à revoir dans sa totalité;* "In the light of developments in Rwanda and Zaïre, French government policy towards sub-Saharan Africa needs to be completely revised."

subsidiarité (f.) Principle incorporated into the **Traité de Maastricht** whereby whatever can be done more effectively at the national rather than the European level will be left to the member countries to do; somewhat similar to the principle of states' rights in a federal system.

suffrages (m. pl.) **exprimés** Votes cast during an election. *Sur la totalité des inscrits, les suffrages exprimés représentent 69%; le taux d'abstention est donc de 31%.* "Out of the total number of registered voters, 69 percent actually voted and 31 percent abstained."

suivi (m.) Follow-up. *S'agissant de crimes sexuels, nous préconisons d'abord une systématisation du programme des soins pour les détenus, puis, à la sortie de prison, un suivi médico-social rigoureux;* "To deal with sex offenders, we urge that once they are behind bars a systematic program of treatment be applied to them and then, once they are released, that a serious medical and social follow-up be applied."

super (m.) Leaded gasoline. *Après-demain le prix du super augmentera de six centimes le litre. Le (super) sans plomb,* unleaded gasoline; see **sans plomb.**

supercagnotte (f.) The big jackpot. *Si vous jouez au Loto cette semaine vous avez des chances de gagner la supercagnotte de six millions de francs;* "If you try your luck in the lottery this week you may win the super jackpot of six million francs."

Superphénix (m.) A nuclear reactor located at *Creys-Malville* in the *Isère* (southeastern France). Work on it began in 1975, and it was connected with the EDF grid in 1986, five years behind schedule. A number of technical problems and accidents caused various stoppages and restarts. Environmentalists and others challenged the usefulness of continuing to spend money on it: *"Superphénix et (l'usine de traitement de déchets nucléaires de) La Hague sont de vieilles casseroles; elles sont une danseuse que l'Etat continue à entretenir,"* said one *écolo-*

giste in a 1997 radio interview; "'Superphénix and (the nuclear waste treatment plant at) La Hague are old and shoddy; they're like a mistress that the government continues to keep.'" In June 1997 the newly elected Socialist government decided to shut down *Superphénix.* See **La Hague; nucléaire**

supporter (m.) Fan of a sports team, as in *les supporters du **PSG**.* By extension, the verb *supporter* has come to mean what *soutenir* meant (and still means). *Les supporters sont venus nombreux pour supporter leur équipe préférée;* "There was a big turnout of fans to back their favorite team."

suppression (f.) **d'emploi** Almost always used in the plural: *Michelin prévoit 3.500 suppressions d'emplois avant la fin de l'année;* "Michelin plans to do away with 3,500 jobs by the end of the year."

surcoût (m.) Overexpenditure; the fact of going over budget. *Le surcoût de la construction du **tunnel sous la Manche** a été phénoménal.*

surdimensionner To exaggerate, overdo. *"Est-ce qu'on ne surdimensionne pas un peu le problème?"* demandait un commentateur, concernant le passé de François Mitterrand après un interview télévisé avec lui en septembre 1994.* "'Isn't the problem being just a little bit exaggerated?' asked one commentator, with regard to Mitterrand's past, after a TV interview with him in September 1994."

On a 1997 radio talk show on *Les déchets: quelles sont les meilleures solutions?* one specialist stated, *"Pour venir à bout du problème des déchets, il n'est pas utile de surdimensionner les incinérateurs";* "'We don't need to have oversized incinerators to deal with our waste disposal problem.'"

A person or thing can be *surdimensionné(e),* "oversized, larger than life," both literally and figuratively.

surdiplômé(e) Overqualified. *On dit aux jeunes de faire beaucoup d'études et de décrocher beaucoup de diplômes mais ensuite quand ils postulent un poste, les employeurs potentiels leur reprochent d'être surdiplômés;* "Young people are urged to go on studying and getting lots of degrees, but later, when they apply for a job, the potential employers tell them they are overqualified."

sureffectifs (m. pl.) Overmanning; having too many employees for the job needing to be done. *Des effectifs* (m. pl.), staff, personnel. See **dégraisser**

surendettement (m.) Excessive consumer debt; inability of consumers to meet the payments on their purchases (or of countries to pay their debts). *La loi Neiertz, qui prévoit des mesures pour protéger emprunteur et prêteur, porte le nom de la socialiste Valérie Neiertz, Secrétaire d'Etat à la consommation, qui l'a introduite;* "The Neiertz law, which aims to protect both borrower and lender, is named after Valérie Neiertz, undersecretary for consumer affairs in a Socialist government, who sponsored it." *Certains préconisent d'effacer carrément les dettes de gens sans ressources;* "Some people urge that when individuals who are in debt have no income at all and therefore no hope of paying off their debt, it is best just to cancel their debt completely." See **endettement**

surfer To surf, coast, freewheel. *Surfer sur l'Internet,* to surf the Internet. *Internaute* (m. or f.), person who does so; compare *astronaute* (m. or f.) and ***cosmonaute*** (m. or f.). *Le surf sur neige,* snowboarding. *Surfeur(euse),* surfer. See **Internet**

surinformer To overinform. *Aujourd'hui, avec CNN, l'Internet, et tout le reste, nous sommes tous surinformés, soumis à un barrage incessant de gros titres, d'articles, de reportages, d'émissions, d'interviews, de commentaires, d'analyses, de statistiques et pourcentages, de photos—comment faire le tri dans tout cela?* "Nowadays, what with CNN, Internet, and all the rest we're all overinformed, constantly hit over the head by big headlines, articles, programs, interviews, commentary, analysis, figures, and percentages—how are we supposed to sort it all out?" *La surinformation.*

surpuissant(e) Hyperpowerful, as *un réacteur nucléaire surpuissant* or *un liquide vaisselle surpuissant.*

syndicat (m.) Labor union. *Etre syndiqué(e),* to be a union member. *Syndicaliste* (m. or f.), union official. *La CFDT (Confédération française démocratique du travail), la CFTC (Confédération française des travailleurs chrétiens), la CGT (Confédération générale du travail), la CGT-FO (Force Ouvrière), la FEN (Fédération de l'éducation nationale), le SNES (Syndicat national des enseignants du second degré),* and *les syndicats des **cheminots*** are the most influential unions. *La base,* the rank and file. *Nicole Notat est devenue, en 1992, la première femme leader syndical en France (CFDT);* "In 1992 Nicole Notat became the first woman to head a major union in France (the CFDT)."

Chaque année au 1er mai, fête du travail, les syndicats défilent; en 1997, pour la première fois, deux syndicats ont défilé ensemble, soulignant ainsi ce qui est peut-être une tendance nouvelle, vers le rapprochement syndical. "Every year on May 1, which is Labor Day, the unions parade through the streets; in 1997, for the first time, two unions paraded together, pointing to what may be a new willingness among unions to act jointly." See **grogne**

synthèse (f.) *De synthèse,* artificial, synthetic, or computer generated, as in *images de synthèse, intelligence de synthèse. Synthétiseur* (m.), synthesizer.

T

tabac (m.) A source of revenue much valued by the government. But at the same time the health insurance system accuses tobacco of being one of the chief causes of its deficit. *Des lois antitabac ont été introduites au début des années 90;* "Anti-smoking laws were brought in early in the 1990s." *Taux de goudron,* tar. See **SEITA**

Tabarly, Eric The dean of French sailors until he died at sea in 1998. A Breton, he won the *course transatlantique en solitaire* (solo trans-Atlantic race) twice, in 1964 with the *Pen Duick II* and in 1976 with the *Pen Duick VI.*

table (f.) **d'écoute** *Etre mis/placé sur table d'écoute,* to have your phone tapped. *Les mises sur table d'écoute sont un des plus gros scandales perpétrés par le gouvernement;* "Wiretapping is one of the biggest scandals the government has to answer for."

tagueur (m.) Graffiti artist; tagger. *La RATP a dépensé une fortune pour faire disparaître toute trace de l'oeuvre des tagueurs sur les wagons du Métro;* "The *RATP* spent a fortune to remove all trace of the taggers' work on the Metro cars." *Un tag,* graffiti signature.

taille (f.) **unique** One size fits all; usually applies to certain types of mass-produced clothing. Can also apply, by way of criticism, to policies or measures that are not considered sensitive or subtle enough. See **pensée unique**

TAO (f.) *Traduction* (f.) *assistée par ordinateur,* computer-assisted translation. See also **CAO; PAO**

tarte (f.) **à la crème** A pie, of the kind that got thrown in the old slapstick films; by extension, anything that is trite, a cliché. *"C'est une tarte à la crème que de dire que souvent la réalité dépasse le roman,"* noted one participant on a literary talk show; "'It's not very original to say that truth is often stranger than fiction.'"

taux (m.) **de participation** Turnout for an election. Commenting on elections in Japan, one broadcaster noted, *"Cela a été le taux de participation le plus faible de l'histoire des élections nipponnes."*

tchador (m.) Variation on the spelling of **chador,** the Islamic head scarf; see also **foulard** and **voile à l'école.** *Tchadoriser, faire porter le tchador par un mannequin dans un défilé de mode,* to have a model in a fashion show wear the headscarf.

Tchernobyl Chernobyl, in the former Soviet Union, where the nuclear accident occurred in April 1986.

technicité (f.) Technical nature, expertise. *La technicité de ce travail fait qu'il ne peut pas convenir à un candidat ayant moins qu'un Bac plus 5;* "This job is on such a technical level that only applicants who have done at least five years of college will be capable of doing it."

technocrate (m. or f.) Officials and employees in Brussels, headquarters of the European Union, are accused by Eurosceptics of being *des technocrates, des espèces de robots ne s'intéressant qu'à la technologie et aux règlements, et ignorant tout des aspects humains des différents problèmes,* "robots who only care about technology and regulations and who know nothing about the human side of the issues at stake."

technologie (f.) Technology. *Technologie de pointe,* advanced or cutting-edge technology. *Le triomphe de la technologie, c'est ce qui caractérise notre fin du vingtième siècle;* "What stands out at the end of the twentieth century is the triumph of technology." *"Technologie, dévoreuse d'emploi"* was how Nicole Notat, head of the *CFDT* labor union, termed it in a radio interview in March 1998: "Technology devours jobs."

technopole (f.) A big city whose intellectual facilities (universities, research centers, etc.) constitute a natural pole of attraction for high-tech industries.

technopôle (m.) A science park; that is, *un site aménagé afin d'offrir un environnement complet comprenant des universités et des laboratoires de recherche aussi bien que des industries,* a purpose-built site that provides a complete R & D environment including universities and research labs as well as industries. **Sophia-Antipolis,** in the Alpes-Maritimes, is the best-known example in France.

téléachat (m.) Teleshopping by **Minitel;** sometimes abbreviated the way it is pronounced, *TVHA.*

télécarte (f.) Phone card available from any *bureau de poste* or *tabac* as well as from *librairies-papeteries* and *marchands de journaux. Presque partout en France des cabines à carte ont remplacé les cabines à pièces;* "Virtually everywhere in France telephone booths that accept only phone cards have replaced coin booths." *Il en est de même pour les parcmètres;* "The same is true of parking meters."

télépéage (m.) Payment of expressway tolls by remote control. *Au lieu de s'arrêter au contrôle, le conducteur continue et le montant à payer est prélevé sur la carte à puce qu'il a déposé derrière son pare-brise;* "Instead of stopping at a tollbooth, the driver drives through it and the amount due is deducted from the microchip card that he or she has placed behind the windshield and that is read electronically from the booth."

téléphone (m.) *Comme le beaujolais nouveau, le téléphone est arrivé, lui aussi!* Up-to-the-minute telephones and telecommunications—*téléphone à touches, téléphone mobile/portable, téléphone cellulaire, téléphone sans fil, téléphone à répondeur, sans oublier la télécopie, c'est-a-dire le fax*—burst on the scene in France at the beginning of the 1990s, when *France Télécom* was spun off from *la Poste.*

téléthon (m.) Marathon fund-raising TV program during which viewers phone in to pledge money to whatever cause is involved.

télétravail (m.) Telework; telecommuting.

télétraitement (m.) Teleprocessing.

temps (m.) **d'antenne** Air time allotted on radio or TV, especially to a candidate or party during *une campagne électorale.*

temps (m.) **choisi** A possibility that has been raised within the overall discussions about reducing *la durée du travail,* "the length of the work week," in the hope of creating jobs for more people. *Le temps choisi serait la durée de travail préférée par le salarié; ce serait moins rigide que la* **semaine de 35 heures** *pour tous.* "Under the choose-your-hours system, the employee would choose the number of hours he or she wanted to work and the number of days over which they would be spread; it would be more flexible than a thirty-five-hour week for everyone." *Le temps choisi* does not necessarily mean *le temps partiel,* "part-time."

temps (m.) **fort** High point. *Le temps fort de cette visite papale a été la messe dite en plein air à Longchamp devant un million de fidèles;* "The high point of the pope's visit was the mass he said outdoors at Longchamp with a million of the faithful on hand."

temps (m.) **réel** Real time. *Faire paraître le rapport/mener l'enquête en temps réel,* issue the report/conduct the inquiry in real time. *"Les élections en temps réel,"* the radio announces; "'Election results as they happen.'"

tenir son rang To maintain one's rank or status. *Tenir son rang dans le monde* is a major aim of French foreign and military policy: "to enable France to maintain its rank among the nations of the world." See **rôle à jouer**

ténor (m.) In the nonmusical sense, this term means a leader or prominent figure. *Cette campagne a eu lieu par le haut, par les ténors des formations politiques;* "The campaign was led by the upper echelons, by the party leaders." *Un ténor du barreau,* a prominent trial lawyer.

TER (m.) *Train express régional,* a fast train but not as high powered as the *train* (m.) *à grande vitesse (TGV),* high-speed train.

terrain (m.) *Un homme/une femme de terrain,* someone who likes to be out there where the action is instead of sitting at a desk; also, someone who has experience with such action. *Si l'université voulait vraiment remplir sa fonction dans le monde réel,* *il faudrait qu'elle donne aux étudiants une "formation terrain et théorique";* "If colleges and universities wanted to fulfill their true function in the real world, they would have to provide students with practical as well as theoretical training."

terrain (m.) **d'entente** Ideological meeting ground or grounds for agreement. *Le but de toute négociation est de trouver un terrain d'entente.*

terrorisme (m.) One of the government's major causes for concern. *Chaque fois qu'il y a eu ou qu'on s'attend à un attentat terroriste, le Plan Vigipirate entre en vigueur;* "Whenever a terrorist attack has taken place or is expected, the government puts its vigilance plan into effect." *Certains points d'accès à des lieux publics sont fermés;* "A number of entrances to public places are closed." *Les corbeilles à papiers aussi bien en surface que dans le Métro sont scellées;* "Wastebaskets both above ground and in the Metro are sealed shut." *Des barrières sont mises en place pour empêcher les voitures de se garer aux abords des écoles;* "Metal fences are put up to prevent cars from parking near schools." *Faut-il couvrir ou coffrer les sièges du Métro afin qu'aucun sac ne puisse y être caché en dessous?* "Should the lower part of the seats in the Metro be completely enclosed so that no bags can be stowed underneath them?" Signs urge the public, *"Ensemble, soyons tous vigilants." A la poste, au guichet, on vous indique, "Pour tout envoi dépassant 250 grammes, prière de présenter une pièce d'identité;"* "In the post office signs at each window say, 'If your package weighs more than half a pound, please show your ID.'"

tertiaire (adj. and m.) *Le tertiaire, le secteur tertiaire,* the service sector. *L'industrie se tertiairise de plus en plus.*

tétanisé(e) (adj.) Paralyzed, speechless with fear.

tête (f.) **de Turc** A person (or country) whom (which) it is convenient to blame for one's own mistakes, failures or disappointments. *Est-ce que la Grande Bretagne n'est pas un peu la tête de Turc des pro-Maastrichiens quand la construction de l'Europe a du mal à avancer?* "Don't the people in favor of **Maastricht** tend to blame Great Britain whenever the building of Europe seems to be just marking time?"

tête (f.) **de veau** *Une spécialité charcutière qui n'est pas généralement considérée comme très raffinée,* calf's head with French dressing, a dish that is not generally considered a great delicacy. It is one of President Chirac's favorite dishes, the media assured the public repeatedly soon after his election in 1995. Cartoonists and satirists quickly pounced on the phrase to symbolize Chirac himself. The public was also told that he preferred beer to wine.

têtes (f. pl.) **blondes** See **nos chères têtes blondes**

TGB (f.) *La Très grande bibliothèque,* unofficial name of the *Bi-*

bliothèque de France, which was officially opened at the end of 1996 at Tolbiac, east of the *Gare d'Austerlitz* in Paris. It is intended to replace, to a large extent, the *Bibliothèque nationale,* whose august premises had long since become too small to meet the demand for seats and storage.

thalasso (f.) *La thalassothérapie,* the use of seawater as, or as part of, medical treatment. *Selon certains, si la Sécu a un trou aujourd'hui c'est en partie parce qu'elle a remboursé trop de cures de thalasso;* "One reason why the Social Security system is in deficit, say some people, is that it gave too many people refunds for seawater cures."

Théâtre français (m.) Common way of referring to *la Comédie-Française,* the state-supported national theater; its mission is chiefly to perform works in the classical French repertory (Corneille, Racine, Molière, etc.) See **maison de Molière.** *Bon nombre de comédiens et de comédiennes qui par la suite se sont fait un nom au cinéma et ailleurs au théâtre ont commencé au Théâtre français;* "Many actors and actresses who later made a name for themselves in films or elsewhere in the theater started out as members of the *Comédie-Française.*"

Thomson S.A. In October 1996 the government decided to sell the money-losing multimedia communications part of this corporation to the Korean firm **Daewoo** for *un franc symbolique* rather than to Matra, a French firm. Employees at the Thomson plant in Alsace were up in arms over the decision. *Aussitôt on plaisantait qu'un café ça coûtait cinq Thomson;* "The joke went around that a coffee cost five Thomsons." Two months later the European authorities in Brussels questioned the sale and sent the file back to the French government for substantial changes. Daewoo withdrew. In 1997 the Socialist government gave its preference to Alcatel-Alsthom, another French firm, instead of Matra.

tiercé (m.) Highly popular system for betting on the races. You must pick the first three horses, *soit dans l'ordre, ce qui rapporte plus, soit dans le désordre, ce qui rapporte moins,* "either in the right order, which carries a higher payoff, or in any order, which pays less."

Tiers monde (m.) The Third World. *"Ce que nous constatons de nos jours c'est la tiersmondisation de ces régions d'Europe,"* noted one talk show participant; "'What we're witnessing today is the transformation of these regions of Europe into Third World regions.'"

tiers (m.) **provisionnel** The first of three income tax payments spread over the year. *En France l'impôt sur le revenu n'est pas retenu à la source; votre fiche de paie mentionnera le montant brut de votre salaire et le montant net imposable après les prélèvements pour la Sécurité sociale, etc.;* "In France income tax

ÉCONOMIE : C'EST LA REPRISE !

BONJOUR J'M'APPELLE GÉRARD JE SORS DE PRISON, IL ME FAUDRAIT UN FRANC SYMBOLIQUE POUR ACHETER THOMSON S.A. !..

The economy is looking up!

"Good morning. My name is Gérard. I've just got out of jail. I need one symbolic franc to buy Thomson S.A."

(Begging in the Paris Metro.)

by Cardon in *Le Canard enchaîné,* October 23, 1996

is not withheld at source; your payslip will show your gross salary and the net amount that is taxable after Social Security and so forth has been deducted."

En février on paie le premier tiers provisionnel, dont le montant est un tiers de l'impôt que l'on a payé l'année précédente sur les revenus de l'année d'avant; en mai on paie le deuxième tiers, et en septembre on effectue le dernier paiement, qui sera plus ou moins élevé selon les revenus que l'on a déclarés pour l'année précédente. "In February you pay your first approximate third, which is one-third of the tax you paid the previous year on your income the year before that; in May you pay the second approximate third; and in September you pay the remainder, which will be more or less than each of the previous thirds depending on the income you declared for the previous year."

The radio will remind you, *"Vous avez jusqu'à ce soir minuit pour payer votre tiers provisionnel";* "'You have until midnight tonight to make your first tax payment.'"

Tifosi (m. pl.) Name given to Italian soccer fans.

TIG (m. pl.) *Travaux d'intérêt général,* community service. *Suite à* *son Alcootest® positif, il a été condamné à six mois de travaux d'intérêt général au lieu d'une peine de prison;* "After a Breathalyzer® test showed that he had been driving while drunk, he was sentenced to six months of community service instead of a prison term." *C'est un tigiste,* "He's doing a spell of community service."

tir (m.) Launching of a rocket. *Le tir d'Ariane, pourtant prévu à Kourou à 3 heures du matin heure de Paris, a dû être reporté au dernier moment à cause des conditions atmosphériques;* "Although the *Ariane* rocket was scheduled to be launched from Kourou at 3 A.M. Paris time, it had to be postponed at the last minute because of weather conditions."

tir (m.) **d'armes** Shooting (during military or guerilla conflict). *Tir nourri d'armes automatiques,* sustained or heavy firing of automatic weapons.

tissu (m.) **social** The social fabric. *L'Etat peut-il arrêter la désagrégation du tissu social?* "Can the government curb the unraveling of the social fabric single-handedly?" See **fracture sociale**

titre (m.) **de séjour** Residence permit. This is what *les sans-papiers de l'Eglise Saint-Bernard* went on a hunger strike about.

titre (m.) **de transport** Your ticket, season pass, monthly pass, or whatever you show as proof of your legal right to use a particular means of transportation. It can be your *ticket de Métro ou d'autobus,* your *coupon hebdomadaire ou mensuel,* your *billet de train,* and so forth.

toi *Toi* and *tu* are replacing *vous* in more and more ads as they are aimed at an increasingly younger and more informal audience. In the mid-1990s, when Renault brought out its mini-compact Twingo model, aimed at trendy but low-budget singles, couples, and young families, the slogan was *"A toi d'inventer la vie qui va avec";* "'Up to you to dream up the lifestyle it goes with.'" An antialcoholism campaign targeting teenagers asked, *"Tu t'es vu quand t'as bu?"* "'Know what you look like when you've had too many?'" See also **tutoyer**

toilettage (m.) Tidying or polishing up, as applied to a dusty old regulation. *Le toilettage du texte de loi sur le cumul des mandats s'impose;* "The law that forbids the holding of more than one political post at any given time needs to be spruced up." *Toiletter la loi Pasqua, la loi Debré, et ainsi de suite.*

Tonton A nickname that was buried with President Mitterrand in January 1996. An off-the-cuff way of saying "Uncle," it was a journalistic pet name for him, much as *"Qui Nous Savons"* or *"Qui Vous Savez"* denoted the quasi-monarchical de Gaulle, three decades earlier, particularly in the *Canard enchaîné.*

Toulon *Une des trois villes dans le Midi (avec Orange et Marignane) à avoir élu, en 1995, un maire Front national;* "One of the three cities in southern France (along with Orange and Marignane) that voted in a *Front national* mayor in 1995." *Toulon fut aussi la première ville de plus de cent mille habitants à voter FN;* "Toulon was also the first city with a population of over one hundred thousand to vote *FN.*" See **Vitrolles** (1997)

In 1996, in several bizarre episodes, Christian tombs were violated in a *Toulon* cemetery, and crosses were placed upside down in the ground. This was first ascribed to *Front national* influence, just as the violation of Jewish tombs in **Carpentras** had been. Later, however, the Toulon incidents were ascribed to a religious sect.

tour (m.) **de table financier** Syndicate to finance a project. *Lors du lancement de cette société de logiciel, le tour de table financier comprenait trois parmi les plus grandes banques privées;* "When that software company was launched, three of the biggest private banks were among the investors pledging money to it."

tourisme (m.) Suggested by some officials as an alternative or replacement activity for farmers who have been told to stop overproducing and let their land lie fallow. Instead of growing crops, the theory goes, they should offer bed-and-breakfast and rent their land to campers. *Mais souvent les cultivateurs eux-mêmes n'ont pas envie de suivre ces consignes;* "But often the farmers themselves have no desire to follow such instructions." See **paysan(ne)**

tournant (m.) A turning point. *Cette nouvelle politique économique marqua un tournant dans la pratique inaugurée par le gouvernement Balladur;* "This new economic policy marked a turning point in the attitude taken/approach put into effect by the Balladur government."

Attendre au tournant means to be ready to pounce (on someone). *Après tant de promesses électorales, on attend les nouveaux élus au tournant;* "After hearing all those campaign promises, people are just waiting to see the new representatives slip up."

tout à fait Perfectly ordinary adverb, now often used by interviewees and others somewhat like "absolutely," to mean an emphatic *oui.* A variation on the same theme is *complètement.*

tout terrain (m.) Mountain biking. *Un nombre croissant de jeunes Français ne rêvent que d'une chose: faire du tout terrain pendant les vacances;* "More and more, the younger generation dreams of just one thing: mountain biking during their vacation." *Le, vélo tout terrain* (**VTT**), mountain bike.

Touvier, Paul A leader in the collaborationist **Milice** during the Vichy period. In 1944, right after the *Libération,* he disappeared; three times, in absentia, he was sentenced to death, but after twenty years the statute of limitations concerning the crimes of which he was accused ran out. The granting of a presidential pardon aroused a scandal and he hid again; not until 1989 was he suddenly "found" and arrested in a priory occupied by an *intégriste* (extreme Right) faction of the Church. It was known that for decades he had been hidden and helped, especially after 1972, by a surprising number of Catholic clergy. The case was disturbing enough that later in 1989, Cardinal Decourtray took the unprecedented step of opening the archives of the Archbishopric of Lyons to a panel of historians and asking them to investigate the Church's role in *l'affaire Touvier.*

Entre 1992 et 1994 Touvier a fait l'objet de plusieurs procès pour crimes contre l'humanité; d'abord acquitté, il a été ensuite condamné à la prison à perpétuité; "Between 1992 and 1994 Touvier was tried for crimes against humanity; he was first acquitted, then given a life sentence." He died in 1996. See **Bousquet, René; Papon, Maurice; repentance**

toxicomane (m. or f.) Drug addict. *La toxicomanie,* drug addiction. *Parmi les SDF il y a un certain nombre de toxicomanes; beaucoup ont fait des cures mais sont récidivistes/ont rechuté.* "There are quite a few drug addicts among the homeless; a lot of them have been in treatment centers but have relapsed."

TPE (f.) *Très petite entreprise,* a company that has between one and nine employees. *On ne peut pas demander aux TPE de se conformer aux nouveaux règlements sur les 35 heures qui entreront en vigueur en 2002;* "The smallest companies cannot be expected to abide by the new rules on the thirty-five-hour work week that will apply as of 2002." See **PME**

TPS (f.) *Télévision par satellite.*

trafic (m.) **de drogues** Drug dealing. *Trafiquant* (m.), drug dealer. *C'est la Brigade des stups (stupéfiants) qui est chargée de poursuivre les trafiquants;* "It's the Narcotics Bureau that's in charge of hunting down drug dealers."

trafic (m.) **d'influence** Influence peddling. *Untel est mis en examen/poursuivi pour trafic d'influence et abus de biens sociaux;* "So-and-So is being investigated/tried on charges of influence peddling and misappropriation of company property." *Complicité* (f.) *de trafic d'influence.*

train (m.) **de mesures** Not the kind of train where you reserve a seat. Instead, this is a set of measures or steps taken or decided upon. *Le gouvernement a pris un train de mesures pour mettre en oeuvre le nouveau décret sur la provenance de la viande bovine;* "The government has adopted a set of measures by which to implement the new decree concerning beef and where it must come from" (see **vache folle**).

train (m.) **de vie** Lifestyle. *Mener un grand train de vie,* to have a high-income or high-powered lifestyle. *"Puisque l'heure est à* *la réduction des dépenses dans tous les domaines, certains économistes proposent que l'Etat réduise son propre train de vie";* "'Since it's the fashion right now to cut back spending in all areas, some economists suggest that the state should reduce its own rate of expenditure on itself'" (*Marianne,* July 28, 1997).

Traité (m.) **de Maastricht** Treaty that transformed the *Communauté européenne* into the *Union européenne,* signed in 1992. It then had to be ratified by parliamentary vote or by referendum in each signatory country. In Denmark the referendum turned it down, but a second referendum one year later accepted it. In Norway the referendum rejected the treaty. In France it squeaked through the referendum by a majority of barely 51 percent. See **critères de convergence**

traité (m.) **de non-prolifération des armes nucléaires** Signed in 1968 by the United States, Great Britain, and the Soviet Union. In 1976 France decided to apply it without signing it; in 1992 France signed it.

En 1995 la France a procédé à ses derniers essais nucléaires sous-marins dans le Pacifique avant de signer le traité de 1963 sur l'arrêt des essais nucléaires non souterrains; "In 1995 France carried out its final underwater nuclear tests in the Pacific before signing the 1963 treaty putting a halt to nonunderground nuclear testing."

See **Mururoa;** *Rainbow Warrior*

traitement (m.) **de faveur** Special treatment. A term often invoked with regard to *les affaires. Nous exigeons de savoir pourquoi Monsieur Untel a bénéficié d'un traitement de faveur;* "We demand to know why Mr. X received special treatment."

traminot (m.) The driver of a tramway or trolley. *Dès que les conducteurs de poids lourds ont obtenu, après une longue grève qui a presque paralysé le pays à la fin de 1996, le droit de partir à la retraite à 55 ans, les traminots dans plusieurs villes françaises ont réclamé le même droit et se sont mis eux aussi en grève;* "After a long strike that nearly paralyzed the country at the end of 1996, truck drivers won the right to retire at fifty-five; then the tram and trolley drivers in several French cities demanded the same right and also went out on strike."

The word was created by analogy with **cheminot** (m.), *ouvrier des chemins de fer;* **SNCF** employee. *Les syndicats des cheminots,* "the railway workers' unions," are among the most powerful in the country.

tranquillisant (m.) Tranquilizer. *D'après les statistiques, les Français consomment nettement plus de tranquillisants que tous les autres peuples d'Europe;* "Statistics show that the French take far more tranquilizers than other Europeans do."

trans-Manche Cross-Channel. *Le TGV trans-Manche c'est l'Eurostar;* "The cross-Channel high-speed train is called the Eurostar." See **Eurotunnel; tunnel sous la Manche**

transparence (f.) Transparency in the sense of complete clarity and honesty, concealing nothing. A term much used with regard to the various **affaires,** "scandals," on all sides of the political spectrum. *Nous réclamons la transparence dans ces affaires de financement occulte des partis politiques et d'enrichissement personnel;* "We demand that all the facts be brought to light wherever underground payments have been made to political parties and individuals have received large sums of money."

transplanté(e) (m. or f.) Recipient of an organ transplant. *Suite à une greffe du rein, la jeune transplantée se porte bien;* "The girl who received a kidney graft is doing just fine."

transports (m. pl.) **routiers** The trucking industry. *La part du fret transportée par les chemins de fer n'arrête pas de baisser, au profit des transports routiers;* "The proportion of freight that is carried by rail is declining constantly, while truckers are carrying more and more of it." *Camionneur* (m.), *chauffeur* (m.) *de poids lourd, routier* (m.), truck driver. *Restaurant* (m.) *des routiers,* truck stop. *"Les routiers sont sympas"* and *"Je roule pour vous,"* trucks used to proclaim on their rear panels or bumpers, to placate irritated car drivers. *Lors de la grève à la fin 96, les camionneurs installèrent deux types de barrages ou blocages sur les routes: des barrages bloquants et des barrages flottants; ils ont surtout utilisé "l'opération escargot" à base de barrages filtrants.* "When they went on strike at the end of 1996, truck drivers set up total roadblocks in some places and partial ones in others; above all, they carried out 'snail's pace' operations, with roadblocks that filtered car traffic through very slowly." One observer termed these maneuvers *"la démocratie du bitume,"* "'asphalt democracy.'" See **traminot**

travail (m.) **à temps partiel** Part-time work. Although it was long considered as being of interest only to married women or single mothers with children, it has been suggested more and more frequently in recent years *comme un instrument de création d'emploi et donc comme moyen de combattre l'exclusion,* "as a way to create more jobs and therefore to prevent people from being excluded from the job market." See **exclusion**

travail (m.) **au noir** Undeclared or clandestine work; *travailleur-(euse) au noir. Le bruit court que même sur les chantiers de construction de l'Etat une bonne partie des ouvriers travaillent au noir;* "Rumor has it that even on the construction sites for the government's own projects, many of the workers are illegal."

travail (m.) **de proximité** A job in the neighborhood; often a modest job that does not require a college degree. *La garde des enfants ou des personnes âgées constitue deux types de travail de proximité. On tente actuellement de créer davantage d'em-*

plois de proximité afin d'offrir aux jeunes surtout autre chose que les petits boulots; "Attempts are being made to create more neighborhood jobs so that young people especially will have other possibilities besides odd jobs." *Beaucoup de personnes, excédées d'avoir à faire un très long trajet matin et soir pour aller travailler, préféreraient un travail de proximité quitte à être payées moins;* "Many people, fed up with a long commute twice a day to get to work and back, would rather have a neighborhood job even if it meant getting lower pay."

travail (m.) **précaire** Work performed without a contract or on a short-term, not necessarily renewable basis. *J'ai été salarié pendant huit ans mais depuis que je suis au chômage tout ce que j'ai pu trouver c'est du travail précaire;* "I had a steady job for eight years, but since I've been unemployed, all I've been able to find is jobs with no security." See **flexibilité; précaire**

traversée (f.) **du désert** A period of wandering in the wilderness (i.e., a very trying and solitary period). In the life of General de Gaulle this was the period between 1946 and 1958. In 1946 de Gaulle, who had been head of the government since the Liberation of Paris in 1944 and the creation of *la Quatrième République*, resigned. He retired to the family seat at **Colombey-les-Deux-Eglises** and for the next twelve years played no part in French public life, until 1958 (see **treize mai**).

treize mai (m.) This refers to *le 13 mai 1958* when a military putsch occurred in Algiers; as a result, General de Gaulle was suddenly asked, by President René Coty, to form and head a new French government. Within months de Gaulle drafted a constitution for what was to become the **Cinquième République;** it provided for a strong executive branch, and the first elections ever to elect a French president by universal suffrage were held in December 1958; de Gaulle was elected. Hence, *le treize mai* is invoked reverently by members of the *RPR, qui se réclament du Gaullisme,* "who claim to be faithful to the Gaullist tradition."

treizième mois (m.) An annual bonus that was quite common in the days of *le plein emploi,* "full employment." *Un(e) salarié(e) pouvait recevoir un treizième mois de salaire soit en une seule fois à la fin de l'année, soit en plusieurs versements étalés sur l'année;* "An employee could receive a thirteenth month of salary either as a single payment at the end of the year or in several installments spread over the year." Bank employees often received *un quatorzième mois* as well.

Trente glorieuses (f. pl.) The post–World War II economic boom. *Les trente années jusqu'en 1975 étaient une période de plein emploi, et de progrès économique et social;* "The thirty years up until 1975 were a period of full employment and of economic and social progress." (The term was coined by Jean

Fourastié in his *Les trente glorieuses, ou la révolution invisible de 1946 à 1975.*) Compare with *les trois glorieuses,* the three-day revolution in July 1830 leading to the abdication and exile of Charles X and hence the advent of Louis-Philippe, *roi des Français* (and no longer *roi de France*).

trève (f.) Truce. *Pour arriver à un début de solution en **Corse,** il faudrait qu'il y ait une trève entre le FLNC et le FLNC Canal historique;* "If there's ever going to be the beginning of a solution in Corsica, there'd have to be a truce between the two independence movements, the *FLNC* and the *FLNC* Historic Branch."

La trève des confiseurs, the annual lull in strikes, demonstrations, and other forms of political and labor agitation during *les fêtes de fin d'année,* "Christmas and New Year's"; in this phrase, *confiseur* is used loosely to mean the manufacturers of not only candy but also chocolates and other holiday treats.

triangulaire (f.) *Une élection triangulaire* is a three-cornered election, fought among three leading candidates.

troisième âge (m.) Old age. *Le club du troisième âge,* senior citizens' club. *Tout le problème du paiement des retraites dans les années à venir vient de ce que le nombre de personnes du troisième âge va sans cesse grandissant, alors que le nombre de jeunes qui auront un salaire et seront en mesure de cotiser va en diminuant;* "The reason why the payment of retirement pensions in the years to come looks problematic is that the number of elderly people is increasing all the time, whereas the number of young people who will have a steady salary and will be able to pay into the retirement system is declining."

tube (m.) A hit song. *Le tube de l'été,* this summer's hit. See **disque d'or**

tueur (m.) *A l'automne 1997, quand le gouvernment a annoncé la mise en place de la **semaine de 35 heures,** le président du **CNPF** a démissionné, proclamant qu'il faudrait que son succeesseur soit "un tueur";* In the fall of 1997, when the government announced that the thirty-five-hour work week, paid on a thirty-nine-hour bais, would be instituted, the head of the employers' federation resigned in protest, proclaiming that his successor would have to be "a killer."

tunnel (m.) **de Somport** The digging of this tunnel, keystone of a projected *autoroute* through the Pyrenees, was completed in 1997. *Des écologistes contestent l'utilité de l'autoroute en général et du tunnel en particulier, étant donné qu'il traverse une zone où les ours sont protégés;* "Environmentalists challenge the usefulness of the expressway in general and the tunnel in particular, since it goes through an area where bears are protected." *Le Monde* (July 31, 1997) feared *"une autoroute dont le trafic—un couloir à camions comme celui qui mène* *au Mont Blanc dans les Alpes—détruira définitivement le caractère sauvage de la valléé d'Aspe et son économie agropastorale,"* "'a highway that will carry heavy traffic—a truck corridor like the one leading to the Mont Blanc, in the Alps— which will put an end once and for all to the Asp valley's unspoiled natural setting and its economy based on farming and sheepherding.'" The article went on to wonder whether a railway line might not be more useful and less environmentally controversial than a highway. See **Rhin-Rhône**

Tunnel (m.) **sous la Manche** Napoleon's dream come true, a tunnel under the English Channel. A joint Franco-British effort, it was inaugurated in 1994 by Queen Elizabeth II and President Mitterrand. See **Eurotunnel**

turbo (m.) Driving force; impetus. *Est-ce encore exact aujourd'hui de dire que l'économie allemande est le turbo de l'Europe?* "Is it still true today that the German economy is the driving force behind Europe as a whole?"

turbulences (f. pl.) **monétaires** Strong fluctuations in the exchange rates between currencies.

tutoyer The fact of calling a stranger *"tu"*—especially when a person in a position of authority does so and cannot be called *"tu"* in exchange—is generally considered condescending and insulting. *Lors d'un sondage sur le racisme en France et sur le rôle des policiers en particulier, une personne a déclaré à la radio en octobre 1996, "Ce n'est pas parce que quelqu'un est frisé ou qu'il a la peau brune qu'il faut le tutoyer";* "Discussing a poll on race discrimination in France and the role of the police in particular, one person noted in a radio interview in October 1996, 'You can't say *"tu"* to someone just because he's got frizzy hair or darker skin than you.'" See **toi**

TVA (f.) *Taxe à la valeur ajoutée,* value-added tax (VAT). *Quand on a un robinet qui fuit et on fait venir une entreprise de plomberie, on paie, en plus de la facture proprement dite, la TVA à 20,6%, que le plombier, lui, reverse à l'Etat. C'est pourquoi tant de personnes préfèrent engager un plombier au noir.* "If you have a leaky faucet and you call in a plumbing company, you pay the bill itself plus a VAT of 20.6 percent, which the plumber will then hand over to the government. That's why so many people prefer to call in a plumber who moonlights."

Vu la baisse des ventes de voitures neuves ces deux dernières années, les grandes marques de voiture demandent une baisse de la TVA sur les voitures; "Since new car sales have slumped in the past two years, the major car manufacturers are urging that the VAT on cars be lowered."

TVHD (f.) *Télévision haute définition,* high-definition TV.

U

UDF (f.) *Union pour la démocratie française,* a center Right political party founded in 1978. One of the three largest parties in France today, along with *le Parti socialiste (PS)* and *le* **RPR.**

UEO (f.) *Union de l'Europe occidentale,* the Western European Union, created in 1954. Its headquarters are in Brussels. Unlike the European Union (former European Community), it has defense functions. (Nonetheless, it has no standing army.) It is called *le pilier européen de l'alliance atlantique, autrement dit, de l'OTAN,* "the European pillar of the Atlantic alliance (i.e., NATO).

ULM (m.) *Ultraléger motorisé,* microlight aircraft.

Unedic (f.) *L'organisme qui gère les allocations chomage en France,* the body that manages unemployment compensation; it groups the **Assedic** throughout France and the **DOM-TOM.** *Les divers syndicats convoitent le poste de directeur de l'Unedic; en 1996, Nicole Notat, de la CFDT, a été élue directrice.* "The various trade and labor unions covet the directorship of the Unedic; in 1996, Nicole Notat, of the *CFDT,* was elected director." See **syndicat**

université (f.) **d'été** Nothing to do with summer school. Instead, the term designates a political party's informal caucus for the purpose of mapping out nationwide policy. Usually held at or near some resort. *Cette année le RPR tiendra son université d'été à Arcachon, une plage près de Bordeaux.*

URSS (f.) Name of the erstwhile *Union soviétique, l'Union des Républiques socialistes soviétiques.* Pronounced "ursse." Replaced in 1991 by the *CEI, Communauté* (f.) *des états indépendants*—that is, the CIS, Commonwealth of Independent States.

URSSAF (f.) *Union pour le recouvrement des cotisations de la Sécurité sociale et des allocations familiales. Toute personne travaillant en France à son compte cotise obligatoirement à l'URSSAF;* "All legally self-employed individuals in France have to pay a set percentage of their income to the URSSAF." For that purpose, every such worker is supposed to be officially registered with the URSSAF as *un(e) travailleur(euse) indépendant(e). Tous les employeurs aussi versent à l'URSSAF un certain pourcentage du salaire de chaque employé;* "Likewise, all employers of salaried workers pay URSSAF a set percentage of their payroll."

U.S. go home A slogan that first surfaced in the late 1940s, as the continued presence of foreign troops on French soil became less and less welcome and as a number of French brides left for the United States with their servicemen husbands. *Des historiens aujourd'hui rappellent que certains Français à l'époque avaient l'impression que les Américains leur "piquaient" leurs filles;* "Historians today recall that some French people at the time felt as though the Americans were 'stealing' their girls."

The phrase has faded away, but the ambivalent attitude toward America is still there. It has grown in recent years with the arrival of **Eurodisney** and **McDonald's;** *le nombre écrasant de films policiers américains qui passent à la télévision en version doublée à l'heure de grande écoute,* "the massive presence of American detective films in dubbed version on TV at prime time;" the ever-wider acceptance of English as the vehicular language in all spheres including the Internet, *au détriment de la francophonie;* and the perception of America as moralizing, puritanical world cop and of American films as *responsables de la montée de la violence,* "to blame for increased violence."

Ushuaia Also called *le magazine de l'extrême;* a popular late-evening TV show whose forever-young and bold but environment-friendly explorer hero, Nicolas Hulot, swooped down into canyons and gorges, over mountain peaks and plains in the remotest corners of the world to visit and admire (but trying not to disturb) little-known peoples and landscapes, as well as the exploits of daring individuals on land, at sea, and in the air. Ushuaia is the name of the southernmost inhabited place at the extremity of the Tierra del Fuego. The word *Ushuaia* eventually became the name of a line of cosmetics based on leaves, roots, and other natural elements, and the show faded away.

usine (f.) **tourne-vis** Screwdriver plant; instead of manufacturing a product, it assembles parts imported from abroad.

U.V. (f.) *Unité de valeur:* a credit for university coursework. *Il faut avoir acquis un nombre précis d'U.V. pour obtenir son **DEUG;*** "You have to chalk up a specified number of credits in order to earn your *Diplôme d'études universitaires générales.*"

vache (f.) **folle** Mad cow disease, *la maladie de la vache folle,* known to scientists as *encephalopathie spongéiforme bovine,* "Creutzfeld-Jakob disease." It caused a very serious scare, *la crise de la vache folle ou la maladie de Kreuzfeld-Jakob,* early in 1996. See **farines animales.** A number of cows in Great Brit-

PLANTU

He: "Doctor, my wife and I think I've got mad cow disease."

Doctor: "I ought to advise you to go and see a specialist, but that would cost the Sécu too much. Just take some aspirin."

She: "Moo!"

He: "You see? There was nothing to worry about."

by Plantu in *L'Express,* April 11, 1996

ain were found to be carriers of the disease, and it was feared that human beings who ate their meat could contract a similar disease. *L'importation du boeuf anglais a été interdite en Europe continentale;* "A ban was placed on imports of beef from Great Britain into continental Europe." Consumption of beef, even when of French origin, declined sharply in France. *Par conséquent les éleveurs de bovins ont subi une sérieuse perte de revenus et un nombre important d'emplois dans le secteur bovin ont été perdus;* "As a result cattle breeders lost a large portion of their income, and a number of jobs in the cattle industry vanished." It was found that a small number of cows in France also had the disease; *il a fallu les abattre,* "they had to be slaughtered."

variétés (f. pl.) Music hall, light entertainment. *Les émissions de variétés ont presque toujours des scores élevés à l'audimat, et leurs animateurs sont parfois aussi connus que les chanteurs et les comiques eux-mêmes; Michel Drucker en est un bon exemple.* "Variety shows almost always get top ratings, and their emcees are sometimes as well known as the singers and comedians themselves; Michel Drucker is a good example."

Vaulx-en-Velin Suburb of Lyons with a heavily immigrant population and scene of several *débordements de colère chez des jeunes auxquels la police a riposté,* "eruptions of anger among some of the younger people; the police retaliated."

vedettariat (m.) One of those collective nouns—such as like *salariat, partenariat, patronat*—formed by adding the suffix *-ariat* or *-at.* This one refers to individuals who have achieved stardom, *que ce soit en tant que musiciens, comédiens, comiques, présentateurs ou commentateurs à la télévision, sportifs, et ainsi de suite,* "whether it be as musicians, actors, comedians, TV anchorpeople or commentators, athletes, and so forth." A star, whether male or female, is always *une vedette.*

véhicule (m.) **4 × 4** A four-wheel drive vehicle, pronounced *"quatre-quatre"* (f.).

Vél d'hiv (m.) The old *Vélodrome d'hiver,* an indoor bicycle racing arena in the fifteenth *arrondissement* in Paris. It was torn down not long after the war, but for historians, writers, and filmmakers its name still evokes *la rafle du 16 juillet 1942:* during that night thousands of Jews in Paris were rounded up, by French police officers obeying orders from the Nazi occupying forces, and were brought by ordinary city buses to the *Vél d'hiv.* There they remained for some days or weeks, in completely unsanitary conditions. The adults were eventually put on board trains that took them eastward, out of France, to concentration camps; the Vichy government decided that the very small children should not be sent, and they were forcibly separated from their parents.

It is said that *la rafle du Vél d'hiv* marked a critical turning point in the awareness and feeling of the overall French population; many people were horrified by the raid, and from then on the resistance movement within the country developed rapidly. *Au mois d'août 42 Monseigneur Saliège, archevêque de Toulouse, fit lire en chaire par tous les prêtres de son diocèse une déclaration condamnant vigoureusement la politique antisémite de Vichy;* "In August 1942 the archbishop of *Toulouse,* Monseigneur Saliège, had all of the priests in his diocese read out loud to the faithful a statement unequivocally criticizing the Vichy government's anti-Semitic policies." The event still lies at the crux of debate today, in countless talk shows, books, and films, over the country's conduct during the occupation. See **Bousquet, René; Papon, Maurice; Pétain, Philippe; repentance; Touvier, Paul**

véliplanchiste (m. or f.) A windsurfer, someone who uses *une planche à voile,* "a windsurfing board."

velléité (f.) An impulse or tendency that may remain only half-defined, as in *"Les Serbes montrent des velléités belliqueuses,"* said a radio commentator in February 1994; "'The Serbs are displaying warlike tendencies/The Serbs seem eager to go to war.'"

Vendée (f.) Region of western France south of Brittany; scene of repression of royalist and Catholic forces during the French Revolution; see **Chouannerie.** Philippe de Villiers, who hails from *la Vendée,* called attention to the bloody *Chouannerie* episode in 1989, during celebrations marking the bicentennial of the French Revolution. In 1994 he founded a conservative political party called *Mouvement pour la France,* which is considered *de droite mais moins à l'extrême droite que le Front national de Jean-Marie Le Pen.*

La Vendée Globe, launched in 1989, is an around-the-world race for single-hull sailboats.

ventre (m.) **mou** The soft belly or underbelly, as in *La concurrence venant de l'Extrême Orient s'attaque au ventre mou de nos industries.*

verbaliser *Un agent de police (une femme agent) ou un(e) contractuel(le) verbalise contre un(e) conducteur(trice),* "gives a driver a ticket," for *excès de vitesse, problèmes de stationnement,* and so on. Also, *dresser un procès verbal (un PV) contre quelqu'un* or *donner une contravention.* See **zone bleue**

verlan (m.) A type of slang, developed chiefly in *les **banlieues,*** in which syllables are reversed. For instance, *l'envers = verlan, zarbi = bizarre,* **ripou** *= pourri, meuf = femme,* **beur** *= arabe.*

vert (m. or f.) *Un(e) vert* is *un(e) écologiste,* "a member of an environmentalist political party." *Les Verts* (with a capital *V*) is "an environmentalist party," the result of a merger of two other parties in 1984.

vertus (f. pl.) **républicaines** Much is made, in official discourse, of *les vertus républicaines,* which refer chiefly to *la laïcité,* the secular (nondenominational) nature of *l'Etat français. See* **chador; Clovis; foulard; loi Falloux; tchador; voile à l'école**

viabilisé(e) Said of land that has been connected to the water and gas mains, sewage system, and electricity grid in preparation for the construction of residential or commercial buildings. *Terrain viabilisé de dix hectares,* twenty-five acres of land ready for construction.

Vichy A genteel spa in central France that became the seat of the wartime government between June 1940 and August 1944. Its hotels were requisitioned as offices; *le Maréchal Pétain* had his headquarters in *l'Hôtel du Parc.* The town was in the unoccupied zone until November 11, 1942, when all of France was placed under German occupation. The name Vichy has since been taken to symbolize the entire occupation period and the government's activity during that time. See **Bosquet, René; collaboration; nono; Papon, Maurice; Pétain, Philippe**

vide (m.) **juridique** Loophole. *Profiter d'un vide juridique,* to take advantage of a loophole in the law.

vie (f.) **active** *Etre dans la vie active,* to have a job. *Entrer dans la vie active, c'est le but de tous les jeunes;* "Finding a job is what all the young people hope to do." *Retourner dans la vie active n'est pas toujours facile pour une mère de famille qui s'est arrêtée quelque temps pour élever ses enfants;* "When a woman has stopped working outside the home for a while to bring up her children, it is not always easy for her to find another job later."

Vigipirate Name of an antiterrorist plan; see **Port Royal; terrorisme**

vignette (f.) **automobile** A mandatory road use tax collected every year; you pay it by buying that year's *vignette* (a different color each year) in *un tabac* and sticking it on your windshield. The radio reminds you that you must do so by the end of November. The cost depends on the age and horsepower of the car, and it also varies from one *département* to another. The license plate itself, however, *"la plaque d'immatriculation,"* does not have to be renewed or updated each year.

ville (f.) **rose** *Toulouse,* because so much of the old city was built of brick.

Vilvoorde (or **Vilvorde**) Town in Belgium; site of a Renault factory whose closure was abruptly announced by the French management. See **eurogrève**

vingt The traditional top mark in the school system. By extension, in any other context as well, *20 sur 20,* "twenty out of twenty," means "top marks; perfect; head of the class."

Virgin Mégastore (m.) The big record-video-TV store on the *Champs-Elysées* which is the chief rival of *la FNAC.* It is owned by Richard Branson, who built his empire on Virgin Airways. In 1993 the store successfully defied the long-standing law forbidding stores other than food stores to be open on Sunday. See **ouverture dominicale.**

Tickets for rock concerts and other events are generally available through *Virgin* and *la FNAC.*

virginité (f.) When a politician tries to clean up his or her image, it is said that he or she *est en quête d'une virginité* or *essaie de se refaire une virginité.*

vitesse (f.) **grand V** Top speed. *Les nations du sud-est asiatique semblaient se développer à une vitesse grand V.*

Vitrolles Early in 1997 it became the fourth town in France to elect a *Front national* mayor; like the other three (Marignane, Orange, Toulon), it is in the south. The successful candidate was Mme Mégret, wife of Bruno Mégret, a likely successor to Jean-Marie Le Pen at the head of the party. Mégret himself was unable to run since he had been disqualified because of an irregularity during a previous election.

v.o. (f.) *Version originale;* used in talking about a foreign film shown in the original, undubbed version, usually *avec sous-titres* (m. pl.), "subtitled." See **cinéma d'art et d'essai**

voie (f.) **sur berge** The riverbank drive on either side of the Seine in Paris. Since each of them is on *la berge,* "the bank," itself and only slightly raised above the level of the water, virtually every year, when the Seine begins to rise in the winter or spring, threatening another *inondation comme celle de janvier 1910,* the radio announces, *"Les voies sur berge sont fermées à la circulation jusqu'à nouvel ordre";* "'The riverbank drives are closed to traffic for the time being. The date of their re-opening will be announced.'"

voile (m.) **à l'école** One of the most intense controversies of the decade; see **chador; foulard; laïcité; vertus républicaines**

voiture (f.) **piégée** Car bomb. One of the extremists' weapons of choice *en **Algérie** et en **Corse.***

voix (f.) **off** Voice-over.

volant (m.) The steering wheel of a car. *Prendre le volant* or *se mettre au volant,* to take the wheel. *"Dès qu'on se met derrière le volant, on change de personnalité, on devient grossier."* "'As soon as somebody takes the wheel their personality changes; they become a crude, rude individual,'" warn officials of *la Sécurité routière/la Prévention routière. "Pas d'alcool au volant,"* "'Don't drink and drive,'" urges one slogan.

volet (m.) *Les volets* are, of course, "the shutters of a window." But in a more abstract sense, *un volet* is "an aspect or part of a topic that is being discussed." *A la Chambre, le Député a été interrompu avant d'avoir pu aborder le deuxième volet de la* *question;* "In the *Assemblée nationale,* the member who had the floor was interrupted before he or she had time to discuss the second part of the question." *Le volet social et le volet emploi devront être inclus dans la politique communautaire;* "Welfare and employment issues should be covered in policies laid down by the European Union."

Volvo The Swedish car manufacturer. A projected merger between Volvo and Renault was canceled in 1994.

vote (m.) **de protestation** Protest vote; less strong than **vote sanction.**

voter utile Make every vote count; a phrase used to exhort voters not to vote for fringe parties that have no hope of winning and thus not to prevent major parties from winning a strong majority.

vote (m.) **sanction** Vote of disapproval (i.e., voters voting against one party's candidates or policies rather than for those of another party). *Le vote **Front national** est un vote sanction contre le gouvernement;* "People vote *FN* to show their dissatisfaction with the government."

vrai faux passeport (m.) This is what Charles Pasqua, then *Ministre de l'Intérieur,* was said to have issued (or to have had issued) to one of the individuals involved in *l'affaire du Carrefour du développement,* one of the earliest (1986) of the **affaires.**

VTT (m.) *Vélo tout terrain,* mountain bike. *Un(e) VTTiste,* a mountain bike fan. *Piste réservée aux VTT,* trail reserved for mountain bikes.

vu à la télé An advertising tagline: "As seen on TV."

X (m. or f.) A student or graduate of *l'Ecole polytechnique,* one of the grandest of the **grandes écoles,** chiefly in the fields of physics and mathematics. Created in 1794, the school was given military status in 1804. Foreigners are admitted; French students are reserve officers and receive a monthly salary. *Les X doivent porter l'uniforme de style militaire (comportant épée et bicorne) lors de cérémonies officielles;* "At official ceremonies the students of *Polytechnique* must wear a dress uniform, including sword and bicorne." *Une offre d'emploi,* "a job offer ad," may read, *"Cherchons X-Pont,"* "'Seeking graduate of *Polytechnique* and *Ponts et chaussées'*" (another *grande école,* in the field of civil engineering).

xénophobie (f.) Xenophobia, fear or hatred of foreigners. An accusation that is often heard, especially from *la **Licra*** or **SOS Racisme,** whenever any individual, group or party expresses anti-immigrant feelings.

Z

ZAC (f.) *Zone* (f.) *d'aménagement concerté,* an urban development zone, where housing can be built and where businesses are encouraged to set up offices, showrooms, dealerships, plants, and so on. The *zone* (f.) *à urbaniser en priorité* (*ZUP*), an earlier category of urban development zone, was replaced by the *ZAC.* Other variations are the *zone* (f.) *d'activités* and the *zone* (f.) *constructible.*

Zeroual, Liamine A general, and president of Algeria since 1994, at the head of a single-party government. After the 1992 elections the government at that time refused to recognize the votes won by the **FIS;** a wave of fundamentalist Islamic terrorism has engulfed Algeria since then. *En France, certains critiquent le gouvernement français du fait qu'il soutient Zeroual et n'intervient pas;* "In France, the French government is criticized in some quarters because it supports the Zeroual government and does not take any action against the terrorism in Algeria."

zone (f.) **bleue** This term concerns parking in town. If you park in a *zone bleue* without paying, you are liable to be given *une contravention* (familiarly called *une contredanse*), "a fine." See **contractuel(le); horodateur; verbaliser**

zone (f.) **franche** Free zone, in which no customs duties need be paid. But in spring 1996 the then *Premier ministre,* Alain Juppé, gave the term a new meaning when he suggested that, to help to create employment for people living in *les **banlieues,*** *des quartiers et villes difficiles* (or *en difficulté*) could become *des zones franches,* in the sense that businesses setting up there would be given a dispensation from having to pay certain *charges salariales* (see **charges sociales**) or taxes.

zone (f.) **libre** During the first half of World War II, this was the unoccupied zone, also familiarly called *la zone **nono,*** short for "zone nonoccupée." It covered most of continental France south of the Loire River, except a strip running the length of the Atlantic Coast, along which *bunkers* (m. pl.) and other fortifications were built by the Germans as part of their intended Atlantikwall (*le mur de l'Atlantique*) from the Netherlands south to Spain. After November 1942 there was no more *zone libre.*

La zone occupée, beginning in June 1940, included Paris, the north of France and the Atlantic strip; after November 1942 it covered all of France.

Bibliography

Barreau Jean-Claude. *La France va-t-elle disparaître?* Paris: Grasset, 1997.

Baverez, Nicolas. *Les 30 piteuses.* Paris: Flammarion, 1997.

Bourdieu, Pierre. *Sur la Télévision, suivi de l'Emprise du journalisme.* Paris: Liber, Raisons d'agir, 1996.

Bremner, Geoffrey, ed. *Aberystwyth Word Lists,* nos. 1–15. Blennerhasset, Carlisle, England: Gilmour House, 1986–1993.

Brunet, Sylvie. *Les mots de la fin du siècle.* Paris: Belin, 1996.

Crozier, Michel. *Etat modeste, Etat moderne.* Paris: Fayard, 1987.

Deniau, Xavier. *La Francophonie.* Paris: Que-sais-je? 1995.

Ferney, Frédéric. *Eloge de la France immobile.* Paris: François Bourin, 1992.

Filoche, Gérard. *Le travail jetable.* Paris: Ramsay, 1997.

Forrester, Viviane. *L'horreur économique.* Paris: Fayard, 1997.

Fourastié, Jean. *Les trente glorieuses, ou la révolution invisible de 1946 à 1975.* Paris: Hachette, 1979.

Frémy, Dominique and Michèle. *Quid 1997.* Paris: Robert Laffont, 1997.

Halimi, Serge. *Les nouveaux chiens de garde.* Paris: Liber, Raisons d'agir, 1997.

Jelen, Christian. *Les casseurs de la République.* Paris: Plon, 1997.

Joffrin, Laurent. *La régression française.* Paris: Seuil, 1992.

Laïdi, Zaki. *Malaise dans la mondialisation.* Paris: Textuel, 1997.

Maffesoli, Michel. *Le temps des tribus.* Paris: Poche Biblio Essais, 1991.

Minc, Alain. *Le nouveau Moyen-Age.* Paris: Gallimard, 1993.

———. *L'ivresse démocratique.* Paris: Gallimard, 1995.

———. *La mondialisation heureuse.* Paris: Plon, 1997.

Peyrefitte, Alain. *Le mal français.* Paris: Plon, 1976.

Ramonet, Ignacio. *Géopolitique du chaos.* Paris: Galilée, 1997.

Rémond, René, with Jean -Pierre Azéma, François Bédarida, Gérard Cholvy, Bernard Comte, Jean Dujardin, Jean-Dominique Durand, Yves-Marie Hilaire. *Paul Touvier et l'Eglise.* Paris: Fayard, 1992.

Index

The French word or words given after each index entry refer to entries in the main French-English text. Index entries printed in **boldface** indicate that there is an entry for that term in the main French-English text as well. Thus, for example, the entry **euro** points to several locations where you may find information about the euro; the boldfacing indicates that you should also look under the term **euro** itself. The French word(s) following each index entry may or may not be the translation of the term; rather, they are indications of where information regarding the topic is to be found. Since this dictionary follows the principle of association of ideas, the index is organized along the same lines. It is intended to supplement the cross-referencing in the text as well as to provide an English-French key to the text.

A

abortion: avortement; IVG
Académie française: académicien
accident: sinistrose
accords de Schengen: Schengen
addict: drogue; shooté(e); toxicomane
advertising: bonjour les dégâts; BVP; Mère Denis; page de publicité; publireportage; vu à la télé
affirmative action: discrimination positive
Africa: Paris-Dakar; subsaharien(ne)
agriculture: accords de Blair House; agriculteur; gel des terres; jachère; oléagineux; PAC; paysan(ne); révolution verte; tourisme
AIDS: hôpital de jour; préservatif; sang contaminé; séronégatif; séropositif; Sida

aircraft: aéronef; Aérospatiale; Airbus Industrie; avion furtif; avionneur; gros porteur; ULM
airline: ligne intérieure
airport: Beauvilliers; enregistrement
alcohol abuse: abus
Algeria: accords d'Evian; Algérie; événements d'Algérie; fellagha; FIS; FLN; GIA; harki; Maghrébin(e); OAS; Papon, Maurice; pied-noir; porteurs de valises; Zeroual, Liamine
alimony: obligation alimentaire
amnesty: amnistie
animals: poils
answering machine: bip sonore; interroger son répondeur à distance
antiabortionists: avortement; commando anti-IVG
antiracism: Licra; MRAP; pote; SOS Racisme

disincentive: désincitation
disinformation: désinformation
Disneyland Paris: Eurodisney
disposable: jetable
diving: apnée; plongée sous-marine
dogs: moto-crottes
do-it-yourself: bricoler
dollar, U.S.: billet vert
domestic workers: chèque emploi-service
DOM-TOM: outre-; Paca
double affichage: double circulation
doubletalk: langue de bois; parler vrai
down payment: apport personnel
downsizing: restructuration; suppression d'emploi
draft: armée de métier; service militaire
driver's license: permis à points
driving: chauffard; excès de vitesse; pastille verte; quatre-vingt-dix
drought: sécheresse
drugs, illicit: brigade des stups; drogue; narco; seringue; shooté(e); stups; toxicomane; trafic de drogues
dues: cotisations

E

Eastern Europe: pays de l'est
East Germany: Allemagne orientale
échoir: cas échéant
Ecole nationale d'administration (ENA): délocaliser; énarque; pantoufler
economic development: DATAR
economic indicators: Insee
economy: conjoncture économique; crise; croissance; déficit; dumping social; marasme; mondialisation; morosité; pouvoir d'achat; relance

education: enseignement libre; formation continue; IUT; nivellement par le bas; scolariser
education system: académie; admissible; ATOS; Bac + 2 or + 3; chador; classes préparatoires; collège; CP; DEUG; Education nationale; grand(e) admissible; grandes écoles; laïcité; licence; loi Falloux; querelle scolaire; Ravel; Rectorat; sélection
elections: ballottage; blancs et nuls; candidat(e) unique; désistement; dissolution; élections anticipées; élections présidentielles; enjeu électoral; entre-deux-tours; parachutage; parité; région; report; suffrages exprimés; taux de participation; temps d'antenne; triangulaire
electoral district: circonscription
électroménager: produits blancs
éleveur(euse): agriculteur
E-mail: courrier électronique; Internet
embezzlement: détourner
emergency response: cellule de crise; Orsec; Plan Orsec; Samu
emploi de proximité: petit boulot; proximité; travail de proximité
employers: CNPF; partenaires sociaux; patronat
employment: allègement des charges sociales; annualisation de l'emploi; arrêt de travail; charrette; chèque emploi-service; congé annuel; contrat d'insertion professionnelle (CIP); embaucher; emploi de proximité; Etat-patron; exojeunes; flexibilité; gisement d'emploi; insertion; intérimaire; précaire; reclasser; réduction du temps de travail; semaine de 35 heures;

G

H

I

J

K

L